D0758128

The Rape of Mesopotamia

Turkey

Khorsabad
Nineveh □ Tepe Gawra
Mosul ■ □ Tell Billa
Tell al Rimah □
Nimrud ■

Hatra ■
Ashur □

Syria

T I G R I S

E U P H R A T E S

Samarra □

Iran

IRAQ

Baghdad
Tell Harmel
Tell Mohammed
Fallujah ●
Ctesiphon □
Babylon ■

Nippur ■
Isin ■ Umma ■
Adab ■ Umm al-Aqarib ■
Bad-Tibira ■ Girsu ■
Uruk ■ Larsa ■ Lagash □
Dahaila □ Nasriyah ●
Tell al-Ubaid □ Ur □
Eridu □

Jordan

Saudi Arabia

Basra ●

S H A T T - A L - A R A B

Kuwait

Assesed Archaeological Site

■ Looted

□ Unlooted

0 20 40 60 80 100
Miles

0 20 40 60 80 100
Kilometers

The Rape of Mesopotamia

Behind the Looting
of the Iraq Museum

LAWRENCE ROTHFIELD

The University of Chicago Press   Chicago and London

LAWRENCE ROTHFIELD is the former director of the Cultural
Policy Center at the University of Chicago and associate professor of
English and comparative literature. He is the author of *Vital Signs:
Medical Realism in Nineteenth-Century Fiction* and the editor of
*Unsettling "Sensation": Arts Policy Lessons from the Brooklyn Museum
of Art* and *Antiquities under Siege: Cultural Heritage Protection after the
Iraq War.*

The University of Chicago Press, Chicago 60637
The University of Chicago Press, Ltd., London
© 2009 by The University of Chicago
All rights reserved. Published 2009
Printed in the United States of America

18 17 16 15 14 13 12 11 10 09   1 2 3 4 5

ISBN-13: 978-0-226-72945-9 (cloth)
ISBN-10: 0-226-72945-1 (cloth)

Library of Congress Cataloging-in-Publication Data

Rothfield, Lawrence, 1956–
   The rape of Mesopotamia: behind the looting of the Iraq Museum /
Lawrence Rothfield.
       p.   cm.
   Includes bibliographical references and index.
   ISBN-13: 978-0-226-72945-9 (cloth: alk. paper)
   ISBN-10: 0-226-72945-1 (cloth: alk. paper)
   1. Iraq War, 2003—Destruction and pillage. 2. Mathaf al-'Iraqi.
   3. Iraq—Antiquities. 4. Archaeological thefts—Iraq. I. Title.
   DS79.76.R68   2008
   956.7044'31—dc22

                                        2008031053

♾ The paper used in this publication meets the minimum
requirements of the American National Standard for Information
Sciences—Permanence of Paper for Printed Library Materials,
ANSI Z39.48-1992.

For Penelope

When the muçala of the Temple of Ashur . . . had collapsed and was in ruins, I strengthened that place, I reached its base, I rebuilt it with granite and earth from Ubase, I restored it to its place and I set up my tablet. In future days, let a future prince, when that place shall have grown old and fallen into decay, repair its ruins; my tablet, the record of my name, let him restore to its place, that Ashur may hearken to his prayers. But whosoever . . . conceals my tablet, . . . or brings and places it in a dark house, where it can not be seen . . .

May . . . the great gods, all of them, look upon him in anger! . . .

May the ruin of his land, the destruction of his people and of his territory at their weighty command be decreed! . . .

May Adad strike his land with a destructive bolt!

—FROM AN INSCRIPTION OF ADAD-NIRARI, KING OF ASSYRIA

(1307 B.C.–1275 B.C.)

Contents

Preface

This book arose from an intense feeling of guilt. As news surfaced in April 2003 that the National Museum of Iraq had been looted, it struck me that I had been asleep at the wheel. As the director of an academic research institute that studies public policies affecting the arts, humanities, and heritage, part of my job was to be on the lookout for incipient cultural debacles like this one. We had brought a policy-analytic perspective to bear on a number of similar cases: the Brooklyn Museum's Sensation exhibition; the renovation of Chicago's landmarked Soldier Field, which generated intense tension between landmark preservationists and downtown developers; efforts by Congress to impose restrictions on sales of violent video games. Yet I had not thought carefully about what the war in Iraq might portend for the astonishingly rich archaeological holdings there, whether in museums or still in the ground. I was deeply chagrined to realize I had failed to consider that policies, organizations, and leadership to protect cultural heritage in time of war might be so weak that the museum, as well as Iraq's archaeological sites, could be left unsecured.

My unhappy sense that I could have done something to prevent the calamity was compounded when I learned that a colleague, eminent archaeologist McGuire Gibson, had met in January 2003 with postwar planners at the Pentagon and State Department, to no avail. I already knew that several of the key imaginers of postwar Iraq—including Paul Wolfowitz (Ph.D., University of Chicago, 1972) and Ahmad Chalabi (Ph.D., University of Chicago,

1969)—had connections to our institution, the University of Chicago. Rumsfeld's granddaughter attended the university's high school, and her class would even take a trip to Washington in 2004 to meet the secretary of defense. The missed opportunities for linking up Gibson directly to these movers and shakers haunt me to this day.

Nothing can put all the artifacts back into the museum's display cases or restore to us the history obliterated by the trashing of thousands of previously untouched archaeological sites. But we can—we must—try to at least salvage some lessons about what went wrong in the past, or, as Santayana warns, we will be condemned to repeat it. It is with that purpose in mind that I offer this autopsy of a cultural disaster.

Acknowledgments

The sad tale contained in the pages that follow is really a composite of dozens of stories pieced together from those who agreed to share their recollections for this volume. I am profoundly grateful, first and foremost, to McGuire Gibson, who has been a font of useful information and a bridge to so many others. Equally valuable have been the canny advice and perspectives on events offered by Patty Gerstenblith and Matthew Bogdanos.

I also want to thank Arthur Houghton and Joseph Collins for their honorable forthrightness, their candor, and their generosity of spirit in patiently helping me appreciate the sometimes painful complexities of the situation within which the story I am telling unfolded. From the military, Chris Varhola, Joris Kila, Chris Herndon, Corine Wegener, Peter Zarcone, William Sumner, Rick Schwartz, and Matthew Boulay offered vivid glimpses into their Iraq experiences and provided guidance into the intricacies of military operations, planning, and the chain of command, as did archaeologist John Malcolm Russell. Laurie Rush gave me a much better sense of the assets for archaeological site protection that existed within the military but were not actualized. C. Brian Rose, Jane Waldbaum, Nancy Wilkie, and Henry Wright described the various ways in which the archaeological community interacted with the military. John Limbert, David Mack, Chris Hoh, Robert Perito, Scott Feil, Ken Dam, Michael Meese, Richard Jackson, and William Polk helped clarify the murky workings of the foreign and military policy community. For perspective on the national and international dimension of cultural heritage protection efforts, I relied upon the insights of Sultan Muhesen, Rasool Vatandoust, Mounir Bouchenaki, Guido Carducci, Jan Hladik, Gaetano Palumbo, Patrick Boylan, Neil Brodie, Morag Kersel, Harriet Crawford, Eleanor Robson, David Gaimster, Colin Renfrew, Peter Stone, John Curtis, Nicholas Postgate, Lamia al-Gailani Wehr, Joanne Farchakh Bajjaly, Christina Luke, Stephen Urice, Bonnie Burnham, Zainab Bahrani, James MacAndrew, and Don Waters. Timothy Potts, Sharon Flescher, Ashton Hawkins, James Fitzpatrick, and Kwame Anthony Appiah helped me better understand the motives and actions of dealers, collectors, and museums. Wathiq Hindo and John B. Alexander provided important insights into site protection. I owe a special thanks to Elizabeth Stone for generously sharing important research and insights into her struggle to assist Iraqi archaeologists.

For their support of this project at various stages, I am deeply grateful to the Pocantico Conference Center of the Rockefeller Brothers Fund, the Feitler Family Fund, the Otto L. and Hazel T. Rhoades Fund, and Ms. Jamee Rosa. Organizational support from the University of Chicago was provided by the Franke Institute for the Humanities, the Law School, the Harris School of Public Policy Studies, and the Humanities Division. Within the Cultural Policy Center, Charlotte Toolan, Jennifer Chang, Laura Page, and Katharyn Hanson provided superb logistical as well as intellectual support. My colleagues Wendy Norris and Carroll Joynes at the Cultural Policy Center deserve more than mere thanks; without their steadfastness and tirelessness, this book would never have been completed.

This book is dedicated to Donny George.

Introduction

In February 2006 the famed golden dome of the Al-Askari Mosque in Samarra was destroyed in a bombing committed by members of an Al Qaeda in Iraq cell. No one was killed by the blast. Nonetheless, anger among Shiites at the desecration boiled over, and within two days more than 130 were killed and 200 Sunni mosques destroyed in retaliation.

A dramatic act of violence against a target of enormous symbolic importance, the destruction of the dome was a turning point in the war, undoubtedly accelerating Iraq's long slide into sectarian strife. But the Samarra bombing was not the first instance in the history of the Iraq conflict in which a high-visibility act of barbarism inflicted terrible damage on one of the world's most important cultural institutions and changed the course of the war.

The sacking of the National Museum of Iraq in April 2003 was not, of course, an act of insurgency. It was not intended as an assault on religious sensibilities. Nor was it a deliberate assault on cultural sensibilities designed to offend those who believe in the value of understanding how civilization began, in the cleft of land between the Tigris and Euphrates, thousands of years ago. It was the profit motive, not jihad, which led looters to attack the museum, the world's main repository for the archaeological treasures of ancient Mesopotamia.

What made the looting of the museum an early watershed in the Iraq conflict was not the economic loss it represented to the country, though it would be a mistake to underestimate this (imagine the impact in perpetuity on attendance at the Metropolitan Museum or the Louvre if they were denuded of fifteen thousand pieces). However devastating the material cost of the looting, its symbolic cost was far more severe and immediate. At the very moment when the Bush administration was seeking, with some success, to cement the invasion's meaning by staging an act of iconoclasm against the statue of Saddam Hussein, the sacking of the museum offered an equally potent iconoclastic image carrying the opposite message. If the toppling of Saddam's statue was intended to stand for the triumph of liberty over tyranny, the inability to prevent the carrying off of the museum's statues signaled that American-style liberty meant lawlessness, the right of an individual to, in Matthew Arnold's disapproving Victorian-era formulation, "enter where he likes, hoot as he likes, threaten as he likes, smash as he likes."[1]

Iraqis did not need to hear about the museum's trashing on television to know that law and order had disappeared. The news would only confirm just how insecure their country had become with the arrival of its liberators. For the rest of the world, however, the museum's looting raised serious questions about the commitment of Iraq's liberators to the values of civilization. America's enemies had done better in similar situations: Russian communist revolutionaries had secured the Hermitage; the Iranian revolutionaries in 1979 had recognized that the fall of the shah's regime created an atmosphere of chaos that posed a threat to Tehran's museums and sent students with guns to guard them;[2] even Saddam, on the first day of the Iraqi occupation of Kuwait in 1990, had posted guards in front of the Kuwait National Museum to prevent looting.[3] Yet somehow the United States and its allies had failed to take similar steps.

Compounding the error, administration officials responded to the museum's sacking with insouciance. Even hard-line neoconservatives such as former Deputy Under Secretary of Defense Fred Iklé—a protégé of Jesse Helms and a supporter of the Project for the New American Century—recognized the pooh-poohing of the sack of the museum as a terrible mistake. "Some senior officials in Washington chuckled about a 'new spirit of freedom' that had suddenly sprouted . . . among 'grateful,' liberated Iraqis," Iklé commented. "America lost most of its prestige and respect in that episode. To pacify a conquered country, the victor's prestige and dignity is absolutely crucial."[4] By appearing indifferent to anarchy, careless about preserving civilization in its very birthplace, the Americans allowed themselves to be branded as barbarians whose troops stood by while one of the world's most important museums was stripped of thousands of artifacts dating from the dawn of civilization.

How could such a thing have happened? In light of the indifference to the museum's fate on the part of some administration officials, it would be easy to treat this as a rhetorical question. But in reality, the question is far from rhetorical, and the story that holds its answer is far more complicated than it appears. It is a tale of mixed motives and mixed signals; of appalling bureaucratic lassitude and individual derring-do; of a highly visible dramatic disaster building to a climax, and an even worse hidden disaster that continues to unfold five long years later. Its cast of characters is large, including not just, or even primarily, the looters, museum staff, and soldiers who happened to be on the scene in Baghdad on April 8–16, 2003. That dramatic moment—and the massive, ongoing looting of archaeological sites that has followed it—came about because of the behind-the-scenes actions or inactions of a motley crew of agents and agencies. Archaeologists, collectors, cultural bureaucrats, the secretary of state and secretary of defense, Pentagon war planners, generals, Civil Affairs officers, site targeters, ambassadors, and antiquities ministers—all played a part, in some cases laudable, in others less so.

A drama with so many actors cannot be reduced to a simple morality tale. Complicating matters still further is the fact that none of those involved were free moral agents. Acting within institutional frameworks, they were constrained in what they could do, and even in what they could imagine themselves doing. It is important to recognize that the disaster that has befallen Iraq's cultural heritage is the result not of merely personal ineptitude, indifference, and ignorance but of a pervasive policy failure. Organizational arrangements, competing agendas, different ways of talking, the siloing of information, missions and legal frameworks that seemed to but did not really address the threat of looting, the absence of social networks between cultural heritage advocates and war planners: these were all important contributors to what went wrong.

The past tense here, however, is misleading. Most of the structural conditions that made the looting of the museum possible remain largely in place, even as hordes of diggers armed with backhoes and AK-47s devastate what remains of Iraq's heritage, and war planners craft invasion plans for other heritage-rich countries. Understanding how such a thing as the looting of the National Museum of Iraq could have happened is crucial if we are to help the beleaguered Iraqis stem the destruction of their—and the world's—patrimony, and if we hope to avoid repeating the same mistakes in future conflicts. The account that follows is intended to help serve that purpose.

ONE

Cultural Heritage Protection in Iraq before 2003: The Long View

The looting of the National Museum of Iraq and its archaeological sites in the aftermath of the American invasion of 2003 is hardly the first indignity inflicted upon cultural heritage in the cradle of civilization. In fact, Mesopotamia has suffered from the plundering of its cultural patrimony since the rise of the first cities. The taking of artifacts as war booty is recorded as early as 1160 B.C., when the Elamites sacked Babylon and carted back to Susa (a site located today in modern Iran) a stele inscribed with a collection of laws prepared for Hammurabi.[1]

Modern war-related pillaging, however, begins with Napoleon, who carried back for the Louvre as much as he could from Egypt and other countries he invaded. The British Museum's own Egyptian collection, including the Rosetta Stone (discovered by French troops building fortifications in the delta), was founded after the British destroyed the French navy in the Battle of the Nile in August 1798 and confiscated their antiquities.

Both British and French governments, of course, were also eager to acquire artifacts in times of relative peace, either through plunder or other methods of dubious legality. How unscrupulous these efforts were is clear from the blunt instructions issued by the French ambassador in Constantinople to his agent in Athens in 1784: "Take everything you can. Do not neglect any opportunity for looting all that is lootable in Athens and the environs. Spare neither the living nor the dead."[2] Lord Elgin's removal of the Parthenon marbles under a notoriously shady agreement with the Turks belongs to this subcategory of pillage sanctioned by occupation authorities.

As ancient as government-approved or military pillaging, but distinct from both and more relevant to the concerns of this book, is looting of burial grounds for private gain. The filing of a charge of tomb robbery against the mayor of twelfth-century B.C. Thebes shows that looting by individuals was already considered a serious problem thirty-two hundred years ago.[3] In Mesopotamia as well, as this book's epigraph shows, looting was enough of a worry in ancient times to warrant extravagant curses warning of dire consequences to anyone who would disturb a burial site to take and hide artifacts.

The fall of Mesopotamian civilization ensured that its treasures would stay buried, at least until the arrival of Europeans, when looting by locals began to be reported from the earliest days of archaeological exploration. The East India Company "Resident" in Baghdad, Claudius Rich, reported in the 1820s that several years earlier "an immense bas-relief, representing men and animals, covering a grey stone of the height of two men" had been discovered: "All the town of Mosul went out to see it, and in a few days it was cut up or broken to pieces." The fragments turned out to be stone wall decorations from the palaces of Nineveh. Rich himself was one of the very first major antiquities collectors in what would become Iraq, rummaging in the ruins of what was later recognized to be Ashur, the first important Assyrian city. He amassed a small collection that his widow eventually sold to the British Museum.[4]

Rich's touristic interest in antiquities was not at all unusual among the relatively small number of Western travelers to the Middle East in this era. Flaubert's friend and traveling companion Maxime du Camp, for instance, wrote of acquiring a statue in Anatolia, only to have it confiscated by local officials.[5] Mesopotamian antiquities, however, were not to become the object of passion among collectors (at least of modern ones—the Neo-Babylonian kings conducted systematic excavations and rebuilt the temples of Babylonia[6]) until around 1850, after news reached Europe of a spectacular discovery outside modern-day Mosul: the biblical city of Nineveh. Nineveh was already legendary in 401 B.C., only two hundred years after its fall, when Xenophon wrote of passing a vast unknown ruined fortification one hundred feet high and eighteen miles around. By the time proto-archaeologists Paul-Émile Botta

and Austen Henry Layard first viewed the site of the once-mighty center of an evil empire that God had made "an utter end of" as the biblical prophet Nahum had foretold, it was nothing more than vast grass-
covered mounds being used as pasturage by tent-dwelling Arabs.[7] On
top of some of the mounds, a few villages were perched, their houses
often built with walls of giant stone covered with cuneiform writing.[8]
These turned out to be the walls of Nineveh.

Despite knowing as they must have that they were living on top of a
buried city, the villagers at Nineveh were not excavating it when Layard
arrived, not even for bricks with which to build their own houses. (In
this regard, they differed from the inhabitants of Hillah near Babylon,
who had been mining that great city's ruins for ancient baked bricks
for centuries, firewood for brick-making ovens having become scarce
since Babylonian times).[9] A market for looted antiquities had not yet
taken root in the 1840s. Indeed, the bigger threat Layard faced when
his tribal diggers discovered a colossal head was not theft but iconoclastic superstition: the tribe's sheikh decided that the figure was one
of the idols that Noah had cursed before the flood. To prevent tribes-
men from smashing the figure to make sure it was dead, Layard found
it necessary to post guards at the site.[10]

Minor acts of iconoclasm would continue to be a problem as late
as 1909, when Gertrude Bell reported that at Nimrud, where Layard's
excavations had yielded so many important pieces for the British Museum, the unguarded site was being ruined: "Such of the carved and
inscribed blocks as have not been carried away have been left exposed
to the malicious attacks of Arab boys, who hold it a meritorious act to
deface an idol, and to the still more slender mercy of the winter rains
and frosts."[11] But this was a very minor inconvenience. There was no
Taliban-like state-led jihad against antiquity on the part of either local
Arabs or the Ottoman rulers of Mesopotamia. At first the pashas simply did not understand the purpose of the Europeans' excavations—
some thought that the excavators' interest in inscriptions meant they
were seeking to establish a historical claim on the land—but they did
grasp that foreigners were seeking something of value. That antiquities
could be lucrative was enough in itself to make them worth protecting.
The first indigenous anti-looting efforts, in fact, stemmed from sheer
greed: the pasha under whose authority Botta was operating suspected
the Frenchman was seeking gold and insisted that the excavations be
supervised by the Turk's own men, who were threatened with torture
when they reported that no treasure had been found. Restrictions on
exports, of a sort, were also based on greed: when the French failed to

pay protection money in 1855, the local warlord sent three hundred packing cases filled with antiquities from Nineveh, Khorsabad, and Ashur to the bottom of the Shatt al-ʿArab.[12]

By midcentury, laws were passed requiring official permission for digs, and the 1884 Ottoman Antiquities Law stipulated that "individuals and groups do not have the right to destroy and move antiquities under their own land or spaces."[13] No individual could assume ownership of an antiquity without a permit or export without express consent of the Imperial Museum. Such laws, however, meant little without enforcement, and the last absolutist Ottoman sultan, Abdülhamīd II (ruled 1876–1909), was not much interested in clamping down. He considered antiquities worthless unless made of silver or gold, and the Western desire for them a folly to be exploited.[14] "Look at these stupid foreigners!" he once remarked. "I pacify them with broken stones."[15] As a result, most finds were not properly guarded. In one instance, the trustees of the British Museum arranged permission for Charles Fellows to remove "the sculptured stones, lying down, and of no use" from a site. As historian Jennifer Shaw recounts, "In the absence of any mechanism to stop him, Fellows took this as a license to excavate and remove an entire temple to the British Museum." Even after Heinrich Schliemann's egregious flouting of laws at Troy, the Ottoman's Magazine of Antiquities let the most famous archaeologist of his era return, though it did finally post armed guards to watch his sites and teams.[16]

In short, the Ottomans' protection of cultural heritage was relatively weak, under a regime designed primarily to deter foreigners rather than to secure sites from indigenous looting. Even when looting became endemic during the last quarter of the nineteenth century, according to archaeologist Roger Matthews, there was no tightening of regulations or stepping up of policing efforts.[17] Only at the end of World War I, when the British occupied the former Ottoman provinces in Mesopotamia, did protection of antiquities from looting emerge as an administrative problem.

The Great War was the first to be conducted under an international treaty designed to protect cultural heritage from looting during armed conflict, the Hague Convention of 1907. Under this convention (to which the United States is a party), military authorities are obligated to restore and ensure public order, including taking adequate measures to enforce a specific prohibition of pillage by warring parties. Despite its ratification, cultural heritage suffered badly during the war.[18] The Germans burned the library of Louvain in Belgium, bombarded the cathedral of Reims, and assigned art experts to military units to select and remove cultural property under their control. In Iraq the German archaeological team managed to haul many of the glazed bricks from the face of the so-called Ishtar Gate off to Berlin's Vorderasiatisches Museum, where the reconstructed gate remains to this day. The British, for their part, set up a War Trophies Committee to help decide what to do on a case-by-case basis.[19]

In marked distinction from their American successors nearly a century later, the British occupiers of Baghdad Province after World War I were acutely aware of the presence of Mesopotamian antiquities. In fact, as historian Magnus Bernhardsson has shown, they engaged in intense policy debates at the highest levels about whether to treat already-excavated artifacts as spoils of war. The internal fracas erupted when the Victoria and Albert Museum suggested to the War Office that artifacts gathered by German archaeologists that had been seized by the Allies should go to Britain instead.[20] Ultimately, the India Office, the Foreign Office, the Eastern Committee of the Cabinet, the British Museum, T. E. Lawrence, and Winston Churchill all weighed in. The foreign secretary Lord Curzon overruled the British Museum's recommendation that "their custody in a European Museum would be more appropriate than the retention in the country of origin," establishing instead a policy of absolute prohibition on exporting antiquities from Mesopotamia.[21] Curzon and the Foreign Office ultimately were outflanked, however, by Churchill, Lawrence, and the Colonial Office, and the German-excavated artifacts were sent back to England without the Foreign Office's approval. Lawrence himself selected duplicates to be handed back to a future Iraqi government able to house them.

Lawrence's involvement points to a second feature of the British occupation quite different from that of its American successor. Whereas almost no archaeologists could be found in the ranks of the American military in 2003, eminent British archaeologists including Leonard Woolley, Gertrude Bell, David Hogarth, and Lawrence himself all served as undercover intelligence officers. In 1913 Lawrence was directed by the British Museum to leave his site—where he had played a leading role in salvaging artifacts from a cemetery that was being looted—and sent to observe Turkish defenses in the Sinai under the pretense of locating biblical and Byzantine sites.[22]

As the remarks above make clear, it was not just individual archaeologists who were tied in to the military effort, but the empire's most important cultural heritage institution, the British Museum. Its function, however, was the opposite of benign. Museum officials used Turkish prisoners of war as slave labor to help them excavate sites, and then exported their findings back to Britain, despite specific orders from the India Office forbidding the shipment on the grounds that it was "improper for the British Museum to send out people to pillage Mesopotamia under the cover of the military occupation."[23]

Eventually, British occupying forces, in consultation with the India Office, put an end to such depredations and began to take action to safeguard archaeologically important sites such as the fragile Arch of Ctesiphon. "HMG [Her Majesty's Government] will be held closely responsible by the world at large for the proper preservation of these famous monuments of the past," one official noted, a statement almost identical to one that Colin Powell would issue after the looting of the National Museum of Iraq.[24] But unlike the Americans, the British acted vigorously on this insight, despite considerable danger. Some of the areas with important sites were very wild, roamed by nomads whom the Turks had been unable to force to pay taxes; as late as 1920, Henry Breasted, on the Oriental Institute's first visit to Mesopotamia, reported that a British officer was murdered close by the ruins of Ashur.[25] Nonetheless, sites at Samarra and Babylon were put under guard, and a proclamation was issued prohibiting any removal of antiquities without official permission, subject to a steep fine.

These measures, directed as much at locals as at the occupying forces, indicate that indigenous looting in the postwar period was recognized as a problem. Whether the war had led to an increase in such looting is impossible to determine. It does seem that the British edicts had some effect. At least one archaeologist complained that prices for tablets had skyrocketed since the war, "owing to the fact that it's more difficult to obtain antiquities from mounds in Iraq."[26]

With the creation in the early 1920s of Iraq as a client state under the British Mandate, new laws and a new state institution—the National Museum of Iraq—were established to deal with the country's Mesopotamian heritage. Eventually, Iraq's archaeological past would be embraced by its rulers, but that was not the case in the early days of the newly created country. In this regard, Iraq's "invention of tradition" took precisely the reverse path from that followed by Egypt, whose leaders timed the ceremonial opening of King Tutankhamen's tomb to coincide with the opening of the new Egyptian Parliament in 1924 but then gradually turned toward Islamic and Arab identifications.[27] Iraq's new king, Faisal I, in contrast to his Egyptian counterparts, had little interest in pre-Islamic culture: his strategy for legitimating his power was to define himself as an Islamic leader of an Arab nation. On the question of Iraq's ancient antiquities, as on many others, Faisal was more than willing to defer to the writer, traveler, and intelligence analyst Gertrude Bell, who had by this point taken up duties as British envoy, in which position she was to become known as the "uncrowned Queen of Iraq."

A legendary figure in the history of the British Empire, Bell is best known for having helped draw the borders of present-day Iraq. But her nation-building efforts were also grounded in a deep interest in the Middle East, in particular its archaeological past. She excavated ruins in Turkey and Mesopotamia, and wrote newspaper stories about her visits to various sites throughout the Levant. It went without saying, for Bell and for the British, that a modern state should have a national museum. But whereas European museums were designed either as tools for disciplining, civilizing, and nationalizing the working classes or as display cases for the trophies of empire, Iraq's museum could serve neither of these purposes. Instead, it was conceived—and in many ways continues to function—as a depository of pre-Islamic antiquities mostly collected by foreign excavators for the sake of foreigners.

Bell's museum received no support—but also no interference—from the Iraqis. According to the great archaeologist Leonard Woolley, "The Iraqi government was unable or unwilling to incur any expense whatsoever in the cause of its antiquities: the Director of Antiquities was an unpaid volunteer . . . and the Museum consisted of a single room in the Serai wherein the objects were laid out on open tables; even when a special building was allotted to the Museum there was no technical staff employed."[28]

The 1924 antiquities law that Bell crafted reflected the extent to which the disposal of Iraq's Mesopotamian past was left to the archaeologists. Most countries' heritage laws stipulated that all excavated material was the property of the host state, so that any division of finds was entirely at the discretion of the government, to be granted as a reward to foreign archaeologists. In a striking departure, Bell stipulated that after the director of the Department of Antiquities—a post to which Bell had herself appointed—had chosen from the finds those objects needed for the scientific completeness of the museum's collection, foreign archaeologists should be given a representative share of the remaining artifacts. European countries, and within the previous few years Cyprus and India, forbade the exporting of antiquities, but Bell's law gave the director the right to permit any applicant—including buyers from licensed local dealers—to export antiquities, charging a percentage of their value (in lieu of export duty).[29]

This regime ushered in what is often described as the golden age of Mesopotamian archaeology. The findings were stunning: Leonard Woolley's discoveries at Ur, the putative birthplace of Abraham; the German excavation of Uruk-Warka and Jemdet Nasr, where archaeologists came upon the earliest form of writing known; the Oriental Institute's excavations of a sixteen-foot-tall winged bull at the Assyrian capital, Khorsabad, and in the Diyala region; the British digs led by R. C. Thompson and Max Mallowan (with Mallowan's wife, Agatha Christie, in tow) uncovering the temple of Ishtar at Nineveh. At the same time, however, looting continued to be a nagging problem. In the mid-1920s, Bell found "a large party of men, women and children" digging illegally at Warka, and a more organized illicit dig at another more remote site that led her to conclude the diggers must have been commissioned by "some merchant in Baghdad."[30] A half decade later, one of her successors as director of antiquities declared illicit digs a "real catastrophe."[31]

By this time, a truly international illicit market was in place, enabled by the advent of cars, railroads, and transatlantic steamships. We know something about the structure of this network thanks to Bell's immediate successor as museum director, Richard Cooke, who later became a middleman executing commissions for Americans seeking antiquities, Persian rugs, and the like. He was caught smuggling items to Beirut, where the Iraqi truck driver had been told by Cooke to deliver a package to the director of Harvard's expedition to Nuzi, the archaeologist R. F. S. Starr (who, when confronted with the charge that he was smuggling antiquities, claimed that he had merely been doing a favor for a respected colleague who had asked him to take a package to the United States).[32]

Even after formal independence from Britain was implemented in 1932, and despite the scandal associated with Cooke, Europeans continued to head the Department of Antiquities until 1934. Over the next few years, Iraqi nationalists forced a change in the interpretation of the laws governing trade and export of antiquities. The Iraq minister of education, Sati' al-Husri, demanded that division of finds, which under Bell and her successors had been more or less understood as a fifty-fifty split (Bell actually flipped a coin to see who would have first pick), should henceforth be understood as applying only to duplicates. This still left foreign archaeologists in a better position than those in other countries where all exports were banned—a so-called "retentionist" policy not put in place in Iraq until the mid-1970s.

In the decades before the 1958 coup that installed a secularist, pro-Soviet military regime, looting remained a chronic but not severe problem. This changed markedly in the post-1958 period, and especially after 1968 under the police state created by the Ba'ath Party and perfected by Saddam Hussein. Human rights may have been nonexistent under Saddam and the Ba'ath, but Iraq's archaeological sites and museums were extremely well cared for. At least during the period before the Iran-Iraq War, illegal digging and smuggling ceased almost entirely. One reason for this was the regime's ironfisted approach to policing. As one museum official put it, comparing the security situation under Saddam with the lawlessness that followed the 2003 invasion: "'In Saddam Hussein's time, if they caught you looting, they did this,' he said, making a slicing motion at this throat. 'Or they would send you to jail for five, six years. But now there is no punishment. We have policemen guarding the sites but they are very scared.'"[33]

Not all autocratic regimes care so deeply about protecting ancient cultural heritage, but for the Ba'ath Party, and *a fortiori* for Saddam, the Mesopotamian past became an important ideological tool for framing—and, when convenient, reframing—a particular conception of national identity. The Ba'athists of the 1970s pursued a cultural policy that fostered folklore and heritage preservation aimed at unifying Iraq's ethnic communities: there was, Saddam declared, not Kurdish, Arab, Turkoman folklore, but only the folklore of the Iraqi people.[34] Precisely because Mesopotamian civilizations were so alien to contemporary ethnic groups, they served this unifying purpose, while also casting reflected glory on the present-day state, "showing the world that our country, which today is undergoing an extraordinary renaissance, is the [legitimate] offspring of previous civilizations which offered up a great contribution to humanity."[35]

But a selective reading of antiquity could and did serve foreign policy objectives as well as domestic ones. Iraq's war against Iran, for example, gave new propagandistic salience to the ancient resistance of Mesopotamians to the Persians. The Shia of southern Iraq were to cease thinking of themselves as tied to a Persian/Iranian culture and instead recognize their anti-Persian heritage as descendants of the Sumerians. Similarly, Nebuchadnezzar's forcing of the Jews into Babylonian captivity provided a handy analogy for Saddam to promote Iraq as the champion of Arab resistance to Israel after Egypt signed the Camp David Accords.[36]

Above all, however, what led Saddam to embrace archaeology was its usefulness to the domestic cult of personality that he assiduously cultivated after consolidating power in 1979. Saddam saw Iraq's Mesopotamian past as reflecting glory on himself and made a concerted effort to place himself in a line running back to the very founders of civiliza-

1   Baseball cap from Babylon International Festival, with emblem showing Saddam
      Hussein and Nebuchadnezzar. Photo courtesy of Amatzia Baram, University of Haifa.

tion. "Saddam has a conscious sense that he belongs to a history going back to ancient times," notes historian Oleg Grabar. "He believes he is in that grand tradition, so destroying it does not fit in with his self-image."[37] Like the shah of Iran, who linked himself to Cyrus the Great by holding a notorious festival in 1976 at Persepolis celebrating twenty-five hundred years of Persian history, Saddam appropriated Babylon for use as a stage set in a Nuremberg-like rally whose slogan was "Yesterday Nebuchadnezzar, today Saddam Hussein."[38] In later iterations of this festival, Saddam was likened to the baby Sargon (whose origin myth was probably the source for the story of Moses in the bulrushes) and to Hammurabi.

The comparison to Hammurabi was made at an international symposium of archaeologists and lawyers held on site and funded by the Ministry of Information, a reflection of the fact that for archaeologists, the Ba'athist era was the golden age of governmental largesse. Within four years of taking power, the Ba'athists nearly doubled the budget for archaeology and announced plans to build regional museums in every province. When Saddam consolidated control in 1979, he went further still, giving the Department of Antiquities virtual carte blanche. During these decades, Hatra, Nineveh, Nimrud, Ashur, and Babylon all were restored, with the first phase of Babylon alone costing $80 million.

Not money alone, but also attention was paid: Donny George Youkhanna (known as Donny George in the West), at the time head of the research department at the National Museum of Iraq, was quoted as saying that Hussein not only read his reports but returned them with careful notes in the margins.[39] There is no doubt that Saddam's megalomania affected the substance of archaeological work to some extent. New excavations were undertaken in and around the tyrant's hometown of Tikrit. And, in the most infamous example, after being shown a Babylonian brick inscribed with Nebuchadnezzar II's name, Saddam ordered that new bricks used in the restoration he was financing must bear his name.[40]

For the most part, however, the Department of Antiquities operated in a highly professionalized manner. While it is true that in the aftermath of the 1968 revolution, *Sumer* (the official journal of the Department of Antiquities) editorialized with revolutionary fervor, it is not at all the case, as historian Eric Davis claims, that "to read *Sumer* after the Ba'athist coup gave the impression that no significant archaeological activity had occurred prior to 1968."[41] The journal continued to translate the reports that foreign excavators were required to submit at the end of each season. Moreover, under the Ba'ath, new money was allocated to allow for the publication of foreign-led excavations that had been completed decades earlier. Monographs were published on the tablets found at Tell Harmal in the 1940s and 1950s, and the important site of Eridu, dug in 1942, was finally published in 1981 as a book.

The Eridu book was coauthored by an English and an Iraqi scholar, just one indication of the effectiveness of the training Iraqis had been receiving since Bell's time. Education came through fellowship opportunities abroad offered by foreign universities and, beginning in 1952, through their own Department of Archaeology at Baghdad University, as well as on digs. The long investment in archaeological expertise gave the Iraqis a great advantage over other countries and explains why Iraq's antiquities service was considered by most archaeologists to be the best in the Near East, with a well-organized national system of roving site inspectors superintended from the capital by professional researchers. On-site guards were often provided by local tribes, as at Ur, where the same tribe had been responsible for security since the site was first excavated in the 1920s.

Matters began to deteriorate somewhat after the onset of the Iran-Iraq War. Even with budget cuts, however, there was enough money to pay guards, in part because looting was still something more like an unorganized cottage (or caravan) industry than the systematic operation it would later become. Elizabeth Stone, who undertook excavations in Iraq in the decades before the invasion of Kuwait, recalls that what little looting there was on her sites was committed by Bedouins from Saudi Arabia who had been camping in that area for the winter since at least Ottoman times. Using a single shovel, they would dig a few holes in the cemetery area. "They had been doing this long before we got there," Stone says. But the quest for salable artifacts was so desultory, she adds, that "we still found cylinder seals on the surface of the site."[42] To the Bedouins, the nails the archaeologists used to mark locations were as valuable as any artifacts.

The continuing professionalism of Iraq's cultural administration was reflected in the exemplary manner in which it dealt with the objects housed in the Kuwait National Museum during Saddam's occupation of Kuwait. In October 1990, prior to the launch of the bombing campaign by coalition forces, the Iraqi Department of Antiquities notified the UN that the Kuwait National Museum was in danger and that its contents would be evacuated to Baghdad for safekeeping. This was seen by Iraq archaeologists as their country's duty as an occupying power under the 1954 Hague Convention, not a taking of war booty. "We had nothing to do with politics," insists Donny George. "We were archaeologists doing our duty, documenting things, evacuating them, protecting them."[43] The National Museum of Iraq personnel worked with the Kuwait National Museum employees to pack the material, which was stored in the National Museum of Iraq and elsewhere. During Operation Desert Storm, the Kuwait National Museum was burned (probably by retreating Iraqi forces), but the collection had been saved.[44] Within a few weeks of the end of the war, Iraq notified the UN that it would send the objects back. Before the crates were returned, they were opened and the first real cataloging done, revealing that the crates contained twenty-five thousand artifacts (not twenty-five hundred, as the surprised Kuwaiti delegation had assumed).[45]

The aftermath of the 1991 Gulf War took a major toll on Iraq's Ministry of Culture and on the country's cultural heritage, providing a preview of what would occur in 2003. In the uprisings that followed the establishment of no-fly zones in the north and south, nine of the thirteen regional museums were looted, and some were burned. In one case, a mob killed the son of the museum director when he tried to resist the looters—and perhaps also because he represented the hated Ba'ath Party.[46] The virulence of the looting shocked the State Board of Antiquities and Heritage, which had expected (somewhat naively, given Saddam's massive propagandistic exploitation of Mesopotamian imagery) that the strong educational campaign conducted over many years would have made museums immune to the fury directed against government buildings.

Some four thousand items were lost to the looters. To assist Interpol and customs agents in recovering what had been stolen, Western archaeologists working with lists provided by museum staff quickly created fascicles describing one hundred of the most easily identifiable objects (fifty with photos). Only a handful of these artifacts, however, have ever surfaced, several in New York, the others in Japan.[47]

Such far-flung terminus points support various contemporaneous reports that even at this early period at least some of the looting was directly carried out by professionals. The director of the Mosul Museum, for instance, claimed that antiquities dealers had spotters stroll through the exhibition hall snapping photos of items of interest; these photos supposedly were then passed on to Mafia-like gangs that executed the job, moving the pieces north into Kurdish territory.[48] The majority of the early looting of the regional museums, however, is believed to have been conducted not deliberately but opportunistically, because at this point there were very few dealers in Iraq and little general recognition of the potential value of artifacts on the international market. At one point, Kurds took over a cave where the Mosul Museum had stored some of the most precious cuneiform tablets, but they did not even bother to open the crates they were sitting on.

Within a few years, however, what had been haphazard and opportunistic thievery evolved into regularized digging operations. This change was fueled by the increasingly desperate living conditions of most Iraqis under the sanctions. In southern Iraq, the effects of the economic embargo were exacerbated still further by Saddam's infamous 1992–98 campaign to drain the marshes, which destroyed local grain fields and date orchards. Thousands of men were forced to seek what little employment there was to be found in the surrounding towns.

But however impoverished the population, it would not have turned to looting for a living if Mesopotamian antiquities had not suddenly become salable commodities. Looting really took off in earnest after a surge in international demand from collectors, especially but not exclusively for cylinder seals. About the size of a finger, cylinder seals are stones whose surface has been incised with tiny, often remarkably intricate designs and stylized figures that served as signatures when the seal was rolled on wet clay. Seals became the rage on the antiquities market following the sale by auction of the Erlenmeyer Collection in 1989.[49] By 2001 prices had reached as high as $424,000 for one high-quality cylinder seal sold on the New York art market.[50] Unlike large relief slabs—such as those stolen from the Sennacherib Palace Site Museum, which even though already cracked were broken into smaller salable fragments by looters—cylinder seals are highly portable, easily hidden, and available in great enough quantities to give locals hope that by digging hard enough they might stumble across one.[51] Middlemen can play on this hope, generally offering very small sums of around fifty dollars to diggers for good pieces and, if the pace of pillaging begins to lag, paying a single digger a large sum.

Purchasing such items without proper provenance was illegal, but this did not serve as much of a deterrent to collectors. Of course, evidence in this area is sparse, but we do have some signs of what collectors hoped for, and of how they might have gotten it through illegal channels. In 1992 or 1993, at least one archaeologist was approached by antiquities collector Shlomo Moussaieff, who asked whether it would be possible to "clean out the basement of the Iraqi Museum for him."[52] Moussaieff told the archaeologist that whenever he wanted material he simply put it on order, paying for it directly rather than buying it on the art market. In 1994 Moussaieff bought—in what he says was good faith—a Mesopotamian relief in a warehouse at the airport in Geneva. The artifact later was determined to have been looted from Nineveh and was returned to the Iraqi government (which, astonishingly, compensated Moussaieff).[53]

There was little that Iraqi antiquities professionals could do to respond to the rising tide of looting. The State Board of Antiquities' budget had been slashed, and under the sanctions even the most basic registration equipment could not be maintained. At one time there had been some six hundred technicians working for the antiquities service, but as the embargo began biting in the 1990s, layoffs began, and by the start of the 2003 war, only about fifty technicians remained on the job. The 2003 budget for the State Board of Antiquities and Heritage was only 2 billion Iraqi dinars—about $2 million. (By way of comparison, the annual budget of the Metropolitan Museum at the end of the 1990s was over $200 million.) Some one hundred or so local antiquities representatives scattered across the country had not been paid regularly, in some cases not for years, and lacked vehicles to get to the sites for which they were responsible.

Under this policing regime, looting was supposed to be prevented by the power of the government and the Ba'ath Party, which regional antiquities officials, alerted by one of the fifteen hundred local guards scattered on sites across Iraq, could call upon to send out troops if need be. At least this was the theory. In fact, the Iraqi National Police (including border guards), a once respected and professionalized organization, had itself been marginalized by Saddam's security forces and forced into petty corruption by neglect after the Gulf War.[54] Even if it had had the will and the means to dispatch forces, the regime could not do so in much of the countryside: the establishment of the no-fly zones meant that remote sites could no longer be quickly reached by helicopter with forces capable of driving off looters. And as national authority grew weaker, looters grew more brazen: in one incident, looters fought a pitched battle with soldiers for twenty-four hours.[55]

The regime's leadership, moreover, was no longer quite as punctilious about cultural protection as in the 1980s. There were even rumors that Saddam's son Uday had sold several thousand artifacts, and that Ali Hassan al-Majid—the infamous "Chemical Ali"—had built a palace for himself atop an ancient Assyrian site.[56]

By the late 1990s, as a result of the weakening of policing power over the sites and increasing demand from collectors, the pace of looting picked up around the country. Around Mosul, poachers began attacking archaeological sites in earnest around 1999, when ordinary Iraqis found they could sell antiquities on the international black market.[57] "Every day we were hearing about things that were just looted, destroyed, everything," recalls Donny George.[58]

Saddam tried to curb the looting with draconian measures, including staging a televised execution of ten wealthy businessmen from Mosul who had chopped a winged Assyrian bull in pieces and tried to smuggle it into Jordan.[59] Even this had little effect. The only bulwark against looting, under these circumstances, was the moral force of local sheikhs, to whom guards often turned for help in getting items returned. Soliciting such assistance was somewhat problematic, however, insofar as sheikhs themselves were often involved in the looting. They would not only direct locals to dig on specified sites, but also oversaw local antiquities sales. One town, George says, was a particularly big market: "People would come from the north, Kurds would come to there, and people would come from Baghdad to buy and sell things."[60] Kurds, George adds, would also pick up pieces from Baghdad for transport through Iran or Turkey. Such pieces were destined to end up in Kurdish-run galleries in Munich, Germany, or elsewhere, along long-established smuggling routes controlled by tribal networks.[61]

2   Head cut from an Assyrian winged bull, sliced into pieces by thieves. Ten men were
     beheaded in consequence, with rumor having it that Saddam wrote on his approval for
     the execution, "Let their heads be cut as they cut the head of the winged bull." Photo
     courtesy of Cris Bouroncle/AFP/Getty Images.

It is important to note that the local guards hired by the State Board
of Antiquities and Heritage were never expected to be able to defend
sites by themselves, especially against looters authorized by their own
sheikh. Rather, guards were expected merely to "hold the fort" until
the cavalry arrived. A number of guards were armed, but by no means
all, as this was something Saddam was loath to do in general. In any
case, site guards were not security professionals or even police; they
could not be expected to risk their lives protecting a remote site. At the
museums, the guards were even less prepared to fight, though not unwilling: archaeologist Zainab Bahrani describes one guard in his seven-
ties who told her he had used his walking stick to try to beat off looters
in April 2003; another elderly site guard at the Babylon Museum tried
unsuccessfully to hold off the mob there with an old iron sickle.[62]

In the face of these challenges, Iraqi and Western archaeologists did
what they could. To protect their own digs, the Oriental Institute took
up paying for the guards on their site, using Jordanian intermediar-
ies. British archaeologist Nicholas Postgate did the same for a guard at
the Sumerian city at Abu Salabikh, a site Postgate had last excavated in
1989. Local provincial antiquities authorities, unable to reach remote

sites and short of cash to pay their watchmen, began to allow guards to live on-site and farm small plots, a very bad thing to do from an archaeological standpoint.

Even so, by 2000, looting in the no-fly areas had gotten so bad—in some cases, George says, because "a lot of our own workers had been looting the sites"—that the State Board of Antiquities and Heritage decided to try a clear-and-hold strategy. It sent its own staff out to a small number of important sites in one area that was being heavily looted, to protect them around the clock for the next three years. The number of armed guards recruited from local villages with help from tribal elders was beefed up from one or two to fifteen or sixteen on these sites, spot inspections were instituted, and Donny George often spent the night on site with a gun at his side. It was a grueling assignment, but some remarkable discoveries were made in these excavations, even as the armed presence stanched looting in that area. The importance of a show of force was confirmed by a story passed on to George by one of his guards. The man had been sitting in a café next to someone he knew as one of the looters: "He asked him, 'Why you don't go to [the site], they say they are finding very good material there?' That man said, 'No we don't go, now the government is here, we don't go in there.'"[63]

The success of George's efforts dovetailed with what seemed to be a turnaround in the international climate that boded well for the future of Iraqi archaeology. During the 2000–2001 period, the sanctions that had kept foreign archaeologists out of Iraq were beginning to crumble, with the Germans and French the first to return to digs. In 2001 Foreign Minister Tariq Aziz presided over the first meeting involving foreign archaeologists in Baghdad since the Gulf War.[64] And the American Association for Research in Baghdad, a nonprofit organization established by a consortium of American universities just before the 1991 war but never actually installed in Baghdad, began to make plans to set up a program at long last. Its president, McGuire Gibson, among others, visited Iraq and toured Umma, which he was relieved to find had sustained less severe damage from looting than anticipated.

TWO

"Nobody Thought of Culture": War-Related Heritage Protection in the Early Prewar Period

Much has been written about the U.S. military's failure to prepare adequately for the post-combat phase of the 2003 war and about the disastrous impact such shortsightedness had on virtually every sector of Iraqi society. The failure to take steps to prevent the looting of the National Museum of Iraq in Baghdad—and the less publicized, though far more devastating, ongoing looting of Iraq's archaeological sites—must be understood within this larger short-term context of failure to protect any number of arguably more important assets. Secretary of Defense Donald Rumsfeld's well-documented desire for invading forces to go in lighter and faster required jettisoning supposedly inessential forces from the first wave, and this meant there simply would be too few boots on the ground in Baghdad to be able to spare tanks to guard buildings, including but by no means limited to the museum. Undoubtedly, too, the rush to war meant that postwar planning would be foreshortened and truncated, in ways that made it difficult for cultural heritage protection—and any number of other important postwar tasks—to even be put into the planning agenda, let alone included in operational orders.[1]

But it would be a mistake to assume that Rumsfeld's strategic preference for speed, the rush to war, or even the tactical decision to punch into Baghdad were the only factors sealing the fate of the museum. There were also deep-seated, longer-term structural impediments, within both the military and the Bush administration, that blocked the development of assets capable of being deployed to protect museums and archaeological sites, had Pentagon policy makers or United States Central Command (USCENTCOM) planners wished to do so.

Soldiers consider themselves warriors, not police, and the American military in particular has traditionally placed a much lower value on the mundane tasks of patrolling or guarding areas than on combat operations. Peacekeeping and stability operations are thankless jobs, lacking the glory associated with the phrase "Mission accomplished." The military's relative indifference to this aspect of their work is reflected in the failure to establish standing units of civil-military officers or trained units of paramilitary police, even after the Gulf War, Bosnia, and Kosovo made clear that such troops were needed.[2] Although it was obvious to any analyst of these conflicts that the U.S. military needed, at the very least, the capacity to train indigenous police as well as other specialized civil-military units, policing within the military continued to be funded in an ad hoc manner, through cumbersome supplementary budget requests coming from the State Department. As Robert Perito notes, while the military engaged in serious lessons-learned reviews that improved combat operations, "no similar effort at efficiency on the post-conflict side was made by relevant U.S. civilian agencies and executive-branch departments [nor, one might add, by the uniformed military]; they simply had not adopted post-conflict stability as a core mission."[3]

In this the U.S. military differed considerably from its NATO allies, for several reasons. First, our European counterparts had experience operating national police and paramilitary security forces and were comfortable with their functioning in tandem with regular military. In contrast, America has never permitted the development of a national police, reflecting the distrust of centralized power that has characterized America since its founding.

But U.S. constabulary functions at the start of the Bush administration were also less robust than our allies' for a second set of reasons having to do with NATO war-fighting strategy developed for the Cold War era. As policy analyst Scott Feil explains:

NATO doctrine called for member nations to take care of their own populations in the event of conflict with the Warsaw Pact. Since the expected conflict would take place largely on the continent, the U.S. military was somewhat absolved from the responsibility for large-scale governance and reconstruction duties. Those would be handled by the NATO allies' governments, and U.S. military responsibilities were to conduct war according to the accepted law of land warfare. That meant moving civilian populations out of the way of conflict, taking due care not to unnecessarily create civilian casualties or destroy non-military targets, etc. But the large-scale governance, constabulary, and reconstruction capabilities that existed at the end of WWII were, to a substantial extent, allowed to atrophy.[4]

The uniformed military's congenital predisposition against policing, the absence of a national police, and the historically ingrained war-fighting posture of American forces all contributed to the neglect of postwar planning for securing sites. None of these conditions, however, would have been as debilitating as they turned out to be, had they not dovetailed with the Bush administration's pre-9/11 desire to get the military out of the business of peacemaking operations. Bush's foreign policy team, National Security Advisor Condoleezza Rice and Secretary of State Colin Powell, came into office suggesting they preferred civilians to handle post-combat policing, a desire that meshed nicely with Rumsfeld's vision of a leaner and more mobile military. The president's first national security directive accordingly nullified all interagency groups, including the Peacekeeping Core Group that the Clinton administration had set up in an effort to grapple with the problem. Clinton's policy directives on peacekeeping were suspended pending review, leaving no clear policy on what assistance the United States should provide for restoring public order, who was to be responsible, how interagency programs should be coordinated, or where funding should come from.

In this environment, responsibility for policing fell to the State Department's Bureau of International Narcotics and Law Enforcement Affairs (INL), in particular to a small group of midlevel officials acting with almost no oversight and no standing forces upon which to draw. Recruiting for UN peacekeeping missions was therefore contracted out to a firm that hired police officers looking for some easy money and adventure, leading to a scandal in Bosnia when several American officers were accused of involvement in sexual trafficking.

The devastating effect America's abdication of responsibility for peacekeeping could have on cultural heritage was demonstrated in Afghanistan, where an international security force authorized by the UN began to deploy only in January 2002, a month after the establishment of an interim government. But even this deployment was limited to

Kabul, with responsibility for maintaining security elsewhere left to the Afghans. The Afghan Northern Alliance already had a 4,000-strong police force that was dispatched to Kabul when the Northern Alliance occupied it. The long-term goal was to train 70,000 police officers. Citing the Marshall Plan in a speech on the issue, Bush raised hopes that the administration had recognized the necessity for nation building. But the U.S. policy was immediately clarified by Donald Rumsfeld and Paul Wolfowitz. Both men remained opposed to using American soldiers as police and envisaged building a national Afghan army and police force, using international peacekeepers in Kabul, and sending Special Forces teams to work with regional warlords.

The European Union nations did have experienced peacekeeping forces that might have done the job. Moreover, they also maintained specialized paramilitary units trained to deal with cultural heritage protection, in particular the Italian Carabinieri (a standing force), NATO's smaller CIMIC Group North Cultural Affairs unit, and national reservist teams from the Netherlands and Poland.[5] Iran also might have been able to provide militarized cultural guards, if this had not been a nonstarter for obvious reasons.[6] But with the UN initially restricted to Kabul, instability growing in the countryside, and tensions growing with Europe over American unilateralism in other policy areas, European countries resisted the United States' suggestion that they should take primary responsibility for peacekeeping on far-flung archaeological sites, where looting had increased a thousand-fold under the Taliban. German forces assisted civilian experts in the heartbreaking task of conserving what was left of the Bamiyan cliffs and niches, under the auspices of UNESCO and the International Council on Monuments and Sites (ICOMOS), but the remainder of Afghanistan's sites remained unsecured.

By December 2003, the news from UNESCO on the situation in Afghanistan was grim:

Positive signs of more vigorous international cooperation [in post-Taliban Afghanistan] face one major challenge in reversing the tragic process of impoverishment of Afghanistan's cultural heritage, namely the continuous looting of archaeological sites and illicit traffic of cultural property outside of the country. The Ministry of Information and Culture of Afghanistan estimates that ongoing looting and illicit traffic are of an amplitude comparable to that endured during the Taliban regime. Means available to counter looting remain limited, especially in provincial areas where the security situation is still volatile. Earlier this year, the Ministry of Information and Culture requested the deployment of five hundred armed guards at the most exposed archaeological sites in the country. So far, resources available to restore law and order throughout the country have been insufficient to meet this demand.[7]

Much of the disaster being suffered by Afghanistan's archaeological heritage can be laid to the policy decision to permit warlords to police their own areas in lieu of a robust coalition military policing presence. On one important newly discovered site, the local warlord banned government officials while his troops plundered it. When the government sent police officers to another site that was also being looted by a warlord, four were murdered.[8] Consequently looting in the countryside has reportedly grown completely out of control: between 2004 and 2006, the British government seized three to four tons (!) of plundered items smuggled into the United Kingdom from liberated Afghanistan.[9]

UNESCO's monitoring of the travails of Afghan heritage protection efforts reflected the international organization's commitment, formalized in the 1972 World Heritage Convention, to work through governmental agencies to induce militaries to reduce war-related harm to antiquities. Unfortunately, despite the ratification of the UNESCO Convention by the United States, there was little UNESCO could do on its own to affect an indifferent military. Any influence would have to be exercised indirectly, through interlocutors within the State Department or other American agencies that might have a stake in cultural heritage protection.

Identifying precisely whom that might be, however, was no easy matter. Such was the degree of disorganization and disinterest about cultural heritage issues inside the government that it puzzled even so astute and seasoned a policy player as Arthur Houghton. Houghton was one of a very small number of people with inside experience of both Washington bureaucracy and the higher levels of the cultural sector. A blueblood scion of the founder of the Corning Glass Works, he had spent thirteen years in the State Department as a Foreign Service officer and six years as an international policy analyst in the White House under both George H. W. Bush and Bill Clinton. But he also had served as acting curator during the early years of the Getty Museum (where he had suffered the unfortunate experience of purchasing a kouros later determined to be fake),[10] and as a member of the president's Cultural Property Advisory Committee.[11] His own collecting passion was Seleucid coins, on which he is one of the world's leading experts.

In late spring 2002, Houghton was approached by Ashton Hawkins, the former executive vice president and counsel to the trustees of the

Metropolitan Museum—and, like Houghton, a proponent of liberalizing antiquities laws to make it easier for antiquities to be exported from countries of origin. Hawkins asked his friend to nose around Washington to find out what was being done by officials and heritage advocates in preparation for what was looking increasingly likely to be a war against Iraq.

Houghton had assumed that there would be an office somewhere in the Defense Department or State Department where the war-related dangers to Mesopotamian sites and the National Museum in Baghdad were already being thought about. "What I discovered," he recalls, "was, lo and behold, nobody was handling the issue, there was no one I could find who was tagged with the responsibility for dealing with the protection and preservation of culture, material culture in Iraq, anywhere in the U.S. government."[12]

In an earlier epoch, someone like Houghton—Harvard educated, urbane, and well connected—might have been able to bring the concerns of Hawkins and others to the attention of policy makers at the highest level simply by calling a few friends in the power elite to warn them that attention must be paid to cultural heritage protection. As Lynn Nicholas shows, this is how it was done in World War II in the run-up to the Normandy invasion: the director of the Metropolitan Museum, after consulting with colleagues in Boston, met over dinner with the board of the National Gallery in Washington, which just happened to include Chief Justice Harlan Stone and the secretaries of state and the treasury. The chief justice offered to serve as chair of a national committee and sent a memo directly to Roosevelt, who responded in favorable terms.[13]

But the old-boy network was a thing of the past, and Houghton found it necessary to hunt through the bureaucracy for months in search of someone who would pay attention.[14] His long quest for an interlocutor inside the government over time would bring him in contact, directly or indirectly, with the Defense Department, the National Security Council, the CIA, State Department elements such as the U.S. Agency for International Development (USAID), as well as various think tanks.

Houghton and Hawkins were not wrong, however, to assume that somewhere there was already some group pulling together plans for postwar Iraq. In May 2002 the Middle East Institute (MEI), a Washington think tank with close ties to the State Department, was beginning to serve as the administration's unofficial host for the Future of Iraq (FOI) Project.[15] And the Future of Iraq Project itself was the outgrowth of months of work. With clearance from the Pentagon and the vice president's office, the State Department's Bureau of Near Eastern Affairs had begun thinking about the aftermath of a "transition" in Iraq as early as October 2001, cobbling together a list of postwar jobs and topics to be considered. The idea was to ask Iraqi exiles to craft a future set of institutions and policies for post-liberation Iraq. In March 2002 the Middle East Institute announced the lineup of working groups to develop plans for Iraq's public sectors.

But even with the green light from Vice President Dick Cheney and Secretary of Defense Rumsfeld, this initiative still faced stiff opposition from the Senate Committee on Foreign Relations, and especially from its chair, aging archconservative Jesse Helms. Helms wanted to promote Chalabi's Iraqi National Congress (INC) above the dozens of other exile groups solicited for experts by the FOI Project.[16] At Helms's insistence, Congress had forbidden any official involvement with exiles by the State Department; housing the project at the Middle East Institute was a way of getting around that stricture, but it was also a risky venture. For that reason, the FOI Project's organizers—Ryan Crocker, later to become U.S. ambassador to Iraq but at that point serving as deputy assistant secretary of state for Near Eastern Affairs; Thomas Warrick, a senior advisor on Iraq serving under Crocker; and David Mack, director of the MEI—made sure the project kept a very low profile. They buried their announcement in the midst of a news cycle dominated by Afghanistan and pulled working groups together quietly—so quietly that the project's existence remained essentially unknown to anyone from the cultural heritage community. Even Houghton, who had at one point served on the Middle East Institute's board, knew nothing about the initiative.

One might have expected those involved in defining the sectors for the Future of Iraq Project to have included culture among the set of public goods to be attended to in planning for the future of Iraq. After all, these were highly cultivated current and former State Department hands, working together with Iraqi exiles who cared deeply about their homeland and who brought expertise about health care, the environment, and other objects of governmental concern. Groups were established on sixteen topics, ranging from "Transitional Justice" to "Water, Agriculture, and the Environment." And yet, as Houghton eventually discovered, "nobody thought of 'culture' as being an independent stand-alone issue that needed to be looked into, and nobody had experience in that area that would suggest, 'Well, we ought to form another working group,' so none was formed."[17] Mack recalls that someone did raise the issue of culture at one meeting, but "the Iraqis said, 'Nah, nah we don't need anything on culture, we don't. What are you going to do, try and save the Iraq Symphony Orchestra?'" None of the Iraqi exiles was an expert on cultural heritage: "People knew that there were some antiquities being stolen, probably under the aegis of the Saddam regime, but they didn't know that it was going to escalate after a change."[18]

There were, of course, other experts—though none among the exiles gathered for the FOI Project—who did expect a surge in looting. Archaeologists knew that the pillaging of cultural sites after combat "was almost predictable," Mack admits, adding, however, "but on the other hand, they didn't do a very good job of blowing the horn."[19] Mack is correct in his assessment, at least for the early period of prewar planning in which he was involved: archaeological organizations did not focus on the issue until the fall of 2002. As we shall see, once they began to try to get the attention of policy makers, it would take several months for cultural heritage protection advocates to find their way belatedly to the table of various postwar planners, including the Future of Iraq Project. During the crucial early period of May–October 2002, however, no one involved in planning for the future of Iraq had a stake in cultural heritage. It simply did not register as an object of governmental concern, as something about which a policy needed to be designed.

This might not have been the case in many other antiquities-rich countries where cultural heritage enjoys a sustained high-level governmental presence in the form of ministries of culture, antiquities boards, and so on. Those cultural bureaucracies have the visibility, clout, and permanency to enable them to develop standing relationships, educational programs, and even integrated operations with military forces, all designed to promote heritage protection. In Iran, for example, it is possible to fulfill the requirement for military service by serving for two years in the Cultural Heritage Guards unit of Iran's Cultural Heritage Organization. Because stemming the cross-border smuggling of antiquities is a major responsibility of the military and border police in Iran, the Cultural Heritage Organization organized special courses for the Iranian military, during and after the Iran-Iraq War, to educate soldiers about the value of cultural heritage and about how to implement heritage protection laws and regulations.[20]

The United States has fewer ancient sites per square mile to protect than Italy, Iran, or Iraq, of course, though the total number of sites in America may be roughly equivalent. But just as our military posture is different from those of other countries, so is our attitude to our heritage—and more generally, to our culture. American suspicion of governmental involvement in cultural matters is deeply engrained, enshrined in the First Amendment. Indeed, the quasi-official line has long been that America has no cultural policy; when in 1999 the Pew Charitable Trusts announced an initiative to shape one, the foundation was savaged as advocating a Soviet-style ministry of culture.[21] This deep-rooted antipathy is reflected in the absence of any cabinet-level post representing the public interest in culture, and in the relatively minor roles in cultural life played by the National Endowment for the Arts, the National Endowment for the Humanities, the Smithsonian, the Library of Congress, the Institute of Museum and Library Services, the State Department's Bureau of Educational and Cultural Affairs, the president's Cultural Property Advisory Committee, and other minor federal or quasi-federal offices.

Not only are America's cultural bureaucracies weak, scattered, and uncoordinated, but they operate under very restricted mandates dealing with trade, conservation, domestic funding of the arts, and other peacetime issues affecting cultural goods. They are neither responsible for nor designed to address wartime or postwar situations. Consequently, governmental offices administering cultural heritage did not bring themselves to the attention of those planning for the upcoming conflict—even when working within the same agency. So far as I have been able to determine, for instance, the State Department's Bureau of Educational and Cultural Affairs did not communicate with the State Department's Future of Iraq Project until January 2003. Nor did cultural bureaucrats attempt to contact the Pentagon office dealing with postwar stability and reconstruction issues. Deputy Assistant Under Secretary of Defense Joseph Collins, who headed that office, has been widely blamed for not having taken the steps needed to protect the museum and sites. As he points out, however, he was never prodded by anyone in the government to attend to the matter until after the fact. "When we started to have problems, all those people came out of the woodwork," Collins recalls. "We said, 'Wow, this is a part of the State Department we haven't seen before!' because it wasn't the part that we met in the interagency."[22]

The structural shortcomings we have identified within the military with regard to cultural heritage protection were mirrored, then, within the government. Even in the absence of more powerful bureaucracies to register and amplify their concerns, or elements of the military designed to deal with heritage protection, however, archaeological and

3   Deputy Assistant Secretary of Defense for Stability Operations Joseph Collins at
     Pentagon news briefing, February 25, 2003. Collins met at the Pentagon with
     archaeologist McGuire Gibson and members of the American Council for Cultural Policy
     on January 20, 2003. Department of Defense photo by Helene C. Stikkel. (Released.)

preservationist NGOs still might have been able to worm their way into
the post-combat planning process. To do this successfully, they would
have had to have built a track record of working over the years with
the U.S. Agency for International Development (USAID) and liaising
with American armed forces. Humanitarian NGOs had done just that,
in Bosnia, Kosovo, and Afghanistan, and had even formed an umbrella
group, InterAction, to represent their interests. When the Pentagon began planning for postwar Iraq, it turned to InterAction for help, and in
the months leading up to the invasion, 150 or so NGOs met repeatedly
with Collins and USAID. None of these organizations, unfortunately,
had as its mission the protection of cultural heritage.[23]

Post-combat planners were turning to Iraq fresh from the invasion
of Afghanistan, where the destruction of the Bamiyan statues had dem-

onstrated with brutal clarity that cultural heritage was at risk in the region. But the statues had been blown up before the invasion, and the lesson they taught was that the way to prevent further destruction of Afghan heritage was to remove the Taliban regime, the sooner the better. Protecting cultural heritage in the post-combat phase in Afghanistan, Collins recalls, was not even on the radar screen, given the intent focus on the Taliban and the need to go to war on the fly, as fast and as light as possible. As we have already noted, even if the military had gone in heavy, it had no standing military policing forces of its own to deploy, especially for something as insignificant as an archaeological site. What was deployed instead were provincial reconstruction teams established by the military after the defeat of the Taliban. Surprisingly, American cultural heritage organizations did not seek to embed experts in these units, and it is only recently that the military has actively begun to seek out archaeologists for such duty in both Iraq and Afghanistan. At this point, continued instability makes any nonmilitarized efforts at site policing or even palliative support for the National Museum of Afghanistan too dangerous for most cultural heritage NGOs: as late as 2004, the museum had still not gotten the help needed even to do an inventory of its objects.[24] "A lot of people in Afghanistan are asking why the Americans are absent in cultural heritage," according to Omar Sultan, Afghanistan's deputy minister of information and culture.[25]

One stumbling block in the way of American archaeological NGO involvement in militarized activities in both Afghanistan and Iraq was undoubtedly that, in sharp contrast to the hard-core disaster-relief orientation of international humanitarian NGOs like the Red Cross or the Red Crescent Society, the flagship American cultural heritage NGOs are oriented toward peacetime conservation, not toward injecting units into unstable situations where their lives might be at risk.[26] They could and did provide information to the armed forces about the location of sites, and, on an ad hoc basis, could send money and experts to help repair damage and train up curators once a war was over. But they were not designed to think proactively about the dangers posed to cultural heritage in the lawless period of stabilization following armed conflicts—a period that, in Iraq, began with a bang but has turned out to be never-ending. And they had no general interest in things military either, it seems. The Joint Civilian Orientation Conference, a program sponsored by the secretary of defense for American leaders interested in expanding their knowledge of the military and national defense, would have been an excellent point of entry for preservationists wanting to get the ear of the Defense Department. Yet less than two months before the invasion, at a January 28, 2003, meeting of this large group, at which not just Collins but Rumsfeld himself spoke, the only representative from the cultural heritage world was the director of the Graveyard of the Atlantic Museum.

There is a single potential exception to this general rule about cultural heritage NGOs, one organization that does focus on cultural heritage protection in militarized situations: the Blue Shield, an international consortium of national committees describing itself as the cultural equivalent of the Red Cross. If any organization devoted to heritage protection should have found its way to the Future of Iraq Project and/or to Collins's office in the Pentagon, it is the Blue Shield. But, incomprehensibly, in 2002–2003 the Blue Shield had no American committee, and its international body seems to have been preoccupied during this period with implementing its newly established function, under the 1999 Second Protocol to the Hague Convention, of advising an intergovernmental Committee for the Protection of Cultural Property in the Event of Armed Conflict.

In any case, the International Committee of the Blue Shield, linked umbilically to the United Nations, was not free from its end to make contact with American war planners. Nor was it likely to have been welcomed by them. The Pentagon was counting on help only from those in the coalition of the willing, not from the United Nations. This was a long-standing prejudice on the part of the United States, not limited to the UN's cultural organizations, of course. But relations with UNESCO had been particularly chilly for decades. UNESCO had made several attempts to go into Iraq after the end of the 1991 war to assess the impact of the war on cultural sites, but the United States—which had pulled out of the organization in 1984—vetoed those requests.

By giving the cold shoulder to UNESCO, the United States made it far more difficult for that organization's cultural heritage section to evolve ways of working with militaries to address proactively the challenges of protecting cultural sites in situations of armed conflict. That such efforts were stymied is illustrated by what happened in the aftermath of the 1991 bombing campaign, when a policy researcher with an interest in cultural heritage sought a meeting with UNESCO's director-general, Federico Mayor. The objective was to persuade Mayor to develop a capacity within UNESCO to gather and maintain site coordinate information for cultural sites. Such a database could have been drawn upon not just by militaries but by development organizations considering major projects. Mayor, however, feared that discussing any aspect of American military action in Iraq would be seen as a tacit criticism of the American bombing campaign. Offending the United States unnecessarily was not something the director-general of UNESCO could afford to do at a moment when the collapsing Soviet Union had failed to pay its bill and UNESCO was desperately seeking ways to persuade the United States to rejoin. The meeting was quietly scrubbed and the idea forgotten. Consequently, UNESCO's focus over the next decade remained on emergency responses and reconstruction, rather than expanding to include prewar disaster prevention measures.[27]

As the war clouds began to gather in the spring and summer of 2002, then, the archaeological and cultural heritage community was structurally unprepared to work with post-combat planners on either long-term postwar reconstruction issues being dealt with by the Future of Iraq Project or on the short-term disaster-prevention issues that Pentagon planners were beginning to address as part of stability and peacekeeping operations.

THREE

Getting to the Postwar Planning Table

It was not until January 20, 2003, a scant two months before the invasion, that President Bush signed the national security directive creating the Office of Reconstruction and Humanitarian Assistance (ORHA) at the Pentagon, effectively displacing the State Department and its Future of Iraq Project. Three weeks more would pass before ORHA finally appointed someone to oversee reconstruction planning for Iraq's cultural sector. Yet postwar planning, of a sort, had been going on for much longer than that in various areas of the defense establishment. As long ago as March 2002, the CIA had conducted a war game that indicated the likelihood of post-combat disorder. This was not what the Office of the Secretary of Defense wished to hear or to be heard, however, and the Defense Department representatives who had dared participate in the CIA exercise were reprimanded and told not to participate further, according to James Fallows.[1]

What Rumsfeld's deputy Paul Wolfowitz and his lieutenant Douglas Feith envisaged was a post-Saddam Iraq where Americans would be showered with flowers, in which security would be provided by thousands of Iraqi freedom fighters who would enter Iraq trailing the invasion force.[2] This plan raised objections from both the CIA and the State Department, not because of its wild impracticality but because it seemed designed to give Ahmad Chalabi undue influence in the postwar period, something that the Future of Iraq Project had been at pains to prevent. In a scaled-down form, Wolfowitz's plan nonetheless continued to be pursued by Feith's senior aide William Luti, who sought to create a cadre of lightly armed Iraqis to serve as "scouts, advisers, and experts on civil affairs"[3]—including, one must assume, the policing of museums and archaeological sites. Later, as it became clear that these troops were not going to be ready, Rumsfeld had a brainstorm on the issue and dashed off one of his famous "snowflake" memos suggesting that the United States approach Muslim nations to guard Iraq's religious sites. That our Muslim allies were Sunni, while the religious shrines to be protected were mostly Shiite, apparently had not occurred to the secretary of defense.[4] And the notion that nonreligious cultural sites might also deserve protection did not cross Rumsfeld's mind.

The attitude of the uniformed military at Central Command toward the Pentagon's post-combat security plan is well summed up by Tommy Franks's comment to Feith after one of Luti's presentations: "I don't have time for this fucking bullshit."[5] When it became clear that the Feith team's plan was completely unrealistic, the chief planning officer for the Joint Staff tasked Steven Hawkins, a brigadier general from the Army Corps of Engineers, to create the nucleus for a follow-on headquarters but gave him no budget of his own. Hawkins's cell never got beyond the war-gaming stage.[6]

Franks's planners at Central Command (CENTCOM), meanwhile, had their own idea about how to handle the post-combat period: once the dust settled, the Iraqi Regular Army could be used to control the country's borders and take on other security tasks that the overstretched allied troops would be faced with after the war.[7] In the short term, any issues involving policing or other non-combat functions would be dealt with on the fly by commanders in the field, from Franks all the way down the chain of command, who themselves would act based on advice from the tiny branch of the military known as Civil Affairs (CA).

Civil Affairs forces number less than ten thousand, with 95 percent of these reservists. CA officers include experts in a variety of areas: sanitation, policing, city management, law, and—of particular relevance to those concerned for cultural heritage—archaeology. In theory, their expertise enables them to offer combat commanders sound policy advice about what the law of war requires and to provide on-the-ground commanders sound operational advice about a wide range of issues.[8] Normally mobilized only sixty days before deployment, Civil Affairs reservists are sent to Fort Bragg and formed there into specialized units or assigned to the Civil Affairs Command. The objective is to spread the appropriate mix of skills across the minimum number of experts.

So, in principle, CENTCOM would have a Civil Affairs Command officer advising Gen. Franks on general policy matters and requirements, doubled one level down on the Army Central Command's primary staff, where Franks had been advised when he ran a brigade. Below that, Civil Affairs Command, brigades, battalions, companies, and teams would be disseminated all the way down to the maneuver brigade level, with each Civil Affairs level in communication with the levels above. Ideally, says Maj. Chris Varhola of the army's 352nd Civil Affairs Command, an armored brigade commander "would have a Civil Affairs guy whispering in his ear saying, 'Hey, don't forget, in your sector you have the museum; based on the 1991 experiences where all of Nāsirīyah was looted, down to the traffic lights, you should watch out for the museum.'"[9]

That was the theory. In reality, Civil Affairs was hamstrung in ways that created many problems, especially with regard to protecting cultural heritage. First, because Civil Affairs was primarily a reserve operation, it was cut out of the prewar planning process until January 2003, when the 352nd Civil Affairs Command was mobilized, too late to have much effect on the overall war-planning process. Second, even with what turned out to be the largest deployment of Civil Affairs soldiers since World War II, some eighteen hundred troops, the multitude of threats that Civil Affairs was supposed to handle inevitably forced commanders to prioritize and reallocate experts to advise on whatever the commander deemed the most pressing concerns. As a result, one officer noted, "in most of these skill areas, people were not adequately trained. The guy responsible for public works and utilities was a financial planner, the econ and commerce guy was a fireman." Civil Affairs Command originally had recognized the importance of cultural issues, pulling the only two archaeologists in Civil Affairs, Maj. Chris Varhola and Capt. William Sumner, from a subordinate brigade to serve on a Culture Team. But Varhola himself was shifted from protecting cultural sites to preparing for a refugee crisis that never materialized, and Sumner ended up guarding the zoo after antagonizing his superior by pushing too hard on antiquities issues. As a result, according to Varhola, "the Civil Affairs guys, some of them didn't even know they had a museum in their sector." McGuire Gibson, who visited Iraq in May 2003, reported, "You'll hear people say, 'I am in charge of the Babylon district, and I'm supposed to protect the site. What am I supposed to be looking for?'"[10]

Civil Affairs had little voice either in planning or on the battlefield. But even where an officer might get the opportunity to advise, any recommendations about cultural protection considered onerous could be disregarded or quashed on grounds of military necessity. Indeed, the doctrine of necessity might lead Civil Affairs officers themselves to withhold information from those on the ground. For example, one CA officer responsible for targeting told Varhola that "when you have an armor battalion commander fighting a fight on the ground in central Baghdad, even though the museum is being looted, they [Civil Affairs officers] are not going to intervene. They are not going to tell that battalion commander to protect the museum because that's undermining his unity of effort, undermining his command, undermining his authority."[11]

This is, to be sure, a completely mistaken view of the commander's authority, which is limited by the rules of war. It is the Civil Affairs officer's responsibility to make sure that the commander understands those rules. Where cultural property protection is concerned, however, very few Civil Affairs officers understood what those rules were, and even fewer knew much about the cultural property of the country the United States was preparing to invade. As Varhola admits, "We didn't have that level of knowledge and we still don't, quite frankly, in Civil Affairs." In contrast to the military's Foreign Area Officers (FAO), who regularly write information papers to CENTCOM commanders on the subject of culture, CA officers are not required to be educated in foreign cultures. But even if the greatest Mesopotamian archaeologist in America had been called into military service, as a reservist he would have not been assigned high enough up in the Civil Affairs hierarchy to have gotten the message through at the level needed. "The Civil Affairs guys responsible for the arts and monuments," Varhola notes, "were not plugged in, directly, to be talking to Gen. Franks."[12] Franks got his information on cultural issues from the Foreign Area Officers, not from Civil Affairs. And FAOs cared only about understanding contemporary Iraqi customs and attitudes, not at all about archaeology.

Neither Franks nor the Pentagon, in turn, wanted anything to do with the post-combat plans in preparation by the State Department's Future of Iraq Project. Indeed, Rumsfeld specifically forbade any contact with Thomas Warrick, who took over the directorship of the FOI Project from David Mack once it moved officially from the Middle East Institute into the State Department.[13] Instead, at a meeting of top National Security Council staff just after Labor Day 2002, National Security Advisor Condoleezza Rice decided that humanitarian aid and reconstruction planning would occur across several offices, coordinated by Elliott Abrams (convicted of unlawfully withholding information from Congress in the Iran-Contra Affair back in the 1980s but now a senior NSC official) and budget official Robin Cleveland.[14] Among the entities called upon to cope with the immediate aftermath of combat was the U.S. Agency for International Development, which began to develop a Disaster Assistance Response Team (DART). In the first press briefing announcing postwar humanitarian plans, held only in mid-February 2003, Abrams would describe DART as a kind of SWAT team composed of "professionals in the field of humanitarian emergencies from several U.S. civilian agencies": USAID itself; the Department of State's Bureau of Population, Refugees, and Migration; and the Department of Health and Human Services' Public Health Service. Missing from this list was the Bureau of Educational and Cultural Affairs, the Institute of Museum and Library Services, or any other office with expertise on cultural problems.

In its outlines, Abrams's plan resembled the one developed by Wolfowitz, Feith, and Luti, except that where they dreamed of Iraqi exiles doing the job, Abrams was a bit more realistic. Abrams's Disaster Assistance Response Team (in the first wave of the invasion, only one such team was envisioned, made up of only sixty persons) was to "enter liberated areas of Iraq in coordination with U.S. military forces," coordinating relief activities, making grants in the field, and liaising with the military, other donors, NGOs, and international organizations.[15]

USAID's disaster-relief planning agency was only one nexus for postwar reconstruction planning under Abrams. The other was squirreled away two layers under Luti, in a newly rechristened staff office buried within the lugubriously named Office of the Assistant Secretary of Defense for Special Operations/Low-Intensity Conflict. The tiny shop was run by Dr. Joseph Collins, a recently retired army colonel who was still settling in at the Center for Strategic and International Studies in February 2001, when his mentor Wolfowitz asked him to serve as his special assistant. Collins had been chief speechwriter to the chairman of the Joint Chiefs of Staff, and Wolfowitz wanted help in navigating through his confirmation hearing. Once Wolfowitz was confirmed, Rumsfeld appointed Collins as deputy assistant secretary of defense heading the newly rechristened Office of Stability Operations.

Before 2002, Collins's shop had been known as the Office of Peacekeeping and Humanitarian Affairs. Its change of name masked the role it was to play in the run-up to the war, working with humanitarian

NGOs to plan for various disasters (use of chemical weapons, environmental damage from oil-well fires, floods of refugees, etc.). The name change, believed to have been ordered by Rumsfeld, also probably reflected the administration's allergy to the messy concept of "peacekeeping," associated as it was with Clintonesque nation building.[16] Collins himself described the Office of Stability Operations as "the junk drawer of OSD [Office of the Secretary of Defense] Policy."[17]

In late August 2002, Collins's office began working on postwar reconstruction planning, often bypassing his nominal superior to work directly over the next few months for Abrams and Douglas Feith, under secretary of defense for policy.[18] Almost immediately, he ran into a problem trying to convince humanitarian groups outside the government to work with him. Most of the humanitarian NGOs felt more comfortable talking to the State Department than to the Pentagon, even after a decade of relief operations in tandem with military forces in Bosnia, Kosovo, and Afghanistan. To draw in the NGOs, Collins turned for help to the U.S. Agency for International Development's Bureau of Population, Refugees, and Migration. "They advertised it, we ended up doing it," according to Collins. USAID, for its part, preferred to turn over the actual liaison work to Collins's office, because of worries over liability.

As already mentioned in chapter 2, cultural heritage organizations were not part of the humanitarian disaster relief scene and remained completely unaware of the Office of Stability Operations' outreach efforts. Collins's office might have been a mere footnote in this story if its ties with humanitarian NGOs had not drawn the attention of another Pentagon office: the Defense Intelligence Agency (DIA). The DIA's Operational Environment Analysis Division was tasked, under international law, with developing a "no-strike" list of thousands of sensitive locations. This is the one area in which there was a well-established history of cooperation between the military and the archaeological community to protect cultural sites. In 1991 two eminent archaeologists—McGuire Gibson of the Oriental Institute and Robert McCormick Adams, then director of the Smithsonian—had helped supply a protected targets list for CENTCOM; none of those sites was hit. More recently, in the quick run-up to the Afghanistan conflict, Civil Affairs officer Maj. Chris Varhola had called upon Washington-area archaeologists to pull together a no-strike list of cultural and archaeological sites, which was developed and sent on via the DIA to CENTCOM within a few days. In both cases, the no-strike list succeeded in saving antiquities from destruction from bombing, as well as from berm building or other on-the-ground combat activities that might have harmed archaeological remains.[19]

The military had other prewar obligations under international law that it did not observe so meticulously, unfortunately. Under the 1949 Fourth Geneva Convention, for instance, it was responsible for restoring public order, providing security, and ensuring effective law enforcement as part of its obligations as an occupying power. That issue would be sidestepped by the simple expedient of not declaring an occupation to be in effect, even after the president declared on May 1, 2003, that active combat operations were over.[20] Another international rule, the 1954 Hague Convention for the Protection of Cultural Property in the Event of Armed Conflict—with its requirement that parties to it "undertake to prohibit, prevent and, if necessary, put a stop to any form of theft, pillage or misappropriation of, and any act of vandalism directed against, cultural property"—was observed by the United States as a matter of customary international law, although it had never been ratified; but this provision was construed to apply only to warring parties rather than to criminal looting by civilians.[21]

The possibility that the postwar period might involve such obligations was ignored, because the leadership at the Pentagon believed in the magic of self-determination. It was a faith strong enough to survive even the looting of the museum. Asked by an angry Egyptian interviewer why the United States seemed to disdain undertaking a policing function, Wolfowitz insisted that "once we get in there with a small military force the local people seem to organize themselves quite well to do those jobs."[22] Collins admits that "a lot of people in the Defense Department, and I suppose I had caught that disease as well, were thinking that the post-conflict world would be easier than it has turned out to be. So the whole notion of having formations and the military armed, having to police the cultural end of this, wasn't there." Like a lot of good thoughts they should have had, Collins says, it "fell through the cracks."[23]

What Collins fails to add, however, is that these cracks were in many cases not natural bureaucratic ones, but fissures deliberately created by policy makers. Postwar planning efforts under way by fall of 2002 were not simply uncoordinated, but in some cases antagonistic. It was as if the Pentagon, State Department, and uniformed military were deliberately seeking a disunity of effort, the opposite of the unity of effort that policy analysts describe as required for any complex contingency operation. Such coordination is all the more crucial when the operation in question involves an objective such as preventing destruction or looting of cultural heritage, which has no natural bureaucratic champion.[24]

Coordination of planning for the post-combat phase was certainly hobbled by sheer antagonism between the Pentagon, the uniformed military, and the State Department. But it also was made far more difficult than it might have been because in the absence of leadership and forethought from the national security advisor, no procedure was created to manage the process. Instead, post-conflict planning was distributed across and within agencies in unexpected places, in an improvised manner. As Collins points out:

> The whole stability operation, the post-conflict operation, if you will . . . there were a number of different planning sites for. The Abrams-Cleveland crew had only humanitarian assistance and the initial swipe of reconstruction estimates under our control. And as it turns out, the things that we spent most of our time working on, like refugees, turned out to be rather minor problems. Issues like de-Baathification, governance in the province, law and order, what to do about the Iraqi military and police or whatever, that was handled by a completely different group. They [the war planners] made their battle plans in a very coordinated sort of way. The other plans for post-conflict issues were made seriatim and in a very ad hoc fashion. I don't know that there was ever sort of a plan, an organizational plan, to say, OK, you know, these are the twelve issues. There was no matrix.[25]

Under such conditions, it was a major project simply to determine where planning was going on and who was responsible for what.

A third impediment to finding one's way into the process was conceptual rather than bureaucratic or procedural. Planners held to ill-defined yet fetishistically maintained divisions between combat and stability, stability and reconstruction, policing and administering, military and Civil Affairs. These divisions allowed planners to avoid grappling with the notion that one might have to worry more about transitions between the phases of combat, or that stability operations might need to continue even while reconstruction efforts got under way.

Bureaucratically at odds, lacking organizational oversight from above, conceptually blinkered, postwar planning was a disjointed affair that dramatically increased the chances for dropped balls—one of which was the securing of important sites, including the National Museum of Iraq in Baghdad, in the immediate aftermath of combat operations.

None of these shortcomings was in and of itself fatal, and had policy makers at the top level wanted to, they might have forced collaboration or even opened up the process to advice and assistance from outside. But all the planning was taking place in a political atmosphere that encouraged planners to both engage in wishful thinking about the need to plan and to hide what they were doing from the world, rather than welcome input into the policy process.

Little wonder, then, that as Arthur Houghton began to probe in earnest in September 2002, he had trouble locating anyone in government working on the issue of protecting cultural sites in the aftermath of combat. Making contacts outside the government with Mesopotamian archaeologists was a bit easier. Houghton found his way to one of the best, Gibson, at a dinner party held by an old diplomatic acquaintance of both men. The old-boys network was creaky, but it did work to this extent. A few days later, Houghton contacted Frank Cross and James Armstrong at Harvard, to ask them who within the academic world was interested in issues related to "material culture, cultural property protection, etc., in a post-Saddam world," adding that "some thought should be given to what may emerge when it's over."

Over the next few weeks, Houghton followed up by contacting Scott Silliman, director of Duke University's Center on Law, Ethics and National Security (who had reviewed targeting requests during the first Gulf War). Houghton was more specific by this point about his concerns, which he described as focusing on

the consequences of a post-Saddam Iraq, possibly in chaos, to Mesopotamian archaeological sites. In this context, and considering the apparent likelihood of a U.S. attack on Iraq, it seemed to me useful to review also what the U.S. does, or has done, to try to avoid damaging sites of cultural importance during hostilities, and what procedures it has set up to take these into consideration.

Houghton apparently made no mention of the possibility of looting by civilians, and Silliman's reply ignored that issue as well.

At this point, in September 2002, the former curator recalls, "there was no channel that was operative between anyone in the academic community: the Archaeological Institute of America, the American Council of Museums, you go right down the list of who should have been calling the Department of Defense, and not one took the responsibility in picking up the phone. Not one."[26]

Gibson was pushing the matter personally, however, and he and Houghton kept in touch, discussing whom to involve. Houghton, who knew former colleagues in the State Department who were working on

Iraq, suggested it was worthwhile to raise the visibility of the protection issue by going through State Department or White House channels. He probably had in mind David Mack of the Middle East Institute, whom he contacted the following day, October 3. Houghton learned belatedly from Mack that the State Department had set up the Future of Iraq Project, and that, to his surprise, it included no working group on culture. Mack recalls, "Arthur came to me, he said, 'You asshole, you didn't set up a working group for archaeology.' I said, 'Thank you for telling me, Arthur, but it's a little bit late and it's not in my hands anymore anyway. But you can go talk to the people in the State Department.'"[27] (By that point, the Future of Iraq Project had been officially acknowledged by and moved into the State Department.)

Already at this early point in their collaboration, there was friction between Houghton the ex-curator and Gibson the archaeologist. When Houghton broached the idea of including the Metropolitan Museum in the effort, Gibson balked, leading Houghton to retort that "even if one has misgivings about the interests of collecting museums, it is not wrong to have an elephant such as the Met on one's side."[28]

What lay behind Gibson's recalcitrance about the Metropolitan was his deep suspicion of the motives of Houghton and the crowd of wealthy collectors, antiquities dealers, curators, and lawyers he ran with, a group that was in the process of formalizing itself into the American Council for Cultural Policy (ACCP). Gibson's fear, shared by many other archaeologists, was that the ACCP—described by one of its members as "a think tank for collecting issues"—was really interested not in safeguarding antiquities from theft or destruction, but in liberalizing Iraq's strict export laws once the war was over. It was not an unreasonable supposition, especially given Houghton's own comments, mentioned above, urging that "some thought should be given to what may emerge" with regard to "cultural property protection, etc., in a post-Saddam world." The ACCP was well known for opposing "retentionist" policies that prevented the free trade in antiquities across national boundaries from "source" nations like Iraq into collections private and public.[29]

It is easy to see in this position a strong element of self-interest on the part of dealers, collectors, and museums wishing to enrich themselves or their collections. But the ACCP and its defenders frame their mission in much loftier terms, as serving the interests that all people have in what philosopher Kwame Anthony Appiah has called a "cosmopolitan aesthetic experience."[30] "I value collecting, the movement of art across national boundaries, in the same way that I value the movement of ideals and people across national boundaries," explains Gary Vikan, director of the Walters Art Museum in Baltimore.[31] Vikan explains elsewhere that he grew up in Romania, under Ceausescu, "and it seemed to me that the worst thing was that people, and ideas, could not cross borders. So with art. It carries ideas, and it needs to move."[32]

Art may not just be trapped, however, but actively oppressed within a country, so that its need to move may be justified as a matter of survival. The easiest case for this justification of free movement of antiquities comes when they are threatened by the very governments that ought to be preserving them. Under the Taliban, for example, it might have made more sense for UNESCO to have authorized the shipment of artifacts from the National Museum of Afghanistan to a safekeeping repository specially created in Switzerland, rather than blocking it, leaving the items to be smashed to pieces by hammer-wielding mullahs. That extreme example, of course, has nothing to do with the antiquities market, but from the collectors' point of view, what the Taliban did with malign intent is what other "retentionist" countries are doing through incapacity to care for their own patrimony.[33] Under these conditions, as Ashton Hawkins, former chief counsel of the Metropolitan Museum, put it, "legitimate dispersal of cultural material through the market is one of the best ways to protect it."[34]

From the archaeologists' point of view, this argument is absurd, since it lays the blame on governments for failing to address a problem for which the collectors themselves are really to blame. Without their fueling of a market for antiquities that dealers themselves peg, very conservatively, at around £300 million per annum for *legally* traded Mediterranean antiquities alone, there would be no profit in illegal digging.[35] And to think that illegal digging would cease if fewer restrictions were put on the legitimate market strikes archaeologists as at best wishful thinking unsupported by the little we know about how legalized markets work in countries such as Israel.[36]

If the cosmopolitan perspective Appiah associates with collecting really were held by collectors, moreover, one would expect to find wealthy collectors and museums donating funds to assist countries, organizations, or even individuals in their efforts to stem illicit digs. But, *pace* Appiah, collectors show no sign of valuing the knowledge of the past that is being irretrievably lost when sites are despoiled in the quest for the one beautiful artifact. They tend to privilege the individual object while often disregarding the value to be gained from knowing where, when, and how it originally was used. Provenance, for the major collectors, seems to count for very little in the decision to acquire:

one study of seven major antiquities collections exhibited in leading U.S. museums concluded that approximately 75 percent of the 1,396 antiquities in the collections were of unknown origin, with many surfacing for the first time well after the passage of national antiquities regulations.[37]

Small wonder, then, that Gibson suspected that what the ACCP was really after was a chance to lobby for changes in those regulations. Houghton tried to reassure the archaeologist on this score, professing that rewriting Iraq's antiquities laws "is far beyond the interest of the ACCP, which would have no interest in involving itself at this level of advice or intervention." Perhaps not, but the group, which held its inaugural meeting October 9, 2002, at the apartment of Uzbek textile collector Guido Goldman, was certainly no bunch of shrinking violets. Among the attendees were Houghton; outspoken collector Shelby White (soon to come under a legal cloud related to antiquities the Italian government claimed were illicitly acquired); legal scholar Professor John Merryman, author of the classic paper laying out the argument for "internationalism" and against retentionism; and William Pearlstein, a lawyer with a client list that included the National Association of Dealers in Ancient, Oriental and Primitive Art (whose former president, Frederick Schultz, had been sentenced in June 2002 to almost three years in jail for violating the National Stolen Property Act by smuggling Egyptian antiquities).

With the exception of Merryman, all these attendees were power-players, not think-tankers. All may have shared the ultimate goal of liberalizing antiquities trade laws, but the immediate objective was to protect Iraq's antiquities from the effects of war. That required access, and access was something the ACCP understood how to achieve. As Houghton, an old State Department hand, knew, it would take "more than simply a telephone call to somebody in a low-level position" to get the government's attention.[38] What was needed was a full-scale use of communications channels. The ACCP decided to pursue a three-pronged public strategy: op-ed pieces, public statements, and closed-channel communications with the government. The core group consisted of Houghton, ex–Metropolitan Museum counsel Ashton Hawkins, and Max Anderson of the Association of Art Museum Directors, who was approached after this meeting.

Quickly, Houghton set to work, crafting a letter to the secretaries of state and defense and the national security advisor, as well as others in the concerned departments and the Joint Staff. These letters, the first known effort by cultural heritage interests to contact U.S. officials, asked that forces avoid damage to monuments or sites; that upon the cessation of hostilities, soldiers respect the integrity of sites and monuments; that the United States encourage any new administration in Iraq to move quickly to establish security for its own monuments, sites, and museums, especially through reconstituting the antiquities service; and—in a jab based on the difficulties Houghton had encountered trying to find his way in—that "an appropriate governmental planning mechanism be created" before the conflict to focus on these concerns.[39]

Missing from this list of demands, despite the generically expressed concern for post-conflict security, was an explicit, red-flag reference to the looting that had occurred in Iraq's regional museums and on archaeological sites in no-fly zones established after the 1991 war. Worries about post-combat site and museum security, the letter implied, were long-term reconstruction problems that could be taken care of by the Iraqis themselves. The U.S. military's attention, the letter seems to indicate, should focus on avoiding doing damage itself to sites and museums, rather than preventing others from doing so.

Framing the issue this way reflected not just the ACCP's but also the archaeological community's view, at least in the fall of 2002, of what the central threat was and of how postwar securing of cultural sites should be addressed. The ACCP, in fact, had approached the Archaeological Institute of America (AIA) and several other organizations to ask them to endorse their statement.[40] The AIA chose not to sign it—not because it did not emphasize the threat of looting, but rather out of fear that its support of the resolution might be misinterpreted or misrepresented as meaning it supported the ACCP's position on liberalizing Iraq's antiquities laws.

Using his personal connections and working the phones, Houghton made sure that the letters got into the hands of as many high-level officials as possible. The ACCP followed up on its letter-writing campaign with an op-ed piece by Hawkins and Anderson in the November 29, 2002, edition of the *Washington Post*. The op-ed was designed not to promote public awareness so much as to ratchet up the pressure on those officials who had already read the ACCP's letter. "Scholars in the United States familiar with Mesopotamian and Islamic history and archaeology are willing and able to assist in designating sites and locations of special cultural and religious importance," Anderson and Hawkins wrote. "To whom should they speak?"[41] The aim was to get the attention of the White House and to obtain a meeting with high-level officials at the Department of Defense, which Houghton had already learned was tasking a group of targeters to draw up a "no strike" list of key sites. Gibson found this news from Houghton reassuring, imagining that the targeting group would probably be building on the list he and Adams had drawn up in 1991 prior to the first Gulf War. "The main concern we all have is the Iraq Museum in Baghdad, since it is in the middle of so many targets," the archaeologist reminded Houghton, but it was on the 1991 list, so it would have been protected this time around as well.[42]

Meanwhile, Gibson worked his own contacts. Just before Thanksgiving, on November 21, 2002, he sent a letter to Ryan Crocker, an old acquaintance from decades earlier when Gibson had been running digs in Iraq and Crocker had been posted there as a diplomat. Ticklish about getting involved in what could be construed as political advocacy, Gibson described himself as representing an independent research group, the American Association for Research in Baghdad (AARB), rather than the University of Chicago. He was writing, he told Crocker, to make the State Department aware that there was an organized body of American scholars and academic institutions concerned for the safety of Iraqis and feeling a particular responsibility for archaeological sites. Reminding the diplomat that the U.S. military had made a special effort to avoid such sites in the 1991 Gulf War, Gibson urged paying special attention to the National Museum. "Even if the museum survives bombing, in the chaos of war it will probably suffer major looting," Gibson said pointedly, in the clearest and earliest warning of what ultimately did transpire. This was not a paranoid fantasy, Gibson emphasized: "During the period of the Embargo, hundreds of archaeological sites in Iraq have been subjected to unparalleled, systematic looting," which the State Board of Antiquities has been powerless to prevent. He added, "We would hope that the museum would be placed high on a list of buildings to be secured and respected by any occupying force." In the long term, the AARB recommended maintaining and enforcing Iraq's current antiquities law, one of the best in the Middle East.[43]

Although Gibson did not know it, he could not have picked a better target for such recommendations than Crocker, one of the key organizers of the Future of Iraq Project. Yet, inexplicably, Gibson's intercession received no response from the diplomat, and no steps were taken at this point to develop a focus on cultural heritage protection within the Future of Iraq Project.

A similar declaration crafted by the Archaeological Institute of America at their annual meeting in December 2002 and sent to the Pentagon in January 2003 also drew no direct response. In its statement, the AIA mentioned the usual need to protect cultural heritage in the case of war and to help repair and recover cultural goods after the end of hostilities. But, it added,

> it should also be recognized that following the 1991 Gulf War, archaeological sites and museums in Iraq were looted on a large scale, with stolen antiquities appearing on the art markets in Western Europe and the United States. We therefore call upon the appropriate governments to take reasonable actions to prevent such looting in the aftermath of war. This includes assisting with security, as well as rebuilding, of museums and sites, providing training for professional staff. Academically-degreed staff who are now working in neighboring countries must be brought back; guards for archaeological sites and overseers who are responsible for antiquities in larger administrative areas must be rehired or replaced. It also means maintaining and enforcing the strong legal framework within Iraq that today serves to protect its archaeological heritage through, among other provisions, state ownership of sites and archaeological objects.[44]

"We wanted a statement that was more comprehensive and didn't just address the bombing," said Patty Gerstenblith, a DePaul University law professor who, with Gibson, helped spearhead the AIA's efforts. This paragraph certainly addressed more than the bombing. But by not stressing that the 1991 looting began *immediately* after the no-fly zones were created, and by adverting to legal frameworks operating in peacetime, it drew attention away from its point about needing to secure sites from looting during the lawless period directly after the fall of a government.

In any case, it was bombing, not looting, that preoccupied the Pentagon, since only the former was clearly prohibited by international law that the United States observed. As 2002 drew to a close, an Internet news article reporting on the Pentagon's efforts to protect sites made no mention of the potential for post-conflict looting, but focused instead on what the military was doing to avoid targeting cultural sites.

Because the phrase "protecting cultural sites" has no necessary predicate, it was possible for archaeologists and war planners to misunderstand— or willfully ignore—what this might entail. Over the next two months, cultural protection advocates and war planners would dance around the distinction between preventing destruction from active combat operations and preventing looting in a way that left advocates thinking the problem had been flagged.

In late December or early January, the American Council for Cultural Policy's publicity barrage finally began to pay off. Hawkins received a phone call from a local CIA office saying they had seen the op-ed piece and wished to meet with the ACCP. Houghton thought it odd, as from the ACCP's point of view this was not a foreign intelligence issue. In any event, it was a Defense Intelligence Agency (DIA) officer, not a CIA agent, who met with Hawkins and Houghton—not because of the op-ed, but because of the letter they had sent, which had found its way to the Defense Intelligence Agency via channels that are still unclear. Already working on a no-strike list of other kinds of sites, the DIA now turned to the ACCP for help in gathering information about cultural and archaeological ones.

It was an odd choice. The ACCP—an interest group of dealers, curators, and collectors—had no expertise whatsoever on the technical issue of mapping archaeological sites. Moreover, the Archaeological Institute of America, whose membership included many who had actually excavated sites in Iraq, was already gathering information at the behest of the State Department's Bureau of Educational and Cultural Affairs (ECA), which had begun belatedly working the issue on a parallel track with public diplomacy officers from the Bureau of Near Eastern Affairs.[45] Bonnie Magness-Gardiner and Maria Kouroupas of the ECA contacted archaeologists Zainab Bahrani, Elizabeth Stone, McGuire Gibson, and others to compile a list, with geographical coordinates included, of the top ten or fifteen most important sites to be protected from destruction during an invasion.[46] The DIA was unaware of these efforts, apparently.

During this period, Bahrani and other archaeologists began almost daily phone and e-mail contact with British colleagues, primarily Nicholas Postgate and Eleanor Robson, who were organizing their own lists. Like their American counterparts, the British were writing op-eds and letters to the press, and putting up a Web site as well. "A lot of that was done without regard for any government agencies, on our own," Bahrani notes.[47]

But efforts to influence public opinion were highly unlikely to succeed in getting the attention of war planners or politicians. What was needed was lobbying expertise, something the archaeologists sorely lacked. Neither the Archaeological Institute of America nor the American Schools of Oriental Research, financially straitened organizations both, employed a lobbyist or even a policy professional on their staffs, which were located in Boston rather than Washington.[48] The Society for Historical Archaeology and the Society for American Archaeology (SAA) did run Washington offices, and the SAA—alone among the organizations mentioned—had a full-time paid government affairs specialist on its staff. But the SAA's focus was on the archaeological heritage of the Americas (it lobbied for increasing funding for America-based archaeology and on legislation such as the Native American Graves Protection and Repatriation Act), and it took no interest in the Iraq issue until just before the outbreak of the war.

Either because the archaeologists were soliciting the wrong agency (the State Department rather than the Pentagon or military) or not directing their efforts to the government at all, or because the ACCP had been more savvy about its letter-writing campaign, it was the ACCP that ended up getting invited to what turned out to be the highest-level meeting to take place at the Department of Defense during the prewar period regarding site protection of cultural heritage. Well aware that they had nothing concrete to provide to the Pentagon targeters, but eager to press the general case for paying attention to the danger faced by Iraq's heritage, Houghton and his ACCP colleagues turned to Gibson. The archaeologist knew he was the odd man out in the delegation that eventually went to Washington for the meeting. "There was only one archaeologist there—me," Gibson recalls. "The rest were artifact collectors and lawyers, the people from ACCP. I only went along to put my own point of view across, which was to plead for a minimizing of the bombing of known archaeological sites. But I wouldn't have stood a chance of getting a meeting with the Defense Department without the ACCP."[49]

Gibson's relations with the ACCP had become tense at this point, in part because he had agreed to attend the Pentagon meeting only with the proviso that his role not be publicized. "There was a question of my own reputation," Gibson explains. "I did not want to be seen as part of a group that is composed, to a great extent, of ravenous collectors, dealers, and a few museum people. This group has diametrically opposed aims to mine or any other archaeologist." Yet his name was dropped nonetheless and appeared in an Internet article that had been reprinted in Arabic by at least two prominent newspapers, with Gibson prominently mentioned. "I really appreciated that," the archaeologist remarked sardonically to Houghton.[50]

Gibson passed on to Houghton the news that the Archaeological Institute of America was preparing a list to present to Rumsfeld directly through a connection, but no consideration seems to have been given to having AIA representatives join the meeting in Washington, probably because the AIA and the ACCP were, and remain, mortal enemies over the non-war-related issue of the relation between antiquities collecting and looting. Despite being engaged in the same prewar quest for attention to be paid by the U.S. government, the two groups made no contact with each other until after the museum had been looted—a disunity of effort by cultural heritage advocates that paralleled the disunity of effort within the government.

Soon after the spat over the Internet article outing Gibson, Houghton reported to the archaeologist another successful contact by the ACCP with war planners. Hawkins, the former Metropolitan Museum legal counsel who was one of the leaders of the ACCP, had received a letter from Deputy Under Secretary of Defense William Luti. Luti did not mention the meetings with Collins and the State Department but, Houghton said, "suggested that information on cultural sites to be avoided could be sent to them or to [Faisal] Qaragholi in the Iraqi National Congress [INC] in London."[51] (Qaragholi is a petroleum engineer who directed the London office of the INC.) Luti was the highest-ranking American official to respond to the prewar concerns raised by the cultural heritage community. His apparent ignorance about the impending meeting at the Department of Defense suggests that Collins's group was acting on its own mandate from Feith and Abrams to fulfill the military's duty to avoid destroying sites as required by the laws of war, and that Luti was either unaware of or (more likely) indifferent to the existence of Collins's work on this problem.

But Luti's reference to the Iraqi National Congress, as reported by Houghton, is extremely odd. The idea that the INC should be involved in making sure that cultural sites were "avoided" makes no sense, since the INC was playing no role in targeting or troop movement planning. That was being handled by the U.S. military, of course. What Luti may have been thinking about was the post-combat security role that the INC—at least in Wolfowitz's mind—was envisioned as playing. In fact, Luti had met in London with exile leaders in December 2002 to ask them to submit the names of applicants for a force of three thousand pistol-armed Iraqi Civil Affairs officers.[52] But if that was the case, the role of these officers would have been to secure cultural sites, not avoid them.

Assuming Houghton's account of Luti's letter is accurate, it reflects a failure to discriminate between the dangers to cultural heritage and the proper way to address these threats. In hindsight, Hawkins, Houghton, and Gibson all might have taken Luti's letter as a red flag showing that even higher-level policy makers were not registering the need for site protection in the immediate post-combat period. But they were all more concerned, justifiably, with ensuring that no bombs were dropped on the National Museum of Iraq, and no one wrote back to Luti for clarification.

Once the meeting with Collins at the Defense Department was scheduled for January 24, 2003, Houghton quickly shot off a request to William Burns, assistant secretary of state for Near Eastern Affairs, for a second meeting at the State Department. Noting pointedly that the Defense Department had asked to meet with the ACCP to discuss their concerns, Houghton suggested that "it is also important to discuss related longer-range matters, including the creation of an appropriate mechanism that could strengthen measures to protect and preserve Iraq's important villages and cultural monuments."[53] Unlike the letter Gibson had sent weeks earlier to Crocker, Houghton's did the trick, probably because the State Department did not want the Defense Department taking even more control of the post-conflict planning process. Within days a meeting to be chaired by Crocker was arranged for the afternoon of January 24, 2003, following the morning gathering at the Pentagon.

On January 21, just days before the meetings scheduled in Washington with Collins at the Defense Department and with Crocker at the State Department, Gibson got a call from yet another quarter, Civil Affairs officer Col. Gary Wager. Like most of those serving in Civil Affairs, Col. Wager was a reservist who had been mobilized only a few weeks earlier. He was just beginning to pull together information to disseminate to commanders operating on the ground in theater. Wager asked Gibson to send him—what else?—a list of sites in need of protection.

What occurred in the period leading up to the January 24, 2003, meetings at the Pentagon and State Department was a convergence of prewar planners from very different bureaucratic precincts, all with some mandate to attend to the problem of cultural sites in Iraq. The targeting experts in the Defense Intelligence Agency were focused on getting site coordinates; Luti was interested in promoting Wolfowitz's Iraqi-led postwar security force; the State Department's Bureau of Educational and Cultural Affairs had become engaged as well; and Civil Affairs wanted to make sure that site information reached not just targeters but commanders. At the same time, Collins's overburdened Pentagon office, with its links to the U.S. Agency for International Development, also became involved because cultural site protection from harm by U.S. military actions was defined, by whom it is not completely clear, as a humanitarian issue (or perhaps simply as a "phase IV" issue irrelevant to active combat operations).

On the British side, things were just as disjointed, though in a different way. Archaeologists' concerns reached much higher governmental echelons more directly, in part because archaeologists had not just representatives but one of their own in Parliament. Colin Renfrew, a leading scholar of prehistoric cultural innovation in the Near East and Greece, also happened to be Lord Renfrew of Kaimsthorn, a Conservative member of the House of Lords. And Renfrew was not the only member of Parliament interested in antiquities issues. Along with veteran Labour backbencher Tam Dalyell and Lord Redesdale, he led an All-Party Parliamentary Archaeology Group (APPAG) numbering 139 members. (One can only wonder whether the National Museum of Iraq would have been secured if a group this large and powerful had existed in Congress.) The APPAG had been concerned about threats to Iraq's archaeological heritage since at least November 2002, when one of its members had read a letter published in the *Financial Times* by Harriet Crawford, chair of the British School of Archaeology in Iraq. At the APPAG's request, Crawford generated a short memo laying out the threat; she also took the liberty of sending a version of the memo herself, on December 27, 2002, to the head of the Middle East Department at the Foreign Office, Edward Chaplin.

This was a promising beginning. The response of the government, unfortunately, was to give the archaeologists the runaround. Having heard nothing from Chaplin's office after a month, Renfrew enclosed Crawford's memo in a letter sent by the All-Party Group to Prime Minister Tony Blair on February 11, 2003, in which they warned that Iraq's archaeological sites were "vulnerable to looting in the event of civil disorder." Getting no response, Renfrew submitted a question for written answer on February 24 and got a canned answer about legislation. Dalyell, in turn, was assured by Blair that "we will do everything we can to make sure that sites of cultural or religious significance are properly and fully protected,"[54] but again the focus was on protecting sites as obligated by the Geneva Conventions, which do not address the threat of looting.

Dissatisfied, Renfrew pressed for an answer to his concerns. On March 24 he was told that the prime minister had asked the Foreign and Commonwealth Office to respond, but that at this point, with the war starting, no letters could be produced; Renfrew replied asking whether they had at least gotten his point about the vulnerability of sites to looting. On April 2, Renfrew wrote again to Blair, copying the heads of the Foreign and Commonwealth Office and of the Department for Culture, Media and Sport (DCMS). To the latter, Tessa Jowell, he added a note about "the slightly strange situation which has arisen concerning the problem of archaeological sites in Iraq," making Jowell aware that despite his warning, "no specific planning has been made." On the floor of the House of Lords, Renfrew asked Blair's government directly, "Has any detailed guidance been given?" Renfrew had in mind guidance about protecting sites from looting, but once again he got the runaround. Lord Bach responded that the military was observing the relevant Geneva Conventions, had drawn up a list of cultural property, would not attack cultural sites, and would take seriously any forms of indiscipline by UK forces.[55]

Crawford's missive to the Foreign and Commonwealth Office met with much the same fate as Renfrew's appeals. Her December 27, 2002, letter did not actually arrive on Chaplin's desk until January 17, and he did not have time to reply until February 4. Chaplin told Crawford that the FCO was "acutely conscious of this," and that they had passed her letter and attachment on as requested. He did not say to whom, however, and no one from the Ministry of Defence ever contacted her.

Unbeknownst to Renfrew, Crawford, or any of the other officials of the British School of Archaeology in Iraq (BSAI), however, the military had in fact been working in secret with one of their colleagues. On February 2, 2003, Peter Stone, a leading archaeologist but not a specialist in Middle Eastern archaeology, was contacted by a friend who was an officer working in the Ministry of Defence (MoD). Stone was asked to serve as a conduit for passing site coordinates from archaeologists to the military. He turned to Neil Brodie, a specialist on the illicit antiquities trade working at Renfrew's Illicit Antiquities Research Centre at Cambridge University, and to Roger Matthews, BSAI's most recent director. Matthews had already been consulting with Iraqi colleagues about the whole question of protecting sites and museums, and both he and Brodie made sure that Stone warned the MoD that looting was likely at museums based on what had happened in 1991.

On March 31, Stone requested that the MoD hold a briefing session to explain to a select group of archaeologists and politicians all that had been done in secret over the past several months. The MoD confirmed to Stone on April 2 that the American operational plan contained detailed instructions to coalition forces on how to avoid damage to archaeological sites. Stone seems not to have asked the obvious follow-up question: What about protecting them from damage caused by looters after the coalition forces had moved through the area?

That question certainly would have been asked by Renfrew had he been included in the inner circle. But as in the United States, the process was conducted through back channels and with poor consultation with the field. When Renfrew learned after the museum's looting that the MoD had bypassed himself and his colleagues, he was livid. "I am not aware of any individuals with specialist knowledge of Iraqi antiquities currently at the University of Newcastle, nor have I been able to identify which specialist at University College, London, was involved in such consultations," he wrote to Secretary Jowell of the Department for Culture, Media and Sport. "When the history of these unfortunate events comes to be written," Renfrew added tartly, "these matters will perhaps be clarified, and the lack of any direct consultations between Government representatives and the officials of the British School of Archaeology in Iraq who had taken a number of steps to contact them may be explained."[56]

Jowell was a convenient target for Renfrew's rage, but she was merely a scapegoat. Her own department had not been consulted by war planners despite its considerable archaeological expertise. And the archaeologists simply did not have the personal connections with the British military that had been in place for earlier generations of Middle East archaeologists like T. E. Lawrence and Leonard Woolley. As Crawford notes ruefully, "We couldn't find a way into the MoD. We simply couldn't find anybody who we could use as a channel."[57]

Such direct consultations, whether between the British government and archaeological groups or between American war planners and American archaeologists, might have yielded what cultural preservationists regardless of stripe all sought: an effectively organized, unified effort to deal with the several threats that they had identified. That, however, would have required policy intervention from above, within the government, and a unified plan for strategic advocacy by archaeologists and the collecting community. In its absence, what transpired was a tragic series of missed opportunities, misdirected communications, and misstatements, culminating in the looting of the National Museum and the depredation of Iraq's archaeological sites.

FOUR

The Meetings

On January 24, 2003, without having had a pre-meeting to clarify which topics most needed to be addressed, archaeologist McGuire Gibson gathered at the Pentagon with three members of the American Council for Cultural Policy (ACCP)—Ashton Hawkins, former chief counsel for the Metropolitan Museum of Art; former Getty curator Arthur Houghton; and Max Anderson, then director of the Whitney Museum. The group made their way to the Office of Stability Operations. There they were met by its director, Joseph Collins. Collins was accompanied by Caryn Hollis, principal director of his office, and Maj. (now Lt. Col.) Chris Herndon, a Foreign Affairs officer.

The Defense Department, for its part, had a very clear agenda: it had requested the meeting because it needed to fulfill its obligation under international law to protect sites, monuments, and museums from damage or destruction during active combat operations. It was not focused on protecting sites during the post-conflict period—this despite Collins's being charged with attending to post-combat stabilization and reconstruction planning. The ACCP, an organization interested in making it easier to collect and sell antiquities, shared the Pentagon's worry about destruction of artifacts, with looting only a minor concern. (After all, looted antiquities would eventually surface.) Only Gibson—who alone among the participants possessed intimate knowledge as an archaeologist about what had happened and would likely happen again to Iraq's museums and sites in the absence of law and order—

saw looting as a second major threat that the Pentagon needed to be warned to take seriously. This mismatch of objectives between the ACCP and the Pentagon, on the one hand, and Gibson, on the other, together with Gibson's being outnumbered by non-archaeologists, may explain why post-combat looting of museums and sites was treated as a secondary issue.

Just how secondary is a matter of some dispute. The only written record of the meeting is a Memo of Understanding prepared by the ACCP. It makes clear that the central focus of this meeting was on preventing damage or destruction by direct military action, with the issue of looting being raised only at the tail end of the discussion:

Prof. Gibson concluded by mentioning his concern that damage to cultural sites during a possible conflict was likely to be less than what could occur in the aftermath. On one hand, occupying forces might carry away material from archaeological sites, but at least as important was the looting and destruction that could be caused by Iraqis themselves in a situation of political chaos. He noted that in the uprisings that followed the Gulf War, 9 of Iraq's 13 museums were either looted or destroyed. The Baghdad Museum, which he understood was now the collecting point for material from Mosul and perhaps other provincial Museums, was likely to be protected only by a small staff, and was particularly vulnerable.

With regard to the possible looting or damage to sites by coalition forces of occupation, Dr. Collins said he would undertake to have an order issued that he hoped would ensure this did not occur. He noted that orders of a similar nature prohibiting the consumption of alcohol by US forces in certain countries had been effective, and he believed orders preventing looting would also.[1]

Two things are worth noting here. First, the bulk of the meeting focused on Collins's request for geographical information on cultural sites for the Defense Department's "no strike" database. Gibson was left only a fraction of the time to broach the issue of looting, although there is some dispute about how long Gibson spent "mentioning his concern." Houghton recollects the issue of looting as a very minor part of the meeting's agenda: "It must have occupied all of sixty seconds during the discussion."[2] Gibson says Houghton is just wrong on this—"I talked about looting far more than two minutes "—and the archaeologist insists he did so with a specificity left out of Houghton's summary: "I told them that when Baghdad was taken, if they did not secure the bridges over the Army Canal, the poor people in what is now called Sadr City would come over and loot everything that could be moved. I made a special point of mentioning the museum and the sites."[3] Houghton also left out entirely Gibson's explicit dissociating of himself from the ACCP, as well as the archaeologist's discussion of Iraq's record of protecting antiquities (the best in the Middle East) and of the need to retain and strengthen its antiquities organization and laws, something that the ACCP may not have been particularly interested in promoting.

Second, as the memo reveals (perhaps inadvertently), Collins responded to Gibson's warning about the threat of looting by *Iraqis* by referring only to the threat of looting by *coalition forces*. This was a subtle but crucial distinction, since ordering troops not to engage in looting themselves would do nothing to protect the museum or sites from mobs. It is not clear whether Collins intended to deliberately confuse the two issues or simply misunderstood; Herndon, for one, insists that the discussion was about looting by American soldiers, not by Iraqi civilians. Houghton's memo indicates otherwise. What is clear, however, is that both Gibson and the ACCP came away from the meeting with the impression that the Pentagon had agreed to take steps to protect the museum and sites from looting by Iraqis. As Houghton put it, "They listened, they said 'yes.'"[4]

It is also clear, however, that the problem of looting, whether by U.S. forces or by Iraqis, was very low on the agenda: so low, in fact, that news reports of the meeting—most prominently Andrew Lawler's January 31, 2003, *Science* magazine piece—do not even mention that issue.[5] Journalistic accounts instead describe the meeting as focusing on the threat of bombs and troops during battle, with collectors supposedly exploiting the opportunity to push their interest in loosening Iraq's antiquities laws to permit exports. For its part, the ACCP vehemently denies having this end in view, and its official public statements support maintaining Iraq's then-current laws. Lt. Col. Chris Herndon, who was well aware of the ACCP's broader interest in liberalizing antiquities import laws, corroborates that at the January 24, 2003, meeting, there was no effort by the ACCP to bring up any legislative issues whatsoever.[6]

The ACCP eventually released the Memo of Understanding, after taking Gibson's advice on an earlier draft to delete references to working with Iraqi officials in the State Board of Antiquities and Heritage, which Gibson warned would get people killed. After the museum's looting, Gibson's concern for the safety of antiquities officials would be seized upon by conservative apologists for the administration and used to try to discredit him as a Ba'ath sympathizer—even though Gibson's whole point was that the names in the memo should be removed because the Ba'athists were evil enough to be capable of killing Iraqi archaeologists for collaborating with Americans. But in the short run, the criticism came from the opposite side. When news emerged that he was providing site information to the military, Gibson faced some anger from archaeological colleagues. "There were certain people who thought we shouldn't have anything to do with the U.S. government," he recalls, including Robert McCormick Adams, former Smithsonian director and dean of Mesopotamian archaeologists. Adams had collaborated with Gibson back in 1991 to supply site coordinates to the military, but he was adamantly opposed to the idea of invading Iraq. Gibson, he felt, was "way out front of the academic community" and proud of it in a way that Adams felt was wrong.[7]

It is certainly true that anti-war sentiment among archaeologists ran high. Seventy-four scholars felt strongly enough to sign a letter to the editor of the Society for American Archaeology's *Archaeological Record* voicing opposition to U.S. military action against Iraq. Helping the military in any way whatsoever, many felt, would send the wrong signal of encouragement for the Bush administration's project for regime change. Others worried that providing site coordinates would be giving real war-fighting assistance to military action, not merely symbolic support, by making it easier for the military to target places that were not on the site list.[8]

In any case, the Office of the Secretary of Defense got what it wanted from the meeting at the Pentagon: access to good site-coordinates data that would enable the military to comply with the Geneva Conventions by avoiding destruction or damage to sites through bombing or ground action. Over the next several months, right up to the onset of the war, Gibson and others from the archaeological community worked closely with Maj. Herndon and Col. Frank Romano, Collins's uniformed military liaisons, as well as with targeting experts from the Operational Environment Analysis Division of the Defense Intelligence Agency, to identify thousands of sites. These sites were protected from bombing (as were a number of buildings in Baghdad, the National Museum of Iraq among them), a remarkable achievement.[9]

Beyond providing the targeters with coordinates, the Pentagon meeting did have one further effect, though not a happy one. Gibson passed along to the National Museum's research director, Donny George Youkhanna (known as Donny George), news of what had transpired. George then reported it to his superiors, hoping to prod them to start thinking hard about protecting the museum and sites. "I said, 'This is what our colleagues in America are doing,'" George recalls. "'They are putting pressure on the government to avoid any kind of attacks on the museum or the archaeological sites.'"[10] Rather than instilling a sense of urgency, however, George's good deed only deepened suspicion that he was "a friend of the foreigners" who could not be trusted.

Immediately following the meeting with Collins, the ACCP team and Gibson stopped for lunch, where they were joined by Bonnie Burnham of the World Monuments Fund and James Fitzpatrick, counsel for the National Association of Dealers in Ancient, Oriental and Primitive Art and a member of the ACCP. It was an odd social occasion, given the ongoing policy tensions between the parties. As Gibson remembers it, Fitzpatrick started to raise the issue of retentionism at one point but was quickly hushed up by Houghton.

That afternoon Gibson, Houghton, Hawkins, and Anderson, joined by Burnham but not Fitzpatrick, made their way to the State Department for the meeting with Ryan Crocker, the Bureau of Near Eastern Affair's overseer of the Future of Iraq Project. Crocker brought along C. Miller Crouch, deputy assistant secretary for Educational and Cultural Affairs (BECA); Thomas Warrick of the Future of Iraq Project had been expected to attend as well but was detained at the last minute. Assistant Secretary of State Patricia Harrison, Crouch's boss at the BECA, also attended.[11] "What we wanted to get out of it," recalls Houghton, "was the creation of some institutionalized mechanism that would have the issue acknowledged and dealt with."[12] Crocker appeared surprised to learn that of the sixteen working groups in the Future of Iraq Project, none dealt with the problem, and he gave assurances that the State Department would immediately create a new Future of Iraq Project working group on the cultural sector. Asked for some names of expatriate Iraqis qualified and willing to work alongside U.S. participants, Gibson, the only participant at the meeting who could answer such a question, promised to come up with a list of suitable candidates.

If Crocker left the impression of being surprised that no working group had been formed, it must have been either inadvertent or disingenuous, for it had been realized at a very large meeting of working groups in late 2002 that culture had been forgotten, and the Bureau of Near Eastern Affairs had been asked at that point to take the lead in forming a working group on culture. And this was months after the Future of Iraq Project should have been alerted to this missing piece in their nation-building plans. As early as October 3, 2002, Houghton had discussed with David Mack, the Middle East Institute director who had hosted the conference that gave rise to the Future of Iraq Project, the story of an Iraqi jet being placed near the Ziggurat at Ur in the 1991 war.[13] This story alone should have been enough to spur Mack to contact Warrick about setting up a working group on culture, even in the absence of the direct and scathing upbraiding we know that Mack got from Houghton as well for having forgotten about culture. Moreover, as discussed in chapter 3, Crocker himself had been warned in November by Gibson, an old acquaintance, that looting of Iraq's museums and sites was likely to occur if plans were not made to protect them. Yet nothing happened. It was only after the State Department learned that the Defense Department was meeting with the ACCP that diplomats began to focus seriously on the problem.

At this point, events were moving so rapidly that the State Department attendees and Gibson worked on the fly, not even writing up notes about what they had learned from Crocker's convening. Following the meeting, Crouch and Harrison returned to the Bureau of Educational and Cultural Affairs, the only foreign service bureau normally concerned in any way with archaeological interests. Along with other duties, its Cultural Property Office processed requests from other countries to prohibit imports of illicit antiquities under the Cultural Property Implementation Act. Iraq would be in no position to make such a request, either before the war or afterward, but officials in the Cultural Property Office ignored protocol in this exceptional situation and contacted the FBI and Department of Homeland Security to prepare customs to clamp down on imports of Iraqi artifacts after the invasion.

Despite Crocker's command, weeks more would go by before the Future of Iraq Project working group on culture finally convened. A committee including Gibson, Iraqi archaeologist Lamia al-Gailani Werr, legal scholar (and later deputy ambassador to the United Nations) Faisal Istrabadi, and three other Iraqi Americans met at the State Department, along with Marcia Isaacson from the Department of Justice. Their first order of business was not to make sure that sites and museums were secured in the aftermath of conflict, unfortunately. Instead, worried that the ACCP and the Bush administration might use the liberation of Iraq as an opportunity to also liberalize Iraq's stringent controls on the export of antiquities, the group focused on possible changes in Iraq's antiquities laws. They urged Istrabadi, who was also serving on another working group on legal issues, to leave the laws governing cultural property untouched, especially the proviso that declares all antiquities sites and objects to be the property of the state.[14] Although the meeting was supposed to focus on legal issues alone, Columbia University archaeologist Zainab Bahrani managed to add to the agenda the crafting of a wish list of things to be done in the case of occupation. "Number one on that list," Bahrani recalls, "was to put guards at all museums and as many archaeological sites as possible."[15] But it was all far, far too little, too late. By this point, Houghton recalls, "the whole working group apparatus was in the process of collapsing."[16] A State Department official who prefers to remain anonymous recalls, "I only went to one meeting. . . . There were no follow-up meetings [actually, there was one more meeting, just before the war], because there was nothing to follow up on, it's over. I mean, there's a war." The working group on culture produced no report.

It turned out not to matter anyway. As is now common knowledge, Pentagon postwar planners deliberately jettisoned as irrelevant the thousands of pages of analysis and recommendations that were developed by the other working groups for the Future of Iraq Project. "This was a series of seminars, not a plan,"[17] scoffs Collins, a view shared by an independent RAND Corporation review of postwar reconstruction planning. "Although the project enabled the US government to expand its contacts with Iraqi exiles," RAND concluded, "it did not produce plans for Iraqi reconstruction that could be translated into practical action."[18] If L. Paul Bremer III is to be believed, even the Future of Iraq Project's overseer, Ryan Crocker, conceded that the Future of Iraq Project "was never intended as a postwar plan."[19] Some cynics even argue that it was nothing more than a make-work exercise designed to keep the exiles busy.

If the Future of Iraq Project *had* included a working group on culture from the beginning, however; and if this group *had* produced a report that included actionable plans for reconstituting the Iraq State Board of Antiquities and Heritage, paying for guards, and retaining Iraq's strong antiquities laws (all recommended in the letters sent to officials and the op-eds published before the war); and if the Pentagon *had* actually adopted all these reconstruction plans—would the National Museum and the archaeological sites of Iraq been saved from looting? The answer is probably not. Certainly the looting of the museum could not have been prevented by a postwar reconstruction plan focused on bureaucratic and legal solutions, since the museum was overrun in the midst of war, or at least in the window between combat and stability operations, not after the conclusion of hostilities. What was needed during combat and in its immediate aftermath was something much less arcane, indeed something extremely basic: a plan to deploy security forces to prevent sites and museums from being looted. The Future of Iraq Project, a child of the State Department, had no leverage to make the Pentagon heed this need for security in the immediate postcombat period, whether for the museums and sites or anything else.

That basic security considerations had been shortchanged by the Pentagon began to emerge less than two months before the invasion, on February 11, 2003, when the administration made its first formal statement to Congress about its postwar planning.[20] Speaking before the Senate Committee on Foreign Relations, Marc Grossman, the State Department's under secretary for political affairs, admitted that the president had not made a final decision about how to proceed. Grossman offered the committee only the broad-stroke outlines of a three-stage plan for the transition. The first stage, stabilization under an interim coalition military administration, would fall to the Office of Reconstruction and Humanitarian Assistance (ORHA), established only three weeks earlier. This was quite confusing, since normally stability is established before reconstruction begins. Stabilization aims at repressing disorder, a task quite different from that of reconstructing order. The alarm bells set off by Grossman's testimony only rang more loudly after it was clarified by Under Secretary of Defense for Policy Douglas Feith, who followed him to the stand. Feith blithely announced that this newborn agency would be responsible for detailed preplanning for an invasion that everyone knew was weeks away—a signal, perhaps inadvertent, that the administration would completely disregard the six hundred pages of proposals that Grossman proudly reported had been produced by the Future of Iraq Project.

Facing a barrage of criticism following this testimony, administration officials adjusted their public description, announcing on February 20 that the management of postwar Iraq would be overseen by a military regime, with ORHA responsible only for emergency humanitarian aid, and only until that task could be handed off to the UN, whose Department of Peacekeeping Operations was already pulling together a political office modeled on the one it had established in Afghanistan. This was a cleaner structure, in which stability operations—the establishment of security in the immediate post-combat period, which would include the securing of at least some sites and the museums—seemed to have been more clearly placed in the hands of the uniformed military, not the civilian planners at the Department of Defense.

But Tommy Franks wanted nothing to do with the messy and inglorious business of imposing order. His objective, drummed into him by countless harangues from Donald Rumsfeld, was to win, and winning meant toppling the regime. Franks was openly contemptuous of the efforts being made independently by William Luti in the Pentagon, which had finally begun pre-deployment training in Hungary of Iraqi exiles, mostly from the INC, for a variety of post-combat tasks, including that of policing liberated areas, according to Maj. Gen. David Barno.[21] Originally envisaged as generating a force of three thousand—among which, one must assume given Luti's comment to Houghton, at least some soldiers would have been detailed to cultural site protection—this program ultimately would produce a total of only seventy-three trained Iraqi Civil Affairs officers.[22]

In the absence of this force, the administration might have turned to coalition partners to provide military police. NATO, the European Union, and the Organization for Security and Co-operation in Europe had done just that in the Balkans and in Afghanistan after 9/11. But France and Germany opposed the United States' actions this time around, and the two major countries that had joined America's coalition of the willing, Great Britain and Australia, did not maintain constabulary forces.[23] Asked after the invasion about whether war planners could have lined up other countries in advance to provide police units, Secretary of Defense Rumsfeld highlighted the problems this posed, given the way the United States had chosen to go to war:

Most people wanted to defer a final decision until the war—some of them—some of them require a U.N. resolution, they think. Some think they require action by their parliament. Some think they would want to wait until they were in—what do you call it?—stability phase, phase four, as opposed to a kinetic phase.[24]

Rumsfeld's difficulty in recalling the term "stability" speaks volumes about how important phase four was considered to be by senior Pentagon planners.

If militarized police were in short supply in general, military police specializing in cultural heritage protection were even more difficult to come by. Of the two NATO nations with the militarized policing units most capable of addressing the specific security problems of cultural sites—the Netherlands and Italy—only the latter was likely to provide military personnel, but even so, not in the invasion wave. The Dutch (whose CIMIC military cultural heritage experts had deployed to Afghanistan) were opposed to the war and hence loath to commit troops.

The failure to secure commitments for militarized police of any kind from allies meant that it fell to the Pentagon's Office of Reconstruction and Humanitarian Assistance, established only eight weeks before the start of the war, to deal with the problem of post-combat instability. The likelihood of instability had been established in a number of reports issued before ORHA's establishment. Unfortunately, the planning necessary to do what these reports suggested would take the one thing ORHA did not have: time. Postwar planning for other conflicts had taken years, had drawn on many different kinds of specialized expertise, and had involved thousands of troops. At the start of the war, ORHA officials even at the highest levels didn't have such basics as working cell phones and adequate transportation.

Had ORHA been given the time, it is possible it might have developed the capability to field peacekeeping forces, though the structural antagonism between the Pentagon and the combatant command would still have remained a major stumbling block to getting any such force deployed to Iraq in a timely manner. It is important, however, to register that a militarized police force still probably would not have protected cultural sites, given the many security demands it would be fielding. Absent concerted pressure from above and outside the combatant command, the imposition of legal obligations, the establishment of standing specialized military cultural police units, or perhaps all three, it was almost inevitable that those involved in postwar planning would push cultural site protection far down the list of priorities.

The Office of Reconstruction and Humanitarian Assistance certainly did so. Not until three weeks before the war did Gen. Garner even appoint the senior advisor who would eventually be charged with overseeing the cultural affairs of liberated Iraq, as one among several duties. The appointee was not a Civil Affairs archaeological expert or an administrator from the cultural sector, but rather an ambassador, John Limbert. An old State Department Middle East hand and former Iranian hostage, Limbert was highly cultured, having recently published a book on the medieval Persian city of Shiraz and its great poet Hafez. But he had no expertise in Iraq's archaeological holdings or in the hard-nosed practicalities of site protection. Like many of the officials appointed to ORHA, he also had no experience in peacekeeping civil-military operations and had never visited Iraq; his latest ambassadorial posting was to Mauritania.

At first, Limbert was told he would be responsible for the Ministry of Planning, then for the Ministry of Religious Affairs. Only when he arrived in Kuwait a week or two before the war began did the ambassador learn he had been reassigned yet again to tend to cultural matters. When he asked what he was expected to do, the answer was extraordinarily vague: work with existing agencies, providing them with funding to continue operating for sixty days, at which point it was expected that the United States would be ready to turn full authority back over to the Iraqis. Easy enough, thought Limbert. No one, however, could name for him the cultural agencies in Iraq that he should be trying to reconstitute. "I couldn't even find out whether there was such a thing as a Ministry of Culture in Iraq," Limbert recalls. "They said, 'Well, there used to be one; well, we think it might be part of the Ministry of Information but then it split off and we're not sure.'" By the time the museum's looting hit the news wires on April 11, Limbert was still hunting for someone who could provide him this basic information; he was not told about the experts who had been recruited for the Future of Iraq Project working group on culture. "I don't know what they did get done to this day," Limbert recalled in March 2005.[25]

Had Limbert been in the loop—rather, had there *been* a loop—he might have been put in contact not just with the Future of Iraq's working group, but with the two other nongovernmental groups that were already actively involved in the postwar-planning process: the American Council for Cultural Policy (which had met with the Defense and State departments on January 24), and the Archaeological Institute of America (AIA), which wrote in January to Rumsfeld. The AIA in particular was trying hard to play catch-up. Having learned of the ACCP's success in getting into the Department of Defense, AIA advocates began pushing, unsuccessfully, to get their own meeting with Collins. On behalf of the AIA, law professor Patty Gerstenblith had made contact in late January 2003 with Lt. Col. John Moran in the Joint Chiefs of Staff's office. Moran first tried to brush her off by telling her that the Defense Department had already met with the ACCP and had all the information they needed. His reassurance had the opposite effect. Gerstenblith had spent years in political trench warfare against the ACCP, as a public representative on the president's Cultural Property Advisory Committee who also regularly testified before Congress on cultural heritage protection issues. She was not about to trust the ACCP to speak for the archaeological community on something so important. At her insistence, Moran agreed to try to raise the issue with Gen. Garner, who had just been appointed to run the Office of Reconstruction and Humanitarian Assistance.

On February 5, Moran reported that he had tried to see Garner but failed. "I must be honest with you that it looks like they are in the process of standing things up right now," Moran wrote; "for instance, they still haven't received all of the interagency personnel from the various departments."[26] Despite repeated prodding, it was not until March 18,

2003, only days before the war's onset, that the AIA was able to get a message through to ORHA, sending an urgent memo laying out specific concerns about the dangers to sites and museums. The memo—sent by McGuire Gibson to Larry Hanauer, Garner's own special assistant, rather than to Limbert—mentions that archaeologists had provided location information on sites to the military and bluntly states: "The National Museum in Baghdad and the regional museum in Mosul, as well as well-known sites such as Ur, Babylon, Nineveh, Nimrud and Ashur, need immediate security provided by U.S. military personnel to protect them from looting and other destruction."[27] Hanauer, already in Kuwait, may have acted on this information, but he never responded to Gibson, and Limbert was never informed.

Other cultural preservation groups that were belatedly raising their voices also remained unheard. UNESCO's director-general, Koichi Matsuura, had sent a letter to Kofi Annan back in November 2002, after the UN Security Council passed a resolution warning of "serious consequences" if Iraq did not disarm. As described after the fact of the looting of the museum, Matsuura's approach seems almost quaint: the UNESCO head is said to have "draw[n] his [Annan's] attention to the wealth of Iraq's cultural heritage. In this letter, Mr. Matsuura pointed out that this country was a cradle of humanity."[28] It is unclear what effect Matsuura expected his missive to have, especially given the frigid relations between the Bush administration and Annan.

Several months later, as the inevitability of war became undeniable, Mounir Bouchenaki, then assistant director-general for culture at UNESCO, got permission from Matsuura to write to Brian Aggeler, the U.S. observer to UNESCO, and to his British counterpart, warning of the need to prevent damage to cultural heritage should conflict occur and offering to supply a detailed map of the positions of Iraqi archaeological sites and museums prepared by UNESCO's World Heritage Centre. Aggeler replied on March 28, a week after the invasion had begun, assuring Bouchenaki that the State Department had received his information and would take it into account.[29] But there never was a direct contact between UNESCO and the U.S. Army, and it is unlikely that Aggeler, his bosses at the State Department, or the British ambassador to UNESCO could have had any impact on what the military was planning at this very late date.[30]

UNESCO did better in assisting some international organizations to batten down the hatches. It invited Interpol, the World Customs Organization, and the International Confederation of Art and Antiques

Dealer Associations—who must have been unhappy indeed to receive such an invitation—to ensure compliance with the 1970 convention relating to the illicit transfer of ownership of cultural property.

Other organizations besides UNESCO entered the fray. The International Council on Monuments and Sites (ICOMOS), an international NGO dedicated to conserving and protecting cultural heritage places, issued a communiqué on March 6, 2003, calling for all governments to act in the spirit of international conventions protecting cultural property. A week earlier the Society for American Archaeology (SAA), a 7,000-member-strong organization, had also finally gotten involved, writing to Rumsfeld requesting "that occupying military forces make every possible effort to comply with the 1954 Hague Convention for the Protection of Cultural Property in the Event of Armed Conflict and the 1999 Second Protocol [both of which the SAA claimed had been observed in the past] and protect Iraq's unique and priceless cultural heritage housed in museums, cultural institutions, and archaeological sites." The concern in this letter is squarely and explicitly focused on the threat of post-combat looting. "After the 1991 Gulf War," the writers note, "there was widespread looting of museums and archaeological sites." In the case of an occupation, the SAA urged, with breathtaking insouciance about the workings of the military, that units should be established "tasked with protection of Iraq's cultural heritage, including museums, libraries, archaeological sites, and other cultural institutions." These units, declared the SAA, "should ensure that looting does not occur," an obligation set out in article 9, section 1, of the 1999 protocol, which tasks occupiers with prohibiting and preventing illicit digs and trafficking.[31]

Perhaps because it couched its appeal in legal arguments, or possibly because the SAA, unlike other heritage organizations, had a Washington lobbyist, the letter was shunted to the Defense Department's Office of General Counsel, which finally replied on March 18, three days before the start of the war. Its response is instructive. After a bland reassurance that the "Department of Defense recognizes the unique cultural history within Iraq and shares your concerns that this history be protected," the Pentagon lawyers noted that while the United States is not a party to the 1954 Hague Convention for the Protection of Cultural Property in the Event of Armed Conflict or the 1999 Second Hague Protocol, "U.S. armed forces conduct all their operations in accordance with the law of armed conflict, including those provisions of the 1954 Convention and 1999 Protocol that reflect customary international law." What this meant was spelled out in the paragraph that followed:

Contingency plans for Iraq (in the event Coalition action is necessary) specifically address providing assistance to any future government of Iraq to establish protections for Iraq's cultural property. Likewise, during military operations, Coalition forces will operate in accordance with the law of armed conflict and will take the requisite measures to protect Iraq's cultural and historical sites.[32]

While the language here echoes the wording used by the Society for American Archaeology, it fails to specify precisely what Iraq's cultural and historical sites were to be protected *from,* in spite of the pointed emphasis by the SAA upon the need to protect them from looting. The language is deliberately vague on this matter, as well as on the crucial question of what is meant by "requisite measures," again in spite of the SAA's having described in some detail what such measures would entail. It is difficult to read the Office of General Counsel's letter without concluding that at least in that office, the possibility that the museum and archaeological sites might be looted had been understood and responsibility for preventing it evaded.

As war loomed in mid-March, archaeological NGOs took one last stab at publicizing their concerns. In the March 21 edition of *Science* magazine, the Archaeological Institute of America published a "Statement on Cultural Heritage at Risk." At the same time, the AIA sent to the Department of Defense a "Declaration on the Protection of Iraq's Cultural Heritage" signed by almost one hundred archaeologists and a dozen or so archaeological associations from around the world. Perhaps because of the number of signatories involved, both documents are slightly weaker on looting than either the AIA's earlier letter or the SAA's demand that the military ensure that looting did not occur. If the *Science* statement lacked specificity, however, there was more than enough of that in the accompanying opinion piece by Gibson in the magazine's "Policy Forum." For those who read *Science,* Gibson laid out a vivid picture of the war's impact on archaeological heritage:

A new war will mean the damaging of many more sites in the western desert, which is classic "tank country," and if the campaign bogs down for any length of time, sites between the two rivers once more will be the high ground. But the greatest concern of archaeologists, art historians, and historians around the world is for the Iraq National Museum in Baghdad and the Museum in Mosul, as well as our colleagues on their staffs, who will try to protect the collections. Both buildings are close to government buildings that were hit by "smart bombs" in the Gulf War. Even if they survive the bombing, any period of chaos or uncertain control during or after the fighting will render both institutions vulnerable to looting.[33]

Unfortunately, *Science* was hardly a journal likely to get the attention of a war planner, especially at this point, and neither the AIA's statements nor Gibson's op-ed had any discernible impact.

On March 19, 2003, the International Committee of the Blue Shield finally issued a statement as well. It urged working within the spirit of the Hague Convention for the Protection of Cultural Property in the Event of Armed Conflict to prevent damage to or destruction of cultural heritage, stressing the prohibition against using cultural property for military purposes or to shield military objectives (probably a reference to the possibility that Iraq might place jets near archaeological sites, as was done in 1991). While the statement did mention looting in the aftermath of war, it did not call upon governments to take steps to prevent it from occurring, instead suggesting that "in the case of looting of cultural property, detailed plans by trained experts should be prepared for the repatriation or restitution of the property concerned, with the involvement of Iraqi scholars and heritage professionals."[34] This is a depressingly weak approach to the problem of looting by what is supposed to be the leading international organization devoted to war-related cultural heritage issues, amounting almost to an abrogation of responsibility.

Did all these warnings have any effect? Yes, but if the military is to be believed, not much. Questioned after the looting of the museum, Gen. Richard Myers, chairman of the Joint Chiefs of Staff, recalled a warning but indicated that he believed it had been about bombing alone. "And we did get advice on archaeological sites around Baghdad and in fact I think it was the Archaeological—American Archaeological Association [*sic*]—I believe that's the correct title—wrote the Secretary of some concerns," Myers said. "Those were passed to Central Command, and those sites around Baghdad were obviously—we tried to avoid hitting those."[35]

———

While the NGOs issued broadsides aimed at the top of the hierarchy, to little avail, those involved at the operational level were working feverishly in the two months before the onset of the conflict to accomplish what they could before it was too late.

Within the government, a small panic about cultural heritage protection seems to have broken out in several offices that had not been involved before. Shana Dale, chief of staff and general counsel at the White House Office of Science and Technology Policy, was tasked—by whom it is not clear—with pulling together a no-strike list of archaeo-logical sites, despite the fact that this was already well under way in Joseph Collins's office. On January 28, Dale phoned Gibson to ask for a prioritized list of important sites, clearly unaware that he was already helping prepare one for the Defense Intelligence Agency. When Gibson told her he needed to know what the list would be used for in order to be able to prioritize, she refused to tell him. Gibson took offense at this and broke off the conversation, leaving her unaware that Collins's office was involved.[36]

Dale had somewhat better luck with her second call that day. At the suggestion of Dr. John Yellen, archaeology program director at the National Science Foundation, she phoned Henry Wright, curator of Near Eastern archaeology at the University of Michigan Museum of Anthropology. Professor Wright suggested it would make the most sense to have the military send maps or images on which the archaeologists could then simply mark the site locations. Dale agreed to try. She appears to have consulted with her boss, Dr. John Marburger, the president's science advisor, before contacting the National Security Council for help in getting the maps Wright needed. In the meantime, however, Wright attended a meeting in Chicago, where he learned from Gibson that a list had already been compiled and passed on to Collins. A somewhat-miffed Wright politely informed Dale about Collins's efforts, and the following day he got a reply from Dale containing an e-mail message from someone named Tom at the NSC. Tom had spoken to Collins, and they had agreed that it made most sense for Dale to let Maj. Chris Herndon in Collins's office continue to be the point person handling the site-coordinate collecting job.

Though the e-mail trail between Wright and Dale contains no references to the possibility of looting, Wright recalls that he did raise the issue in his final phone conversation with her. "I said the real problem was the museum," Wright recalls. "She said, 'Really? What are you talking about?' She hung up the phone and I never heard from her again."

At around the same time, in early February, Gibson heard from another new office—in this instance new in the literal sense. CENTCOM had realized, at long last, that while it had been focusing hard on planning five different iterations for the first three phases of war (preparation for combat, initial operations, and active combat), it had neglected to plan for phase IV: post-combat stabilization. To rectify this problem, the Joint Forces Command set up a joint task force and sent it off to work on its own in Kuwait, from where Lt. Col. Kraig Kenworthy (one of a tiny number of Marine Corps Civil Affairs officers) contacted Gibson several times to ask for a list of sites in Iraq and for a list of experts on matters cultural.[38]

Adding to the crazy quilt of efforts, by this time the military's Civil Affairs Command had been sensitized to the danger of civil unrest and its potential impact on the museum and archaeological sites. In February the Center for Middle Eastern Studies at the University of Chicago held a two-day crash course for Civil Affairs personnel, organized by historian John Woods at the request of Col. Gary Wager. In McGuire Gibson's presentation, he stressed, among other concerns, the potential for rioting in Baghdad. Wager later passed on to Gibson the good news that this danger had been flagged as well in an early March briefing given by two officers of Iraqi heritage. A few days later, on March 10, 2003, Wager wrote again to Gibson, assuring him that most major commands now knew about the major sites and museums.

Back in Baghdad, the National Museum staff was well aware that looting might break out. "If the Americans attack," Donny George (then director of research at the museum) had warned in February 2003, "the looting of historic sites will be infinitely worse than in 1991. . . . The looters have had time to organize their trade network and build up an international clientele. They are powerful and armed."[39] George had warned the directors of Iraq's State Board of Antiquities and Heritage in December or January, and then again in February, that the museum might be a target of looters. "I suggested doing exactly what the Lebanese did for their museum," George says. "They put everything in the cellars, they sealed all the doors with concrete and iron and kept it there. Over sixteen years of civil war in Lebanon, nothing was lost from the main collection that was hidden."[40]

The Iraqis had themselves evacuated their showcase pieces twice before.[41] But publicly at least, the board was not about to do anything at this point that might imply it doubted their leader's power to protect the country. George recalls:

At another meeting almost a month before the war, I started begging the people, "Please, for God's sake, we have to do something. Now you see that the war is coming." And they said, "You are exaggerating everything. Since Saddam is here, nobody will dare to come to Baghdad." This was their reply. And this for me at that time meant, "Shut up, or we will report you." That is what this meant for me. But I said, "Okay, I have warned you because I am sure if anything happens then the museum will be targeted," and it happened.[42]

4   Some of the artifacts from the National Museum of Iraq that were placed by museum staff in storage containers for safekeeping before the invasion. Photo courtesy of Joanne Farchakh Bajjaly, archaeologist-journalist.

Although the State Board of Antiquities and Heritage pooh-poohed the danger in public, the Ministry of Culture quietly began to take steps to address it nonetheless. A group of five employees was secretly given permission to pack up what they could of the museum. A total of 8,366 of the museum's most treasured objects were removed to an air-raid shelter, with the employees taking an oath on the Qur'an not to reveal their location until it was safe to do so.[43] Donny George, whose friendship with foreigners made him suspect to some of his colleagues, was among the many at the museum who were kept in the dark.

Like the United States, Iraq had no Blue Shield organization to coordinate cultural protection efforts with its military, which in any case had its hands full preparing for the invasion. Instead, the Ministry of Culture sent down orders to supplement the small number of regular museum guards by dragooning the museum's sixty to seventy young archaeologists. Everyone at the museum, including the female director, Dr. Nawala al-Mutawalli, was given a uniform and an AK-47, and units began taking overnight shifts guarding the building.[44]

The museum is located just across the street from a telecommunications center that was bombed in 1991, showering the museum building and garden with debris. Worried that the same target might be struck again this time around, the museum staff dug two shelters on the lawn in front of the building for people guarding the museum to duck into to protect themselves from possible shrapnel. Iraq's minister of culture, Hamid Yousef Hammadi, came by the museum several times to check on these efforts and to make sure that everyone understood what they were being told to do. As Donny George recalls, Hammadi said, "Look here, if the American forces are here, you are not going to defend the museum with these weapons. It's impossible. Your main duty will be protecting the museum if the locals attack it."[45]

While the museum in Baghdad began to batten down the hatches, the same thing began in earnest at other museums around the country. In early March, employees quietly began to consolidate materials, removing everything possible from the Mosul Museum and from Babylon, and depositing forty thousand manuscripts in a bomb shelter. But it was only two weeks before the start of the war that the National Museum of Iraq finally received official permission from the State Board of Antiquities to pack up or sandbag the museum's own vastly larger holdings. Only five people—Donny George not among them—were authorized to take down everything they could carry (there being no elevator in the building). Much was protected as a result, but in the rush several important pieces were left either sitting out or in desk drawers.

The museum's lack of resources for this last-minute effort points to a failure not only by Iraq's government, but also by the international community. The world had recognized, in the 1999 Second Protocol of the Hague Convention on the Protection of Cultural Property in the Event of Armed Conflict, that governments facing war would require financial resources and know-how to take the measures needed to protect their cultural property. The Second Protocol provides for the setting up of a fund for just this purpose. But as of March 2003, the protocol itself still had not been ratified by the twenty states required for it to come into effect. It only came into force in March 2004, and in the four years since then the fund itself, dependent on voluntary contributions from governments or private sources, has received no donations. Even had the protocol been ratified and a fund put in place, however, the international community could not have provided financial assistance directly to the government of Iraq without violating the UN's own sanctions put into effect after the 1991 Gulf War.

While the hands of international organizations may have been tied to some degree, they showed remarkably little initiative in exploring other channels to reach either the Americans or the Iraqis. Despite the publicity accorded the meeting at the Pentagon by the press, for instance, Gibson was never contacted by the World Monuments Fund, ICOMOS, or the International Committee of the Blue Shield. Nor did antiquities ministries or museums in the Middle East contact the National Museum of Iraq. The sole exception was UNESCO, whose assistant director-general for culture, Mounir Bouchenaki, provided Gibson with information about Iraq's sites.[46]

Among neighboring countries, only Jordan maintained contact with Baghdad, reporting a spike in seizures of illicit antiquities from Iraq in the months just before the start of the war. The increase in artifacts seized reflects what archaeologist Elizabeth Stone's careful analysis of satellite photos has revealed to have been a tremendous surge in looting at archaeological sites in January–March 2003.[47] Despite the imposition in November 2002 of new and more severe criminal penalties for archaeological looting (compensating for the Iraqi regime's redeployment of forces away from policing and toward the impending war), the sites were almost totally at the mercy of diggers.

The key concern at this point in the United States, however, was not the sites but the museum. Gibson was happy to learn from a March 14 Reuters report that the building had been sandbagged, with movable items put in storage, and that the museum staff was planning to remain on the premises to guard the collection. This last bit of information raised a new worry, however, which Gibson passed on to Collins, Herndon, and Wager. The source for the Reuters report, Donny George, "is well known to me," Gibson wrote, "and he will, in fact, stay there and if looters come he will try to repel them." Gibson's point was not to alert Collins and the others about the possibility of looting, something Gibson believed was already being addressed for the museum and the sites, both by the U.S. military and, from inside the museum, by its own staff.[48] Rather, it was to make sure American troops entering the museum would not mistake George and other staffers as enemies.

Gibson's certainty that troops would in fact enter the museum and secure it is reflected in his reminder, in the same letter, about the need to not bomb the Central Bank building where treasure had been moved before the 1991 war. Had the treasure stayed in the museum, then "it would have been in no danger" of being destroyed or stolen, he believed. In the Central Bank vault, by contrast, bombing and looting were real threats, and Gibson pleaded for "a way to guarantee that the building is not bombed again and that it will be secured very quickly."

(Ironically, Gibson later discovered that he had been referring the military to the wrong bank building.[49])

Six days later, on the very eve of the war, Collins responded to Gibson's e-mail. The Pentagon planner ignored the question of looting, focusing solely on the targeting issue. There is no guarantee, he told Gibson, that locations will be put on a no-strike list, but the need for occupation and subsequent participation in reconstruction does add weight to the appeal for caution and care in targeting. Collins had forwarded Gibson's message to the Defense Intelligence Agency for the database, he said, but he added pointedly that he was sending it also to CENTCOM intelligence personnel working on Civil Affairs issues and to the State Department. The implication was that the looting problem was not his but theirs.

His reticence was understandable, especially at this point: having just returned from a trip to Kuwait and Turkey to assess preparations for humanitarian relief, he was worried enough to express concern to his superiors about what his memo to them labeled a "Rear Area Forces Gap." The plan, he worried, envisioned deploying "a small attacking force in the South that may have insufficient stay-behind units to maintain law and order behind the advancing troops." He reiterated what he had mentioned in an earlier report, that "all want Carabinieri or gendarme or guardia civile troops for rear area use, during and after combat."[50] No such troops were available, as Collins surely knew.

None of this trepidation, of course, was shared with Gibson, who was led to believe that the troops likely to advance at least had been alerted to secure the National Museum and the bank. Col. Wager informed Gibson on March 19 that he had passed on Gibson's information both to his higher-ups at headquarters and to some Civil Affairs contingents attached to forward units most likely to reach Baghdad first. He warned, though, that in such a fluid situation it is unknown who would reach the museum and the bank first, so he promised to do what he could to get word out to maneuver units and major ground forces commands.

What Wager left out of this already troubling caveat was that Civil Affairs was itself in a state of flux that ultimately would prevent word about cultural site protection from getting out in quite so efficient a manner as he described. As Civil Affairs officer and archaeologist Maj. Chris Varhola describes it, "On the eve of the war, I was the cultural affairs officer and then I was yanked out and we put everybody into population resource control in preparation for a mass exodus."[51]

As war clouds gathered, a few civilians, not trusting either the museum itself or American forces to provide adequate protection, took, or tried to take, direct action. In February William R. Polk traveled to the Middle East on a private diplomatic mission. A member of the State Department's Policy Planning Council in the Kennedy and Johnson administrations who went on to found the Center for Middle Eastern Studies at the University of Chicago, Polk went to Iraq in desperate hopes that he might somehow work out a deal with the Iraqis that would persuade the Bush administration not to attack. He also wanted to safeguard the museum's holdings, however, in the very likely event that he failed. Sometime early in 2003, Polk contacted Arthur Houghton with the idea of saving the National Museum's collection by moving it out of the country. Asked by Houghton about this possibility, Gibson responded that he was afraid there was not much to be done: the Iraqis were pretending there would be no war, and there was no way they would allow the collection to be sent out of the country. He added, "I have repeated numerous times to the military that the museum is vulnerable to looting, and I hope that they have a plan of action for securing the museum, and the one in Mosul."[52]

Polk forged ahead nonetheless. He secured an informal agreement with William P. Carey, head of the W.P. Carey Foundation, that the foundation would underwrite the packing and shipping of the museum's materials, at a cost Polk estimated at only $30,000–$50,000. Then he made his way to Baghdad, stopping first in Amman to feel out the Jordanians to determine whether they would agree to custodianship of the museum's holdings. Polk's plan was to line up the directors of the Smithsonian, the Oriental Institute of the University of Chicago, the Metropolitan Museum, the Museum of Natural History in New York, and the British Museum, then ask the king of Jordan to serve as honorary chairman and agree to house the collection in Amman. He was told, unofficially of course, that Jordan would not consider doing this unless the Iraqis requested that they do so.

In Baghdad a month before the invasion, Polk visited the museum, noting that nothing had been done to protect the collection. Asked why, a museum official with whom he met, recalls Polk, "simply raised his hands and eyebrows in a gesture of resignation, saying, 'What can I do?'"[53] Polk then met with Deputy Prime Minister Tariq Aziz. "I said I was worried [about the museum's safety]," Polk recalls, "but he brushed it aside, saying they had more important things to think about"—an understandable attitude, given the imminence of the conflict. Nothing came of the effort. "If I had been there a month before, it is conceivable I might have gotten something done to ship things out," Polk says now, ruefully.[54]

Wathiq Hindo, a Chicago-based Iraqi businessman who ran a company in Iraq providing security for Gibson's sites, had a less grand but more practical idea than wholesale removal of antiquities: Arm the local guards directly and proactively. Traveling to Iraq just weeks before the invasion, he struck a deal with a local tribal leader to provide eight guards to protect the Mesopotamian city of Kish, in exchange for $300 and a Kalashnikov assault rifle.[55]

Hindo's tactic worked for Kish, but there was neither time nor money nor means to set up any similar arrangements elsewhere. Looting of unguarded sites was already well under way before the start of the war, but even those that had substantial numbers of guards were newly vulnerable with the outbreak of hostilities. On the day the war began, March 20, 2003, guards from Umma came to Baghdad to report that dozens of men had arrived at the site, driven off the thirteen guards there, and begun to loot it. Umma, located south of Baghdad, is, like Isin, a perfect site for looting: only thirty miles north of the main highway, but an hour and a half out in the desert along a track road.

News of this event almost certainly did not reach ORHA's postwar reconstruction planners, who were being literally kept at a distance from CENTCOM in Kuwait, where they were to languish until mid-April. It is also possible that ORHA did not know about another episode of looting that took place on the first day of the invasion in the Iraqi border town of Safwan, where an elementary school was ransacked as American tanks and troop carriers rolled past.[56] By March 26, however, they must have been well aware that looting in the liberated areas behind the coalition advance was endemic: journalists who had been bused in to Safwan to watch aid be distributed by the Kuwaiti Red Crescent Society were attacked by a mob of young men who stripped their bus of its contents in minutes.[57]

At this point someone at the Office of Reconstruction and Humanitarian Assistance finally sent the commanders at the Coalition Forces Land Component Command (CFLCC) a list of sixteen institutions that "merit securing as soon as possible to prevent further damage, destruction and/or pilferage of records and assets." Had Gibson seen the list, he would have been very pleased: the national bank, where Gibson believed some of the museum's treasures to be secreted, is first on the list, the museum second. The Ministry of Oil, which ultimately was guarded, is sixteenth. With a sense of urgency, the memo noted that the National Museum "contains literally thousands of priceless historical objects" and predicted that "[it] will be a prime target for looters," who "should be arrested/detained." "Coalition forces must secure these facilities," the memo warned, "in order to prevent looting and the resulting irreparable loss of cultural treasures."[58]

The prominence of cultural heritage sites on this priority list probably reflects the success of Maj. Chris Herndon, who had attended the Pentagon meeting in January with Gibson and the ACCP and who had assiduously pushed Gibson's recommendations to both the military operations staff and to reconstruction planners in ORHA. It turned out to make no difference whatsoever. More than two weeks after the March memo was sent, ORHA officials would be told it had not even been read.[59]

What CENTCOM *had* read, however, was the operational order stipulating that under international law the military was required to take steps to avoid destroying cultural property through military actions. One touchy question for coalition forces would be what to do about Iraqi military equipment positioned on protected cultural sites. At a briefing in Qatar on March 26, Brig. Gen. Vincent Brooks showed a slide of Iraqi communications vehicles parked on the ruins of Ctesiphon (whose ancient standing arch is the largest in the world), near the museum building, the roof of which sported a blue shield. Although, as one official noted, under such conditions protected sites, even those marked as such, "are legally subject to attack," Brooks went out of his way to reassure reporters that this would not happen. "We remain committed to preserving the rich culture and heritage and the resources of the Iraqi people," the general said. "The regime continues to put them at risk."[60]

Brooks's remarks were reported in the next day's *Wall Street Journal,* in an article that quoted Gibson, Gerstenblith, and archaeologist John Malcolm Russell on the risks to Mesopotamian heritage not just from military action but also from post-combat looting. Readers might well have missed the latter emphasis, however, given the article's title, which highlighted the archaeologists' fear that "Fighting in Iraq May Destroy Trove of Mesopotamian Antiquities" without indicating that looting was also a concern.[61] Nor was that anxiety voiced at Brooks's briefing by journalists, who for obvious reasons were more concerned about loss of life in the bombing of Baghdad.

By April 4, with U.S. forces having reached the outskirts of Baghdad and taken control of the airport, two things seemed clear: the combat phase of the war would soon be over, and the military was successfully avoiding causing damage to cultural sites both from the air and on the ground. A Pentagon spokesman had gone public with this policy, adding that the military had distinguished between "no fire" areas that should be kept immune from bombing or missile attacks, and "restricted ordnance" sites that could be attacked if Iraqi troops or irregulars were occupying them, but not with heavy weapons.[62]

The war seemed nearly over. Gibson took the opportunity to write to Collins at this point, recapitulating the prewar efforts that had been made by those concerned about protecting antiquities and other cultural heritage. He did this in order to alert Collins—and through Collins, Luti, who was suspected by archaeologists of having secret dealings with the American Council for Cultural Policy[63]—that "to let the ACCP have influence in the reconstruction of Iraq is to allow the fox into the hen house."[64] Any offers of technical help by the ACCP, Gibson wanted Collins to know, would be matched by AIA-affiliated museums and university groups, and the American Association for Research in Baghdad (AARB). The archaeologist reminded Collins that it was in the name of the AARB that Gibson—not the ACCP—had provided the site coordinates sought by the Pentagon.

Gibson also sought in this e-mail to warn Collins, in the most graphic terms yet between the two, about the likely looting of sites, which he noted needed to be stopped by the United States in accordance with the 1954 Hague Convention. Looting and smuggling had been going on throughout the period of the embargo, Gibson pointed out, and probably were occurring even while the war continued. "If the guards run from their duties," he wrote, apparently unaware this had already happened at Umma, "especially on isolated sites in the desert between the rivers in the south, the looters will go right in and resume their work with front-end loaders."[65] Gibson even suggested a quick fix: helicopter flyovers guided by State Board of Antiquities members would halt the looting.

Gibson had in mind the deployment of American troops accompanied by one or two Iraqis to show them where to fly. But his suggestion about working with the Iraqi State Board of Antiquities and Heritage gave Collins the opportunity to once again pass the buck on looting from Stability Operations to Civil Affairs. He sent Gibson's message on to Col. Frank Romano, who had taken over as liaison officer for Chris Herndon. Romano let Gibson know that he had in turn forwarded the archaeologist's e-mail to the Civil Affairs staff at CENTCOM and to the Defense Intelligence Agency targeters involved in mapping sites for the humanitarian relief effort. "As you know," Romano told Gibson, "cultural relations is one of the functional specialties for Civil Affairs."[66]

FIVE

A Punctual Disaster: The Looting of the National Museum of Iraq

Beginning on April 5, a small but lethal force of twelve thousand soldiers—with not a single Civil Affairs military officer in its ranks—punched into Baghdad in a series of "thunder runs." Over the following few days, the tank crews secured only two buildings, the Palestine Meridien Hotel (where foreign journalists were holed up preparing to report on the toppling of the statue of Saddam on April 9) and the Ministry of Oil.

Even as the battle for Baghdad was being joined, CNN reported on April 8 that looting in Basra was already rampant and that mobs were beginning to loot on the outskirts of the capital. Asked about what the United States planned to do in Baghdad to prevent this from spreading throughout the city, Brig. Gen. Vincent Brooks responded with a generality, a litotes ("It's not unexpected"), and a disavowal:

We know that there is often in liberated areas a vacuum in terms of control, especially when you've had as tight a grip as this regime has had on its people for so long. When that's pulled out of the way, humans make decisions about what they're going to do next and what opportunities may be presented to them.

I think as time goes on more law and order will be established, ideally that goes by way of the Iraqi populations taking care of themselves. That's how we see this, not something that's a military control over top of all people, and this will settle down as time goes on. It's not unexpected. We might see it anywhere where there's a temporary vacuum that forms and law and order is pulled away.[1]

Brooks was correct to note that liberated areas in which there is a power vacuum often experience looting: the United States had its own experience of this in Panama City after the overthrow of Noriega, in the no-fly zones of Iraq in 1991, and in the suburbs of Sarajevo in 1992.

But if looting was "not unexpected" in any such situation, what about this one? The puzzled reporter followed up by asking whether this meant that the U.S. military expected Baghdad to be looted. Brooks responded by reiterating his position in an even more passive form and more ornate litotes: "I think anywhere that we have circumstances like this and there is a removal of structures of control there will be decisions that are made by members of the population. We would certainly discourage that, but I can't be certain that it won't happen in this case."[2]

Back in Kuwait, William Sumner was growing anxious. A Civil Affairs reservist in the army's 354th Civil Affairs Brigade, Sumner had been called up a few months before the invasion and tasked with handling arts, monuments, and archives (one of sixteen so-called "special functions," a catchall area covering civil functions other than government, economics, and public facilities). His master's degree in archaeology gave him a leg up on most of his fellow officers. "In most of these skill areas, people were not adequately trained," Sumner recalls. "The guy responsible for public works and utilities was a financial planner, the econ and commerce guy was a fireman. I was an oddity because I actually had skills in the area I was assigned to." He was told that his unit would be established in Baghdad and that his job would be to assess the city's monuments, sites, and museums (as well as the national zoo) to determine what was damaged and what was required for repairs or conservation. This information was supposed to be passed up to the supporting division via his commander. Sumner also controlled a discretionary fund of $200,000 for use in Baghdad. None of this touched on security, however, which would have to be worked out through requests made to combat divisions on the ground. Sumner himself had no firepower whatsoever for securing sites or even for his own safety: "We had a couple trucks, a few pistols, and a rifle if we were lucky. Armored vehicles were science fiction; my truck was stripped down as much as I could so it could go faster. Our philosophy [in Civil Affairs] is to break contact and get out of the area as fast as possible."[3]

Not that Sumner had thought much about security for the museum as a problem with which he would have to deal. He had been working since February to compile his own maps of monuments, sites, and museums with many archaeologists, including Harriet Crawford, Eleanor Robson, and Nicholas Postgate from the British School of Archaeology, as well as another archaeologist from the British Museum whose name Sumner can no longer recall. None of the archaeologists had raised the possibility that looting might occur, and Sumner did not ask. "I thought there would be plans to take care of securing the museum," he explains.[4] But such plans had not been developed by either Sumner's Civil Affairs superiors in the army or those of his counterparts in the marines. According to marine Lt. Col. Peter Zarcone, commander of the Civil Affairs detachment for the First Marine Infantry Division, the postwar Civil Affairs planners at corps headquarters in Kuwait "didn't foresee the marines as going out and assigning marine units as security." He adds, "The issue of archaeological sites was considered a targeting problem" to be dealt with by those flying bombing sorties.[5]

Once the war began, Sumner remembers, "we saw what was going on," and around April 8, Sumner started asking to be sent forward to begin assessing the state of affairs in Baghdad, even though combat operations were still ongoing. Worried that the museum might have been forgotten, Sumner went to see army Brig. Gen. John Kern, commander of the 352nd Civil Affairs Command, and asked him point-blank what the plan was to secure the museum. Kern, recalls Sumner, "looked at me and said, 'Captain, if you don't think that commander is securing that museum, you don't know what you are talking about.'"[6]

Like Sumner, the archaeological community grew increasingly alarmed about the fate of the museum as word began to leak out about growing and unchecked chaos in Basra. As radio reported that the looting had spread to Basra's banks on April 10, archaeologist McGuire Gibson e-mailed Lt. Col. Kraig Kenworthy, a marines' Civil Affairs operations officer who had been assigned to deal with cultural issues (among others) by the Combined Joint Task Force in late January. Gibson made clear what a similar sacking of Baghdad's banks might mean: "If the mobs hit the safe-deposit vault of the Central Bank," he noted bluntly, "they will have access to the most important objects from the Iraq National Museum, and they will see them as mere gold to be melted down."[7]

Concern also touched on what might ensue at Nineveh, Babylon, Ur, or hundreds of other fabled Mesopotamian ruins. Joining forces, the Archaeological Institute of America (AIA) and the American Association for Research in Baghdad (AARB) shot off a letter to Powell, Rumsfeld, Bush, and Blair urging that "the United States and Britain undertake emergency measures to protect the cultural heritage of Iraq from destruction through the looting of archaeological sites. These sites, located throughout Iraq, are now presumably unguarded unless the Coalition forces immediately provide the necessary security." The letter specifically called on coalition forces to "provide immediate security, where necessary, for museums and major archaeological sites, to make public statements condemning the looting of sites and museums and warning that cultural objects removed from Iraq are stolen property; and, where necessary, to make appropriate shows of force to stop looting until a revived Department of Antiquities can reestablish normal controls."[8]

These steps, the AIA and AARB argued, are prescribed by the 1954 Hague Convention, which imposes the duty to undertake to "prohibit, prevent and, if necessary, put a stop to any form of theft, pillage or misappropriation of, and any acts of vandalism directed against, cultural property." The writers noted that the Department of Defense had publicly stated they would observe this convention, citing the language used in the Defense Department's response to the Society for American Archaeology: "U.S. armed forces . . . conduct all their operations in accordance with the law of armed conflict, including those provisions of the 1954 Convention and 1999 Protocol that reflect customary international law." This reminder seems to have been meant not just for Bush et al., but also for James Burger, the Defense Department's general counsel, to whom a copy of the letter was forwarded. Unfortunately, the context of the provision cited makes it clear that it was intended to cover theft or pillage by warring parties, not civilians.

A copy of this letter was also e-mailed to others involved more directly in operations, including Larry Hanauer at the Office of Reconstruction and Humanitarian Assistance, Donald C. Leins at OSD-Policy, and Maj. Chris Varhola of the U.S. Army Civil Affairs Command. Varhola, an anthropology graduate student interested in archaeology, was already in the Middle East at this point but hardly in a position to issue the kind of orders required. He could only gnash his teeth at the cover message Gibson had added. Gibson stressed "the necessity of halting and preventing looting of archaeological sites, monuments, and museums in Iraq" and urged "that coalition forces be made aware of the necessity for guarding sites and museum and doing their utmost to prevent looting and desecration of sites and the plundering of the cultural treasures stored in Iraq's museums, and in particular the National Museum in Baghdad, which is especially vulnerable to the chaotic situation in Baghdad at this moment."[9]

Waking early on April 10, Gibson sent a similar message to Capt. John Gurney, one of the targeters with whom he had worked, reiterating that the main priority was securing the National Museum of Iraq and one of the buildings of the national bank. If possible, helicopter flights should also be dispatched to seven specified sites that Gibson noted "are being looted even today, while the war is going on." Gibson also e-mailed Lt. Col. Kenworthy, Civil Affairs Col. Gary Wager, and Col. David Undeland of CENTCOM, who had contacted him and Elizabeth Stone in February for targeting coordinate information. "The looting in Basra and Baghdad is appalling and completely predictable," Gibson wrote, adding anxiously, "I am particularly concerned with the Iraq National Museum, which should have been taken yesterday or today. Can you tell me anything about it and our colleagues, the museum staff who are inside and who will try to repel looters? I am getting lots of questions about the museum and would like to stop speculation about it."[10]

That same morning, Gibson and fellow archaeologists John Malcolm Russell, Lamia al-Gailani Werr, and Henry Wright also received an e-mail message from Ambassador John Limbert at the Kuwait headquarters of the Office of Reconstruction and Humanitarian Assistance. By asking journalists in Kuwait, ORHA's senior cultural advisor had finally found his way to the archaeologists who had been dealing for months with the Pentagon, the Defense Intelligence Agency, Civil Affairs, and CENTCOM. Limbert was seeking "advice on the question of maintaining the integrity of Iraq's cultural heritage in the aftermath of the current fighting." He asked Gibson and Wright how to find qualified Iraqi specialists but added, "I would also like to find someone knowledgeable in the international trade in antiquities, who could help the new Iraqis recover stolen and looted works of art."[11]

This was a red flag for both archaeologists. Wright replied on April 11, urging that the museum be protected. "There is an international antiquities mafia," he explained to Limbert, "and they are prepared to strike on days like today."[12] Gibson, who wrote back immediately, was more blunt. He assumed the museum had been taken two days ago, when the Americans had charged into the center of Baghdad. "If looters get in," he remarked, "it is going to be a disaster."[13] In fact, the looters had probably already broken in, first entering the compound on the evening of April 10, Baghdad time.[14]

By that point, the museum had been almost completely undefended for several days. Although the Ministry of Culture had done its official duty before the war by dragooning museum staff to serve as an impromptu guard force to defend the museum from looters, it now recognized the futility of trying to do so in the name and uniform of a government under military attack. Once it became clear, very early in the fighting, that the war was coming to Baghdad, museum employees were told to shuck the uniforms they had been ordered to wear just weeks earlier. They did not need to be asked twice. Donny George hung his uniform in his locker, while others just tossed theirs anywhere willy-nilly.

The plan to protect the museum in shifts stayed in effect, but it began to fall apart as the danger of traveling through the city became clear. George himself was dissuaded from going to the museum on April 5 by friends who told him of a fierce fight in progress on his route. The next day he picked his way back to work through an obstacle course of charred vehicles.

The museum's leadership had arranged to take turns staying overnight at the museum, but when George tried to return home by the same route he had taken the previous day, he was stymied by American forces driving through the streets firing at any movement. Forced back to the museum at around sunset, George found the minister of culture there checking in briefly with the museum's director, Nawala al-Mutawalli, who had taken over from George for that night.

That evening George was awakened around 2:00 a.m. by the sound of three huge blasts. Missiles had struck the telecommunications center across the road, just as had happened back in 1991. The next morning, April 7, several busloads of journalists arrived to view the damage, including the debris that had showered the garden. After they left, the telecommunications center was struck again by two more missiles.

At this point, George says, "I decided to stay because now it's war. . . . For me personally, the museum was a part of my life. As director of research, I could have gone and stayed at home, but I could not." George's commitment to the museum's safety was shared by Dr. Jabir Khalil Ibrahim, the chair of the State Board of Antiquities and Heritage, who courageously remained with George in the building. The museum's director, Dr. al-Mutawalli, found it too dangerous to stay (not an unreasonable view, considering the risks to women in war zones). She stopped by the museum that morning to say that her family was fleeing and she was going with them. According to George, she was asked point-blank by Khalil, not once but twice, "Doctor, all the doors are locked?" She answered yes, handed Khalil the keys, and left.[15]

She was not the only one fleeing. The units of archaeologists, a total of forty employees, assigned to protect the museum had mostly melted away already, and with bomb blasts and shooting in the streets on April 7, the remnants took off as well. The Ba'ath security police, who were supposed to be protecting the museum but in actuality had always been seeking various ways to "crack the strong wall of senior professional archaeologists" on the State Board of Antiquities and Heritage, had run away before anyone else.[16]

As George and Khalil hunkered down for the trouble ahead, George recalls, "little by little everybody that day just disappeared." By the next morning, only five persons remained: George; Khalil; Muhsin, an employee who lived in a shack behind the museum; his son; and Abdul Rakhman (the museum's fifty-seven-year-old live-in guard). A driver waited outside. George recalls:

We understood that the American tanks were here, very close to the museum. And people started disappearing. But I told the chairman of the board, "I will stay here, whatever happens. We have water. I have some biscuits in my room and some bread. We can take everything, now you have the keys, we can take everything. We should go downstairs, down into the cellars of the museum. We can stay there until everything is clear." And he decided, "Yes." He said, "We will stay here."

When George returned with the food and water, around 11:00 a.m., Khalil stopped him and told him they would have to leave. Puzzled, George asked why. "Come and have a look," Khalil replied. Peering from the window, George saw three men in the museum gardens wearing civilian clothes, carrying rocket-propelled grenades (RPGs) and machine guns. They were aiming at the American tanks approaching the museum area, George believes. "It's impossible," Khalil declared, "we will be in the crossfire. We have to go."

Leaving behind only Muhsin and his son, who locked themselves in their house, George, Khalil, and Rakhman hurried out the back through a small glass door to the car, making their way to another complex of museum buildings on the other side of the river. At around 3:00 p.m., they decided to try to cross back over the Tigris to return to the museum. In the middle of the 17th July Bridge, they were stopped by townspeople and warned that the Americans were controlling the whole area, shooting anything or anyone that moved. At that point, George says, "We decided we can do nothing since the Americans are controlling the whole thing." Dora, the district where Khalil and George both lived, was now swarming with American forces, so Khalil had the driver drop him at his brother-in-law's home. George himself spent the next several days holed up in his aunt's house.

Khalil's worry about being caught in the middle of a battle at the museum was well justified. The non-uniformed Iraqi fighters George and Khalil had spotted in the museum gardens were preparing to engage American forces in tandem with Special Republican Guard forces, whose headquarters was located across the street from the museum. Their objective was to deny the Americans control of the strategically important al-Ahrar Bridge across the Tigris, only half a mile down the road. A makeshift command post was quickly set up in the back of the museum compound, and at least one sniper took up a perch at a window in the museum's aboveground storage room. Iraqi fighters also ensconced themselves in the foxholes the museum had dug earlier as bomb shelters, turning them into fighting trenches, complete with candy cane–like aiming sticks for directing machine-gun fire. A ten-foot-high wall running along the western side of the buildings had been erected two years earlier as part of an uncompleted project to protect the museum from car bombings or RPG attacks that had struck the capital; now this wall provided cover for fighters to move unseen from the front to the rear of the building.[17] Last but not least, fighters armed with rocket-propelled grenade launchers climbed to the roofs of the Children's Museum (in the front gate of the museum complex) and the museum's library building.

Fighting not far from the museum broke out on Tuesday, April 8, probably just after George and Khalil left the museum, as the army task force assigned to the sector, a tank company operating with eleven tanks, expanded its perimeter to encompass the train station, parliament, and several other government buildings. The museum itself was a half mile up the road, and, as task force commander Lt. Col. Eric Schwartz would tell an NPR crew later, it "initially . . . just did not fall into anyone's area of responsibility."[18] A day earlier, on April 7, Schwartz's unit had forced its way into Zawra Park, rumbling under the well-known crossed-sabers monument there after running a gauntlet of machine guns, AK-47s, rocket-propelled grenades, and suicide car bombs, all of which scarred but did no real damage to their tanks. They had had enough breathing room that afternoon to take almost an hour to wait for a Fox TV News crew to arrive and determine the most telegenic way for a tank crew to fire a round toppling a statue of Saddam on horseback.

Now, on April 8, probably soon after Donny George and Jabir Khalil

5   Sandbagged machine-gun firing positions on the museum compound. Photo courtesy
      of Col. Matthew Bogdanos.

had left the museum, the tank company again faced a barrage of
rocket-propelled grenades, including some fired from the roof of the
Children's Museum, as well as occasional sniper shots, mortar rounds,
and suicide car bombs at their checkpoints. By late afternoon, however,
the fighting had died out in the sector, leaving the Americans in control of the intersection, though still subject to sporadic fire. On April 9
they methodically cleared the government buildings now under their
control. As they moved on from one cleared building to the next, tank
commander Capt. Jason Conroy recalls, "the civilians would come in
right behind us, carrying, rolling, and hauling away anything that was
not anchored in steel or cement."[19]

Either on that afternoon (in Conroy's account) or, much more probably, the morning of April 10 (in the official, multiply sourced investigative report prepared by marine Col. Matthew Bogdanos), the unit
also reported looting in the area of the museum, together with occasional AK-47 and rocket-propelled grenade fire. Iraqi soldiers were seen
cutting through the museum grounds changing positions. It is not
clear whether it was this sighting that prompted Col. David Perkins,
Schwartz's commander, to inform Schwartz that the museum was in

his area and was his responsibility. Journalist Andrew Lawler reports that a U.S. senior officer, who prefers to remain anonymous, made a request to U.S. Central Command on April 10 to move forces quickly into position to protect the museum. According to Lawler, CENTCOM acknowledged the request and told the officer that U.S. forces were on their way.[20] In any event, Schwartz says that "any direction from Perkins is time-sensitive" and would have been acted on by him in minutes. "At the same time, other battles are going on," Schwartz recalls. "I take Jason [Conroy] out of all that and say your focus is getting to the museum." According to Conroy, Schwartz told him: "I need you to tell me if you see people carrying stuff outside the museum."[21]

When Conroy's platoon tried to move forward, it met heavy but ineffectual fire, including from the museum grounds. It was at this point that the tank crew returned fire, knocking a hole in the Children's Museum and spraying a window in the museum's storage room where a sniper had been operating. Under the laws of war, firing on the museum in this situation was perfectly legal. In turning the museum into a military position, the Iraqis had violated the absolute prohibition against using protected cultural sites for military purposes. Any cultural site suffering such an unfortunate fate loses its protected status.[22] Nonetheless, Schwartz ordered his forces to regroup out of direct-fire range rather than continue to engage the enemy.

This decision effectively foreclosed any further action by the tank unit. Though Schwartz insists that he instructed Conroy to "keep visibility on that museum," no further probes were made to find out whether Iraqi forces had melted away (as they did elsewhere), or to investigate the danger that the museum might be prey to looters. Schwartz's concern about that possibility was trumped by the decision, passed down to Schwartz by his brigade commander, Col. David Perkins, to neither condone nor try to stop the looting that had broken out all around his forces beginning on April 9. On the afternoon of April 8, Baghdad was "dead quiet," Schwartz recalls.

I remember looking up and seeing people in their apartments looking down at us and us looking at them. When twelve hours went by and nothing happened for twelve hours, all hell broke loose. It started as a celebration and then it transitioned to "grab everything you could possibly grab." I contacted Perkins from the bowels of Baghdad and told him, "This thing is absolutely uncontrollable. What should I do?" I remember Perkins saying to me something to the effect that these people have got to get this out of their system. The control factor is just not there, you can't do anything about it.[23]

6   Tank posted next to Children's Museum. U.S. forces responded to sniper fire from the
     museum's archway by blasting the hole shown. Photo courtesy of Joanne Farchakh
     Bajjaly, archaeologist-journalist.

On the morning of April 10, Schwartz passed along Perkins's order to
the troops to ignore looting, sparing them the unpleasant truth about
their not being in full control of a city they were supposed to be mop-
ping up, and merely saying, in Conroy's recollection, "We are not into
stabilizing the civilian community."[24] This order was not specific about
the museum, and Schwartz insists that "at no time did I tell anyone
that looting from the museum was acceptable." But the message received by the troops was that it was enough at this point to preserve
as much as possible of the area they had already taken, which Conroy recalls Schwartz describing without apparent irony, in an analogy
probably borrowed from Perkins, as "the heart and soul of Iraq, the
Washington Mall of Iraq."[25] No one pointed out that the Iraqi equivalent to the Washington Mall's National Gallery—the National Museum
of Iraq—was not under American control.

     To be fair, however, it must be added that even the area in which the
American forces were operating was not really under their control. As
has already been noted, Iraqi looters were following directly in the U.S.
soldiers' footsteps as they cleared buildings in their area. If the American forces had returned to the museum, then they might well have

succeeded in clearing the compound of fighters without harming the museum's treasures or putting soldiers' lives at great risk.[26] But what they could have done to counter mobs of looters showing little fear is another question. A major show of force by platoons trained in crowd control might have succeeded in deterring or dispersing looters, but the military had no such stability police forces in its force structure, or even a minimally adequate number of infantry troops to do any such thing. Schwartz recalls that he had deployed an infantry company of 140 to secure the Al-Rasheed Hotel, but they were pulled off for a couple of hours to do something else, and when they returned a few hours later, the hotel had been looted.

Lacking any of the basic off-the-shelf tools of crowd control (tear gas, batons, shields, riot MPs, etc.), the tank units were ill equipped to deal with this sort of situation. A tank and ground troops in front of the museum would be an imposing sight, but by April 10 civilian looters no longer feared that American soldiers would open fire on them. The unwillingness to use a whiff of grapeshot to disperse mobs was not based on indifference to the value of what was being looted, but on fear of being court-martialed. Shooting unarmed civilians is considered murder under the Uniform Code of Military Justice. Firing a warning shot is not a war crime; it was prohibited, however, by the rules of engagement set by the American military for the 2003 invasion. All soldiers were given cards specifically and emphatically instructing them that if required to fire their weapons, they "must [f]ire only aimed shots. NO WARNING SHOTS."[27] Moreover, warning shots would only be effective if those firing were separate from the mob being fired upon. Schwartz remembers having "an image in my mind of Conroy's tank approaching the museum surrounded by thousands of people."[28] Firing aimed shots into or over the heads of such a crowd would have been not just extraordinarily irresponsible, if not criminal, but foolhardy to boot.

Had the military or the cultural heritage community invested before the war in a small amount of research and development or even some simple reflection focused on what would be needed to secure a building like the National Museum of Iraq from looters, a set of relatively cheap, portable, and easy technological fixes might have been devised. For instance, the tank crew might have been equipped with canisters containing either sticky foam or slippery foam, substances the military already has in its arsenal. These could have been quickly sprayed on doorways and windows to render it very difficult for intruders to get in, without requiring the tank unit to remain stationary. Another simple, low-cost solution for troops moving through an area would be malodorants, or in laymen's terms, stink bombs, used by police in some U.S. cities to keep vagrants from squatting in abandoned buildings. More high-tech solutions under development or available in 2003 for military use include painfully high-intensity sound machines and even a heat ray.[29]

None of these was at the disposal of Conroy and his soldiers. They did not even have the foam rubber riot-control rounds that marines had used at an air base elsewhere in the country to drive back looters a few days earlier; for some reason these were not available in Baghdad.[30] The tank units did not even have maps identifying the exact location of the museum, although the archaeologists had provided such coordinates many times, and Sumner had made up maps for precisely this purpose. The army report on battlefield operations in Baghdad touts how thorough the mapping of the city was:

By the time V Corps entered to the heart of Baghdad on 5 April, all major systems within the city had been dissected, studied, and targeted. Every building and section of the city were mapped and numbered. Everyone working in and around the city, on the ground or in the air, used the common graphics and systems data for targeting, thus maximizing lethality while minimizing collateral damage and fratricide. What started as an internal V Corps' planning concept for urban warfare permeated across joint, coalition, and interagency realms to make the total force more efficient and lethal.[31]

If this seamlessness is real, then the absence of cultural monuments from maps is all the more puzzling. But whatever the cause, this was one more way in which policy and operational planning failed the troops on the ground.[32]

"I have high confidence that a single building could be protected (or destroyed)," if so ordered, Joseph Collins insists. But this order from headquarters would need to be communicated to the troops on the ground, via the captains and sergeants in that sector, who, in turn, must retain the flexibility to carry this task out in its appropriate priority order. "All of this," Collins notes, "is a huge set of complicating conditions," given that "protecting cultural sites is among many, many other priorities. When small units are fighting for their lives, working to prevent loss of life among indigenous people, preventing looting of hospitals, etc., cultural site protection may be way down the list."[33] As Brian Barnella, sergeant major of the Third Infantry's Task Force 164, puts it:

There at the time was not a clearly defined objective of securing the museum, and to be honest, in a combat operation, that's not the first thing that's important, and as a combat force, in a commander on the ground that has orders to neutralize an enemy, those orders would never include, "and oh by the way, take away from your combat strength to guard a building." We were being shot at, and we were going out and destroying that enemy while other Iraqi citizens were looting the museum.[34]

And in the case of the units fighting in Baghdad, Collins adds, "there was a disconnect between these forces and their higher headquarters." The Third Infantry Division had no stability operations plans, nor did the marines operating in the other area of Baghdad, because "both assumed they would be evacuated after the 'real' fighting stopped."[35]

Inside the museum itself, the scene was pandemonium. Sometime in the morning of April 10, Iraqi fighters decamped from a small concrete building at the back of the museum, leaving behind Kalashnikovs and RPG launchers. A few hours later, looters broke through a window a few yards from the weapons cache, some grabbing guns on the way. The one live-in guard remaining described how a shouting crowd waving axes and iron bars rushed through the building, undeterred by his feeble attempts to beat them back with his walking stick:

They said there was no government; that everything belonged to them. There were women and children. They stuffed the pieces into bags and I couldn't talk because there were too many of them.

So I stayed in my room. They were yelling that there was no government and no state and that they would do whatever they liked.[36]

The administrative offices were the primary focus of the rampaging mob. Computers, air conditioners, chairs, desks were all dragged off. Worst of all, the museum's index cards documenting its holdings were ransacked and many burned. This would prove a devastating blow, hobbling later efforts to identify which artifacts had been stolen, since there were no backups to the index cards: the sanctions regime had prevented the museum from computerizing its antiquated recordkeeping system or even photographing most of its items.

Passing by a storeroom containing 100,000 tablets, including one containing a flood story similar to that found later in the Bible, some of the looters made their way into the public rooms and the restoration room. This second group of looters was less interested in wanton destruction than in thoughtfully executed looting. All of the 451 public

7   The museum director's office door, smashed in by looters. Photo courtesy of Joanne
     Farchakh Bajjaly, archaeologist-journalist.

display cases except those holding the famed Bassetki Statue and a Ne-
anderthal skeleton had been emptied by staff before the war, and only
twenty-eight cases ended up being smashed. What drew the attention
of the looters were the larger statues, steles, and friezes too large for the
staff to have moved. Leaving copies and less valuable pieces untouched,
these discriminating looters made off with forty of the museum's finest
artifacts, ranging from cuneiform bricks to a headless limestone statue
carved in Lagash 4,400 years ago. Among the most painful losses were
six works of the highest caliber that museum staff had brought to the
restoration room but failed to move down to the basement store hold:
several plates from the royal tombs of Ur; a large Assyrian ivory-relief
headboard; a ninth-century B.C. wheeled brazier from Nimrud; the
5,000-year-old Mask of Warka, the first naturalistic depiction of a human face; and an exquisite eighth-century B.C. ivory depicting a lioness
attacking a swooning Nubian.

    If the looters in the public galleries and restoration room knew what
they were doing, the same cannot be said of those who pilfered three
thousand items from the museum's aboveground storeroom. Despite
having been facilitated by an insider—the door, which Donny George
had locked before leaving, showed no sign of forced entry—the looting

8   A smashed display case in one of the public rooms of the National Museum of Iraq. Most display cases had been emptied by museum staff before the war. Photo courtesy of Karim Sahib/AFP/Getty Images.

9   Broken head of an Assyrian-era (1984–1881 BC) lion, damaged during the looting of the museum. Photo courtesy of Cris Bouroncle/AFP/Getty Images.

10   Smashed display case showing the base of the Vase of Warka, which was stolen and
      later recovered in pieces. Photo courtesy of Joanne Farchakh Bajjaly, archaeologist-
      journalist.

here was clearly the work of amateurs. Shelves containing invaluable
artifacts remained untouched, even as thieves emptied others holding
fakes.

It was in the museum's basement where the worst looting took
place, again at the hands of professional thieves. The museum staff had
bricked up the rear entrance to the underground rooms, but that wall
was broken through, and the intruders wasted no time in making their
way directly to the corner of one room. They rifled through one hundred suitcase-sized plastic boxes on the floor, making off with 5,144
cylinder seals and a roughly equal number of other small items (beads,
glass bottles, amulets, and jewelry). What the thieves were ultimately
after, however, were some of the museum's finest cylinder seals and

11   Donny George, Col. Matthew Bogdanos, and unidentified marine survey damage in the Sumerian room of the National Museum of Iraq. Photo courtesy of Col. Matthew Bogdanos.

thousands of coins, locked in a set of otherwise innocuous storage cabinets. Somehow the looters had gotten hold of the keys to these cabinets, and they also had been told where they were located. It was sheer luck that saved these priceless artifacts from ending up in some collector's inner sanctum: in the darkness the thieves accidentally dropped the keys into the detritus they had made on the floor, tried to burn some foam padding to give them light to look for them, and ended up abandoning the room because of the fumes the padding generated.

On the morning of April 11, the BBC broke the first reports of an attack on the museum, and scenes were broadcast of looters trying to get into the bank. McGuire Gibson immediately wrote in desperation to Kenworthy and Limbert. "If they get into either place," the archaeologist warned again, "the international condemnation of the ineptitude of the U.S. forces will be devastating." "Since late January," he reminded Kenworthy,

I have been cooperating with the army to try to save archaeological sites. In every conversation I have had, and in a lot of e-mails, I have put first in importance the Iraq National Museum. I even pointed it out on a map to a group. I was told that a special effort was to be made to protect it. I also mentioned the importance of one of the buildings of the Central Bank. Again, I was assured that something would be done.

For the last three days, I have been waiting to hear that the museum had been secured. I started to send special messages two days ago, to everyone I had contact with in the Army. Now I see on the wires that the museum has been badly looted. The U.S. forces had to have been on the street right in front of the museum in the past three days. Why was the building not secured?[37]

The next day Limbert replied that he had heard the BBC reports and had spoken with contacts in Central Command Headquarters in Doha emphasizing the same points about a catastrophe in the making. Thanking Gibson, Limbert added sadly, "I only wish I could do more."[38]

In reality, Limbert was trying to do more than he shared with the archaeologist. "I was screaming at everybody I could back in Washington," recalls the ambassador. "I don't think I've ever felt quite so helpless." The response from the State Department's Bureau of Near Eastern Affairs, from ORHA's head Gen. Jay Garner, was the same: hand-wringing. The only entity capable of doing anything to secure the museum was the military. And the response given by the political advisor at Central Command, Limbert says bitterly, was "not a priority."[39]

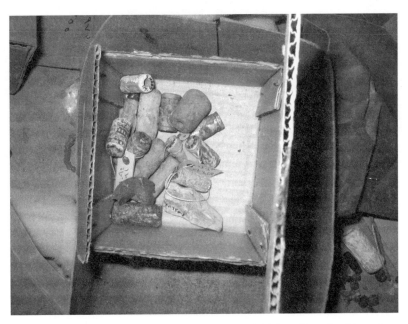

12 Cylinder seals looted from the museum but recovered. High-quality seals sell for up to $100,000. Over five thousand were stolen from the museum, and most are still missing. Photo courtesy of Col. Matthew Bogdanos.

As Gibson was getting word that the museum was being looted, Patty Gerstenblith received an e-mail from a British colleague, Kathy Tubb, alerting her as well. Gerstenblith immediately forwarded the news to Varhola, who replied that he was stressing the issue hard to the ground commander via his staff section and would probably be flying into Baghdad that night from Kuwait City.

Meanwhile, Eleanor Robson—an English archaeologist who played a central role in efforts by the British archaeological community to persuade the Blair administration to protect Iraq's archaeological heritage—woke up archaeologist Zainab Bahrani in New York with the news. Bahrani immediately phoned Maria Kouroupas, executive director of the Cultural Property Advisory Committee in the U.S. State Department's Bureau of Educational and Cultural Affairs, who had worked with Bahrani on the aborted Future of Iraq Project working group. Kouroupas told Bahrani she didn't know what happened: her office had given the Pentagon the information; they just didn't pay attention.

SIX

The World Responds

The State Department was indeed at a loss. James Fitzpatrick, counsel for the National Association of Dealers in Ancient, Oriental and Primitive Art and a member of the American Council for Cultural Policy, reports that around this time "my law partner Jeff Smith, who is a former Defense Department official and former general counsel of the CIA, got the call from someone at the State Department [in reality the call was from Arthur Houghton, who was a retired Foreign Service officer] saying, 'Can you help us? The Baghdad museum is being looted, and we're not making any progress in terms of getting DoD to respond.'"[1] Smith quickly dispatched a letter to Paul Wolfowitz. He received no reply until a month later, when the Defense Department sent a pro forma response.

McGuire Gibson got a call from the State Department as well, on April 11, to let him know that they had persuaded the army to fly troops up that coming evening to protect the museum. Unfortunately, the military did not know where the museum was located, in spite of Gibson having sent maps at least five times to different people in the Pentagon and Central Command. Gibson passed this information on to John Limbert in Kuwait and went on to warn the diplomat that with the appearance of looted items on the antiquities market, Limbert was likely to get entangled with the American Council for Cultural Policy, which Gibson felt sure would be pressing its agenda to liberalize Iraq's antiquities laws.

Limbert still had no idea where the ministry he was

supposed to be administering was located. He only found it by accident, several weeks later, on April 24, after being ordered by Secretary of State Colin Powell to make his way up from Kuwait to Baghdad to give a press conference at the National Museum of Iraq in order to show the world that the United States was responding to the disaster. As he was being driven through the streets to the museum (which still had not been put on military maps, requiring his driver to pull over so that the ambassador could solicit directions from street urchins), Limbert happened to look out the window at one of the many trashed government buildings. "It had been picked to the bone by the looters to a degree I've never seen—not a stick of furniture, not a piece of wire, not a pipe remained," he recalls. With a start, Limbert read the name on the building: "Ministry of Culture."[2]

The Ministry of Culture building had been looted and set afire around the same time that the museum was being looted, despite Civil Affairs' Maj. Chris Varhola's best efforts. Varhola had arrived at the Ministry of Culture to try to protect the Iraq Museum of Modern Art located within it:

I went in there with two other guys and we were chasing out the looters and we got nine pretty pathetic looters—taking everything from art to the screws out of doors. But after we caught about eight of these guys, I guess some of the looters got upset, so they lit the building on fire underneath us.

Outside the Ministry of Culture building, Varhola encountered thirty U.S. soldiers making no moves to prevent the ransacking going on before their eyes. Varhola rushed up to the sergeant in charge and yelled in frustration, "What the hell? Hey, sergeant, why aren't you stopping it?" "Sir," the sergeant replied, "I have strict orders not to leave this intersection, I'm guarding this intersection, it's a traffic control point, I'm not allowed to stop looters from the ministry."[3] Varhola was on his own.

Nor could the plucky Civil Affairs officer rely on backup from his superiors, who probably would have regarded his actions as foolhardy rather than courageous. Col. Gary Wager, who had organized the prewar information session for Civil Affairs at the University of Chicago in February 2003, told Gibson that at this point most Civil Affairs units were not being allowed out to do much due to a fear by higher-ups that the lightly armed Civil Affairs reservists might be taken hostage by Iraqi holdouts. Varhola continued to show courage, though of a different kind, when Gibson passed on word that the bank building containing the vault where some of the museum's most precious artifacts were stored had not yet been secured, even after the museum's looting had become public. What happened at the museum, Varhola told Gibson, was a national disgrace, and he had bypassed his chain of command (always a risky thing to do in the military) to pass on the message about the bank vault to Brig. Gen. John Kern, commander of the 352nd Civil Affairs Command in Iraq, also copying the director of civil-military operations (John Kuttas) and John Limbert. Kern had responded, according to Varhola, by instructing the forward command post to attempt to provide protection for the bank. This exercise seems to have been of no avail, however, as the bank was still unsecured as of April 16, several days later.

Meanwhile, Gibson's Civil Affairs contact in Kuwait, Lt. Col. Kraig Kenworthy, focused on immediate palliative steps that could be taken, asking Gibson if offering rewards to thieves to turn in stolen artifacts was a good idea. Gibson approved, adding that "if a message about returning stolen antiquities, especially if the population had been prepared by messages from the Shia mullahs about how Muslims should not rob, it might work to some extent. But it has to be done right away (not a week from now), because the stuff will be out of the country in a week."[4]

Enlisting the clerics was a strategy that Donny George had thought of as well. The hawza, the seminary-like institutions of Shiite religious authority, had been unable to protect Iraq's ministries from being gutted, but their imams did manage to protect some of Baghdad's hospitals from looters and might be willing to help now to salvage the museum's artifacts.[5] Accordingly, later in the month, after the museum was secured, George fanned out with his staff to local mosques begging the imams to urge citizens to return looted items. "It worked!" George recalled. "I got my computer printer back, and a good number of the Nimrud ivories, some of them gilded."[6] But time was of the essence in getting the word out, and Gibson suggested to Kenworthy that the United States should broadcast appeals over radio and television telling people to turn in items at the museum or a neutral site like the Sheraton Hotel. Kenworthy jumped on the idea, asking for operational details. What form of compensation (in dollars, dinars, food, clothing) would be appropriate? Who would authenticate the items being turned in? It would take time, he noted, to get U.S. dollars committed. "Are there foundations in the U.S.," he asked, "that would help fund this initiative until the U.S. could spin up on this issue?"[7]

The answer, sadly, was no, at least not in the short term. Eventually, some funds were forthcoming, at least from the British side. The

British School of Archaeology, in a drive spearheaded by its chair, Harriet Crawford, raised about £45,000 from its own membership and one very generous outside donation. The British Academy also chipped in approximately £12,000 to help the museum restore its library. In September 2003, the Dutch government's Prince Claus Fund established a new Cultural Emergency Response fund of 120,000 euros.

Those with far more wherewithal—wealthy antiquities collectors, dealers, and museum directors—also responded to the emergency but gave little more than words. An umbrella organization representing auction houses, antiques and art fairs, art brokers, and others in the Netherlands arts world issued a statement deploring the looting but did nothing more. The American Numismatic Society provided help to reconstitute some of the archaeological book losses that the Iraqi museums and libraries had suffered. The Association of Art Museum Directors called for an amnesty program with financial incentives but made no contribution. Philippe de Montebello, director of the Metropolitan Museum, told Fox News that he was personally urging UNESCO to create an amnesty fund, which it did; the Metropolitan gave nothing to it nor to any other initiative aimed at helping the National Museum of Iraq. Nor did the American Council for Cultural Policy or any private collector, so far as can be ascertained.

A former ACCP member with an enduring interest in institutional behavior and misbehavior explains why his group opted out:

The AAM [American Association of Museums] held a big meeting of concerned groups with State [Department] and others in attendance, but pointedly did not invite ACCP to send anyone, and instead selected attending groups from a list that was not inclusive. Yes, of course we talked about what more we could do, but having opened the door, some of us felt, the ACCP was now being asked to stay outside.

Beyond that there appeared to be a mounting level of vituperation [from archaeologists] about what our "real purpose" had been, which in their stated views was to curry favor with Iraq and manipulate the new order there in an attempt to change retentionist laws and make it possible for a market in Mesopotamian antiquities to flourish.

I think most of us threw up our hands at this and said, "Well, fuck it. We did the best we could," we thought.[8]

Annoyance at petty indignities was enough, apparently, to trump the needs of a museum in shambles.

There was one telling exchange at around this time between the moneyed interests and the archaeologists. Archaeological Institute of America president Jane Waldbaum and AIA legal advisor Patty Gerstenblith had published an op-ed piece in the *Washington Post* on April 27, 2003, warning that while museums and dealers had backed many of the proposals made by archaeologists to help recover the museum's looted objects, "the less scrupulous dealers, private collectors and even some museums will simply wait out the current focus on the issue and then proceed with the secret sale and purchase of these cultural treasures." If prominent collectors truly wanted to help, Waldbaum and Gerstenblith suggested, they should "make available to law enforcement agencies images of the ancient Mesopotamian objects in their collections and inventories, as well as the documentation of the sources of these objects."[9] This, the authors added, would provide information on how objects move through the international market and thus would help authorities in tracing any taken out of Iraq.

The implication of this tongue-in-cheek suggestion was clear: Waldbaum and Gerstenblith were all but accusing collectors of being at one end of a supply chain that was handling illicit antiquities. Astoundingly, the insult almost bore fruit in spite of itself. The day following the appearance of the op-ed piece, former curator Arthur Houghton called Waldbaum offering a counter-suggestion as inflammatory as hers had been. If the AIA thought documentation important, should the archaeologists not be publishing and recording their excavations? After all, a number of the cuneiform tablets that were lost from the museum had never been recorded. (Houghton was fond of quoting Sir Mortimer Wheeler's remark that a site that is excavated and unpublished is a site that is looted, but did not do so here).

That idea, both Waldbaum and Houghton knew, was going to go nowhere. But then Houghton added in passing that he was speaking for Shelby White (one of the wealthiest collectors and a member of the ACCP), who despite being a lightning rod for criticism still wanted to get things done. That same day Waldbaum was contacted by someone acting as an intermediary for White, with a question: if White went along with the AIA's suggestion to provide images and documentation of the sources of her pieces, would she have to give them back? In asking the question, and in having Houghton approach the AIA, White was clearly signaling a wish to do something other than simply handing over information about her collection to the police. Given the dire need for funding to help the museum and the Iraq State Board of Antiquities to get back on its feet again, one would have thought the

AIA might have pursued the conversation, but no further exchanges occurred. A few years later, White would donate $200 million to NYU to create a new graduate-level research institute for the study of the ancient world. Addressing the problem of antiquities looting is not on the institute's agenda.

The response from American foundations and other nongovernmental entities also was much less robust than one might have expected. To my knowledge, no major foundation, group, or individual philanthropist stepped forward with a pledge of immediate help, with the exception of the National Geographic Society (which at Gibson's request pitched in $2,000 to hire a bus to transport Iraqi women safely to and from the museum to begin inventorying what was left).

The only major gifts, in the short term, came from the Mellon Foundation and the Packard Humanities Institute. After the news broke of the looting of the museum, Mellon's president (William Bowen) and the foundation's trustees asked program officers to explore ways that the foundation could be helpful. (Mellon had done the same thing after 9/11 to assist New York's hard-hit cultural institutions.) But it turned out to be a personal connection that determined Mellon's choice of projects. Bowen remembered that one of his friends at Princeton, the late historian Lawrence Stone, was the father of an archaeologist specializing in Mesopotamia. So it was that Elizabeth Stone ended up persuading Mellon to provide her with a small initial grant of $12,500 at the end of May 2003 to do what she thought most important: quickly develop an inventory, audit the losses, and compile a reliable list of the objects missing from the museum.[10]

Unfortunately, the much larger commitment of $1 million in funding by the Packard Foundation to help recover actual artifacts and protect sites ran into red tape. An AIA officer contacted by David Packard recommended that he try to move the money through the State Department so as to avoid violating the sanctions, which were still in effect, or the graft and corruption that would have been involved in passing out such funds independently. Packard himself contacted Condoleezza Rice (with whom he had served on a board in Palo Alto) and secured her help in expediting the process. Despite this high-level lip service, the State Department moved so slowly that any chance of injecting the monies effectively in a rewards program or any other immediate recovery efforts was completely squandered. It was not until June 2004 that the Packard gift finally arrived in Baghdad in the form of twenty pickup trucks.

For his part, Gibson offered to see if some funds could be found to pay for the objects stolen from the museum, but he noted that "there are people here who think it is a bad idea, that it might increase the looting of sites in the desert."[11] He reiterated his refrain that the military should start patrols or helicopter flights to stop the looting at the sites. But to clamp down on the trade in Baghdad, Gibson now recommended conducting a few raids on the more than one hundred antique and jewelry shops that had sprung up since the embargo. Already, days after the attack on the museum, artifacts were reported to be available on the black market in Paris, showing, Gibson said, some planned rather than haphazard looting. To stop the outflow of stolen antiquities, Gibson strongly urged searching all vehicles at border points heading to Amman, Kurdistan, Iran, and Syria. Syrian border police and security could not be trusted to turn items over: they would search hard, keep things for themselves, and sell them to dealers in Beirut. The desert route to Saudi Arabia, he added, is harder to patrol.

Gibson's suggestions about raids, helicopter patrols, and border security were not taken up right away, but his hectoring on other matters did bear fruit almost immediately. As archaeologist Eleanor Robson learned on April 13 from Capt. William Sumner, whose Civil Affairs cultural unit was finally about to leave Kuwait for Baghdad five days into the occupation of the city, the military's "psy-ops" unit had been ordered to broadcast messages asking for objects to be returned for the good of the Iraqi people, and the military would be approaching religious establishments for assistance as well. Equally important, Limbert had complained to Kern, and due to his complaints, Sumner assured the archaeologists, the museum was now secured.

That was something of an overstatement. Donny George and Jabir Khalil, chairman of the Iraq State Board of Antiquities and Heritage (SBAH), had secured the museum by themselves on Sunday, April 13, without any help from the American military. The previous evening they had heard over the BBC that the museum they had locked down four days earlier had been looted. That morning the two men made their way by car to the Palestine Meridien Hotel, headquarters for the marines, who were in charge of that part of the city (though not of the sector where the museum itself was situated). It was a painfully slow trip, taking four hours rather than the normal thirty minutes, and once inside the building the two officials waited several more hours before finally being ushered into the office of Lt. Col. Peter Zarcone, the Civil Affairs officer for the First Marine Infantry Division. George explained that they had come from the National Museum of Iraq. "We know the museum has been looted, and we need protection," George told Zarcone.

This was not news to Zarcone. "When I met with him," the officer recalls, "I already knew there was looting of the museum, and I was concerned." But there was little he could do, since the museum was in the army's sector, not the marines'. Zarcone then asked George if there was anything left in the museum. Yes, replied the archaeologist, adding, according to Zarcone, that museum officials had safeguarded the most precious stuff already. "That definitely lessened my anxiety," recalls Zarcone.[12] Nonetheless, he told George that now that the military knew there was something to protect in the museum, it was their duty to protect it. "We will take the museum and I will send a unit now to the museum," George recalls Zarcone saying. Just to be certain, George asked, "Are you sending them now?" Zarcone told him yes, asked him to point out the museum's location on the wall map, then scribbled a note with the coordinates on it authorizing George and Khalil to pass through checkpoints unimpeded. "Once you are in the museum— maybe before you—we will have the unit there," Zarcone told the relieved official.

"I said, 'This is wonderful!'" recalls George. "We went to the museum— there was no one there."[13] In fact, the military would not arrive at the museum until three days later, on April 16. Zarcone notified the army that the museum was in their sector and that it was their responsibility to safeguard it, but it is unclear what became of that message.

It was left to George, SBAH chairman Khalil, and two guards, assisted by a couple of staffers from the neighborhood, to secure the museum as best they could. The looters had left the premises on April 12 when reporters arrived, heralding—or so the looters must have imagined— the imminent arrival of U.S. forces. To deter the mob that continued milling around the main gate, the museum staff chained the front doors, stood guard in front of the building with clubs and pieces of aluminum, and posted a sign warning that American troops were in the museum and would shoot anyone who entered.[14] Several times during the next two days, George recalls, minibuses filled with men brandishing Kalashnikovs drove by the museum, yelling "We'll be back!" at them. George recalls that "at that moment we were afraid that there will be more waves to come to the museum and set fire to the whole building because this is what they did for all governmental buildings. After looting, they come back and burn everything." The National Library and Archive, containing historical documents including the old

To ALL US MILITARY PERSONNEL;
Dr JABIR KHALIL AND
DR DONNY GEORGE ARE
MUSEUM OFFICIALS FROM
THE IRAQ MUSEUM IN MUSEUM
SQUARE (MB 428 878).
THEY ARE COOPERATING WITH
COALITION FORCES FOR THE
RECONSTRUCTION OF IRAQ.
PLEASE ALLOW THEM TO PASS
THROUGH SECURITY CHECK POINTS
WITHOUT DELAY.

Lt COL A.A. ZARCONE
1ST MARINE DIVISION
CIVIL AFFAIRS OFFICER

13   Handwritten note provided to Donny George by a Civil Affairs officer after George went to marine headquarters begging for help to secure the museum from further looting. Photo courtesy of Donny George.

14   Deputy Museum Director Mushin Hasan holds his head in his hands as he sits on
destroyed artifacts, April 13, 2003. Photo courtesy of Mario Tama/Getty Images News
Collection.

royal archives of Iraq, had been set ablaze, as had the library of Qur'ans
at the Ministry of Religious Endowment. Alerted by journalist Robert
Fisk to the burning of the Qur'anic library, the marines could do nothing but watch it burn, having no firefighting capacity.[15]

As George and Khalil returned to the museum on the afternoon of
April 13, the State Department was jumping into the fray. Gibson and
Gerstenblith received a call from Carol Thompson, a Foreign Service of-
ficer at the State Department working with Thomas Warrick (late of the
Future of Iraq Project). Thompson asked for information about museum
inventory lists and international property law that could assist the return of artifacts. Gerstenblith pointed Thompson to Bonnie Magness-
Gardiner in the Cultural Property Office of the State Department and to
UNESCO officials Mounir Bouchenaki and Guido Carducci for advice
on international legal instruments that could be used in this situation.
The most effective one, she added, was the 1970 UNESCO Convention
on the Means of Prohibiting and Preventing the Illicit Import, Export
and Transfer of Ownership of Cultural Property, which prohibits the import by states' parties of cultural objects stolen from museums and other
cultural institutions, allowing for seizure and return of looted items.

That same day, Gerstenblith, who had e-mailed Limbert on April 12 urging several immediate steps, also got a call from him in Kuwait. The ambassador wanted a more formal set of recommendations from the Archaeological Institute of America about what could be done to set things right. She sent him a "wish list" (among other things, the AIA urged sealing off borders, using helicopter overflights to establish short-term security at sites, providing funds to rehire and train new Iraqi guards, and using the American military to establish a security perimeter around the museum so that Baghdad police forces could inspect houses in the vicinity), as well as a draft statement invoking the United States' National Stolen Property Act.

Limbert and Thompson needed this information to help prepare Secretary of State Powell for an exercise in damage control, following Defense Secretary Donald Rumsfeld's famous belittling of what had transpired at the museum. Responding at an April 11 news conference to the broadcasting of scenes of looters at the museum, Rumsfeld had remarked pettishly:

The images you are seeing on television you are seeing over, and over, and over, and it's the same picture of some person walking out of some building with a vase, and you see it 20 times, and you think, "My goodness, were there that many vases? Is it possible that there were that many vases in the whole country?"

Too much fuss was being made for what was after all a normal part of life, Rumsfeld continued. After all, even American cities had seen riots. "Stuff happens!" the exasperated defense secretary railed. "But in terms of what's going on in that country, it is a fundamental misunderstanding to see those images over, and over, and over again of some boy walking out with a vase and say, 'Oh, my goodness, you didn't have a plan.' That's nonsense. They know what they're doing, and they're doing a terrific job."[16]

By April 13, in a *Meet the Press* interview, Rumsfeld was no longer joking, but he continued to disclaim any responsibility for preventing the looting at the museum, which he blamed on the chaos that ensues "when you go from a dictatorship" to a new order. "We didn't allow it. It happened. . . . There's a transition period, and no one is in control. There is still fighting in Baghdad. We don't allow bad things to happen. Bad things happen in life, and people do loot."[17]

Rumsfeld's characterization of the losses at the museum as merely a bit of "untidiness" was the last straw for several members of the president's Cultural Property Advisory Committee. Its chair, Martin Sullivan, immediately resigned, along with Gary Vikan, director of Baltimore's Walters Art Museum, and Richard Lanier, director of the Trust for Mutual Understanding.

On April 14, the morning following Rumsfeld's *Meet the Press* debacle, Colin Powell issued a written statement giving a more considered response to the looting of Iraq's cultural heritage. In addition to the National Museum of Iraq, this list now included the Mosul Museum—looted on April 12, in a replay of what had happened at the National Museum, with professionals taking thirty-four cherry-picked cuneiform tablets and bronzes, followed by a smash-and-grab mob—as well as other cultural institutions and archaeological sites.[18] Drawing on a draft sent by Gerstenblith to Limbert (as well as, to a lesser extent, on materials received from Eleanor Robson's group via Civil Affairs archaeologist William Sumner), Powell invoked the U.S. National Stolen Property Act, affirming that objects and documents taken from museums and sites are the property of the Iraqi nation under Iraqi and international law, and therefore are stolen property.

The secretary of state also took the highly unusual step of speaking on behalf of the Defense Department: "In addition to the well-reported efforts made to protect cultural, religious, and historic sites in Iraq" (a phrase it is hard to read otherwise than as sarcastic), he announced, Central Command had instructed troops to protect museums and antiquities throughout the nation. In addition, U.S. radio broadcasts were encouraging Iraqis to return items, and the Office of Reconstruction and Humanitarian Assistance (ORHA), under Limbert's auspices, would spearhead the effort to restore the artifacts and catalogs. To make clear that a new, multilateral day had dawned, Powell added that the United States would work with UNESCO and Interpol to these ends.[19] The FBI and Interpol announced the following morning that they were dispatching teams to Iraq.

Despite Powell's pronouncements, the National Museum still remained vulnerable to looting a day later, on April 15. This news emerged unexpectedly during a meeting in Paris hastily convened by UNESCO in response to the crisis. As the meeting was getting under way, John Curtis, keeper of the Middle East collections of the British Museum, was astonished to be told by a TV reporter that they had Donny George on the satellite phone. Under Saddam, cell phones with GPS were considered spying equipment, and George had never seen one in Iraq, much less a satellite TV truck. But a reporter from England's Channel 4 who had arrived at the museum with just such a truck happened to know both George and Curtis, and offered to let George use his phone to connect with the crew covering the meeting in the British Museum.

George told Curtis that even at this point, there was still no guard on the museum. Joint patrols of American soldiers and Iraqi police had begun the day before, under the direction of U.S. Civil Affairs officers who had arrived in Baghdad by this time, but no troops had been posted to the museum. George recalls, "I said, 'John, will you please try to do something because I'm afraid there will be more waves [of looters] and they will set fire to the whole museum.'"[20] Prime Minister Blair's office had already been pressuring the White House (though only in a teleconference between spokespersons) on the need to protect the museum. Curtis immediately called the prime minister's office to report the lack of action and demand something be done. He also phoned McGuire Gibson, who relayed the message to Chris Varhola and to John Marburger, the White House science advisor.[21] To Marburger, Gibson added tartly, "Powell's statement of yesterday will look pretty empty if there is more looting." Marburger's assistant, Dr. William Jeffrey, senior director for Homeland and National Security at the Office of Science and Technology Policy, wrote back to Gibson quickly, saying only that he needed Lt. Col. Kenworthy's correct e-mail address to send him some information. Later that day Kenworthy told Gibson he had been contacted by Jeffrey and that Gibson's original message was now going up the chain of command.

As criticism rippled up and down that chain, the response of authorities modulated from flippancy to defensive dismissiveness. At Central Command (CENTCOM), the response to criticism of the failure to secure the museum was twofold: we were too busy fighting, and nobody could have known the museum would be the target of looting, so let's just move along. This was the way Brig. Gen. Vincent Brooks, deputy director of operations, handled the hot potato in a press briefing on April 15:

First, as we entered Baghdad, we were involved in very intense combat, and our focus was the combat actions necessary to remove the regime and any of its appendages. In removing the regime, there is a vacuum that is created—that certainly did occur—and the vacuum will be filled as time goes on. I don't think that anyone anticipated that the riches of Iraq would be looted by the Iraqi people, and indeed it happened in some places. So while it may now be after the fact that that looting has occurred, it's still important to try to restore it as much as possible. It's simply not useful to speculate as to why we did, did not, what could we have done differently. We did what we did, and our operations were focused on objectives at hand at the time.

They are riches. They are important to not only Iraq, but the world, and we have to count on others as well at this point now to assist in trying to bring that back to a degree of closure and protecting those antiquities for the future.[22]

The "no one could have known this would happen" defense was untenable, of course, given that the museum had been identified as second on a list of fifteen buildings to be secured by the military as soon as possible—not to mention the many other warnings detailed in these pages.

That did not prevent Rumsfeld and Joint Chiefs of Staff chairman Gen. Richard B. Myers from denying they had been warned. At a press conference the same day, Rumsfeld did his best to appear to take seriously what he had earlier dismissed with a weak joke. Describing looting as "an unfortunate thing," he compared what was happening in Iraq to riots at soccer games and after athletic events. "No one likes it. No one allows it. It happens, and it's unfortunate. And to the extent it can be stopped, it should be stopped. To the extent it happens in a war zone, it's difficult to stop." Rumsfeld added, "The United States is concerned about the museum in Baghdad, and the President and the Secretary of State and I have all talked about it, and we are in the process of offering rewards for people who will bring things back or to assist us in finding where those things might be." As for taking responsibility for what had gone wrong, the defense secretary continued to demur:

Sec. Rumsfeld: To try to lay off the fact of that unfortunate activity on a defect in a war plan—it strikes me as a stretch.

Q: But weren't you urged specifically by scholars and others about the danger to that museum? And weren't you urged to provide a greater level of protection and security in the initial phases of the operation?

Sec. Rumsfeld: Not to my knowledge. It may very well have been, but certainly the targeting people were well aware of where it was, and they certainly avoided targeting it, and it was not hit by any U.S.—this was—whatever damage was done was done from the ground.

Rumsfeld was edging perilously close here to contradicting his own "Who could have known?" defense with the admission that the military had been in touch with archaeologists. The obvious follow-up question remained to be asked: If the military knew enough to protect the museum from being bombed, how could it not also be concerned with the possibility of threats on the ground as well? Myers sprang to the defense secretary's aid at this point:

15   Secretary of Defense Donald Rumsfeld and Gen. Richard B. Myers at press conference
taking questions about the looting of the museum, April 15, 2007. Department of
Defense photo by Helene C. Stikkel.

Some have suggested, "Well, gee, you should have delayed combat operations to
protect against looting, or you should have had more forces, should have waited
till more forces arrived." To that I would say this: The best way to ensure fewer
casualties on [the] coalition side and fewer civilian casualties is to have combat operations proceed as quickly as possible and not prolong them. And so it gets back
to the—a matter of priorities. And we're dealing with some of those issues that you
just brought up, Jamie, but the first thing you have to deal with is loss of life, and
that's what we dealt with. And if you remember, when some of that looting was
going on, people were being killed, people were being wounded, as I made reference to in my opening remarks. So I think it's, as much as anything else, a matter
of priorities.[23]

Under fire in front of a hostile press corps, Myers's and Rumsfeld's
defensiveness was understandable, but the president of the United
States was not about to adopt such a tone or face such an audience in
talking about what had happened. George W. Bush waited two weeks
before making his only public comment on the museum's looting. In
a triumphalist speech delivered to a largely Arab American crowd in
Dearborn, Michigan, on April 28, 2003, the president began by ex-
pressing regret that he had not been in Dearborn "when the statue
came down—I understand you had quite a party. I don't blame you."

Bush went on to hammer home his main theme: Iraq was in terrible shape, with half as many hospitals as it had in 1990, run-down schools, a power system that could not be relied on, but these were "the dictator's legacy." Now, with the Americans in charge, progress was being made. Rail lines were reopening, oil was flowing, water services were being restored, and land mines cleared. And, Bush added, "we're working with Iraqis to recover artifacts, to find the hoodlums who ravished the National Museum of Antiquities [sic] in Baghdad. Like many of you here, we deplore the actions of the citizens who ravished that museum. And we will work with the Iraqi citizens to find out who they were and to bring them to justice."[24] It was a breathtaking spin: America was not only not responsible for what had gone wrong, but was pursuing the looters with the same righteousness devoted to capturing Saddam.

Conservative media opinion makers would require a few more weeks to take the next step and develop a full-blown counterattack. The original news reports had described the museum as a total loss, with all its 170,000 items stolen. (While the museum has 170,000 catalog numbers, many numbers designate a group of items, so the actual total of pieces held by the museum was more than 500,000.) The 170,000 figure had been provided by a former museum official who could not know that many—though by no means all—important pieces had been secretly moved to an air-raid shelter before the war, and that the actual losses were in the range of 15,000 artifacts, including around 40 pieces taken from the museum's display cases. Seizing on this and other flaws in the original reporting once the figures were revised downward, the administration and its defenders went on the offensive, pooh-poohing the museum's looting as much ado about nothing, or worse.[25] In a briefing on May 9, 2003, Rumsfeld declared that the military had gotten a "bum rap" since, as he would note at a later news conference, "only an estimated 38 items seem to be currently confirmed as still missing."[26] But "it would have been a bum rap even if the items had been looted," the defense secretary insisted, since

it isn't as though you had one task, you invaded the country to go in and protect a single thing. You had a complex set of tasks. And that those decisions cannot be made in Tom Franks' headquarters; they have to give guidelines and then people go out, and colonels and captains and lieutenants and sergeants and corporals and privates make those decisions as to is it more important to save the life of my trooper buddy standing next to me or to provide safety for a mosque or for a hospital or for something. Those are tough calls.[27]

It was left to conservative commentators to savage those who had had the temerity to complain about the museum's fate. Charles Krauthammer, for example, suggested that Donny George had deliberately let the figure of 170,000 stand knowing it was false "because George and the other museum officials who wept on camera were Ba'ath Party appointees, and the media, Western and Arab, desperate to highlight the dark side of the liberation of Iraq, bought their deceptions without an ounce of skepticism."[28] In reality, George had been kept in the dark by his colleagues about any of the details of the plans to remove the artifacts from the museum, because, as George put it, "I was accused of being a friend of the foreigners."[29]

All this revisionism would come later. In the immediate aftermath of the looting, the Pentagon had gotten the message that it should present itself as understanding that the museum should have been protected. That did not mean, however, that there was going to be any real accountability, or even any real urgency to securing the museum, which at the time of the Rumsfeld-Myers press conference still was being defended only by Iraqi museum employees. Replying on April 16, 2003, to Gibson's angry comment that it seemed almost as if all the looting had been deliberately allowed, given that no guards had been placed at the museum as late as April 15, Maj. Varhola agreed that it would certainly seem that way. Varhola then informed Gibson that he had been directed to quit bothering his immediate superiors with this subject, as they had other priorities. "There have been a lot of utter failures in this," Varhola pointed out, in the most succinct description of what had gone wrong inside the military: "CFLCC C9 [the Coalition Forces Land Component Command, responsible for on-the-ground decision making] said they were doing nothing because they were not directed by CENTCOM. CENTCOM said it had a war to fight and that if it was important, it would be directed by the Pentagon. The Pentagon (whoever that is) probably assumed that it was CFLCC's job and couldn't believe that CFLCC said that this was not a high-enough priority to guard."[30]

The tragicomedy was continuing on the ground. As participants continued to arrive in Paris on April 16 for the emergency UNESCO meeting, a rumor went around that the museum still had not been reached by U.S. troops.[31] On hearing this, Bonnie Magness-Gardiner, who as consulting archaeologist for the Cultural Property Advisory Committee had been sent to the UNESCO meeting as Powell's special envoy, immediately faxed the grid coordinates to the military. Five hours later

16   U.S. soldier standing guard during one-day opening of the museum, July 3, 2003.
      The museum was secured by American forces on April 16, 2003, three days after Donny
      George's direct request for assistance. Photo courtesy of Scott Peterson/Getty Images.

she received a fax back saying soldiers were having trouble locating the
museum (which is located in Museum Square!). By that time, however,
at least some American forces had already arrived, securing the complex around midday on April 16.

The George was relieved, not only because a show of force at the museum
would deter any further attacks on it, but also because he knew that
some of his artifacts were in the hands of local Iraqis who were eager
to return them if the museum were secure. Two men had come to see
him anonymously on April 14 or 15 to say that they had gone into the
museum during the looting and taken objects home for "safekeeping."
A few days after the American tanks arrived, the men showed up at the
museum gate carrying some of the museum's most valuable pieces: a
statue of Shalmaneser III, the Assyrian conqueror of Palestine and Turkey; two 6,000-year-old Sumerian reliefs; and other smaller objects.

The apparent ineptitude of the military, even after so many statements by so many high-level officials, made Gibson very uneasy about
the treasures in the bank building, so he sent off yet another urgent
message to John Marburger, the White House's science advisor, copying Lt. Col. Kenworthy at Central Command, urging that guards be stationed there as soon as possible. Even at this late date, after all Gibson's
warnings, Kenworthy still lacked exact location coordinates. He asked

Gibson to send them through secure e-mail or to recommend an Iraqi who could serve as a guide. He also suggested copying a Maj. Hansen at CENTCOM, whose address Marburger's assistant Dr. Jeffrey could provide, noting in caps: "WE NEED TO WORK THIS AT ALL LEVELS."

Jeffrey tried to calm Gibson, telling the agitated archaeologist that the Defense Department had assured Jeffrey that orders to protect the bank and other buildings had already been issued. (Whether executed yet, however, was a question Jeffrey left untouched.) Jeffrey added, in a neat reversal of Kenworthy's assessment: "One element of confusion that is arising is that multiple parties are contacting various parts of the government with information (sometimes inconsistent information). It would be useful—at least in the short term—to have a centralized point of contact for the archaeological community when dealing with the actions in Iraq. OSTP [the White House Office of Science and Technology Policy] is willing to serve as that interface."[32]

It is not clear that this would have been the most effective arrangement for the archaeological community to transmit information to ground forces in Baghdad. In any case, Gibson paid no attention to the offer. He focused instead on ORHA ambassador Limbert and on Powell's emissary, Magness-Gardiner. From Limbert, he wanted action to close down the antiquities market in the capital to make it more difficult to move stolen pieces from the museum. A show of force to the antiquities dealers, he insisted, was essential: "They need to be visited, their premises searched, and things confiscated if they show up. They have to be made afraid of prosecutions and jail. Nothing else will work."[33]

Visits to the antiquities stalls, dangerous work, would have to wait for the arrival of marine Col. Matthew Bogdanos and his combat-hardened Special Forces investigative team later in April, followed by the Civil Affairs units of Col. John Kessel.[34] Bogdanos, a pugnacious Manhattan assistant district attorney in civilian life, had been in Basra gathering intelligence on terrorist networks when he learned that the National Museum had been looted. An avid student of the ancient past (he had earned a master's degree in classics from Columbia while an active-duty marine in the early 1980s), Bogdanos immediately asked to be allowed to take charge of the investigation and recovery efforts at the museum. He requested that he be allowed to handpick a small group to assist him, and that he be given the autonomy he needed to be able to go where he wanted at will without having to go through channels. In a sign of just how deeply embarrassed the military had been, Bogdanos's requests were granted without the batting of an eyelash. His team would spend the next few months sleeping at the museum, fanning out into neighborhoods, drinking tea with Iraqis, and undertaking raids based on tips.

The mobility, autonomy, and authority granted Bogdanos stood in stark contrast to the situation of the man who was supposed to be taking charge of Iraq's culture in the aftermath of the invasion, Ambassador Limbert of the Office of Reconstruction and Humanitarian Assistance. Hunkered down himself in a completely nonfunctional ministry, with little pull with the combat troops on the ground, Ambassador Limbert was in no position to undertake operations at will. Meanwhile, the State Department brought what resources it could on its own to ease the plight of the museum. Because it was, in archaeologist Elizabeth Stone's words, "at war with the Defense Department," the State Department found it difficult to even get into and out of Iraq. Instead, Magness-Gardiner worked with Gibson and Stone (who could enter the country claiming to be journalists for *Archaeology* magazine) and the museum's Donny George to determine what was most needed: generators, air conditioners, safes, vehicles, furniture, and computers for the museum. Only in late June 2003, six weeks after the looting of the museum, would the first of these goods begin to arrive.

Over the next few weeks after the news broke of the disaster, the government pulled itself together. The White House Office of Science and Technology Policy, as Jeffrey had envisaged, took on the role of coordinating a government-wide task force tasked with finding emergency money and help. Including staffers from the Defense Department, the U.S. Agency for International Development, the National Endowments for the Humanities and the Arts, the Library of Congress (responding to the looting and targeted burning of archives in Iraq's National Library),[35] the National Security Council, and the White House, this task force was overseen by Patricia Harrison, assistant secretary for Educational and Cultural Affairs. Harrison may have been tapped for this duty as a kind of booby prize: she had been the only cultural bureaucrat present at the State Department meeting on January 24, 2003, when Gibson had warned in no uncertain terms that the museum might be looted and it was learned that the Future of Iraq Project had no task force focusing on culture.

The State Department also continued to work on the legal side of the problem, now doing a much better job coordinating actions. Foreign Service officer Jane Gaffney announced to Limbert that she was setting up a working group, probably in the Bureau of Near Eastern Affairs, to work further on legal aspects of actions that might be taken. The group would draw on advice from Gibson, whom Gaffney (wrongly) believed had been meeting with the Iraqi lawyer on the Future of Iraq Project's working group on cultural heritage.

The State Department's legal work resulted in the U.S. government's decision in late May 2003 to push for inclusion in UN Security Council Resolution 1483 of a paragraph calling for member states to prohibit trade in or transfer of items illegally removed from the National Museum, the National Library, or other locations in Iraq. Since the United States already prohibited trade in such objects, this was not a huge step forward. It would take more than a year for Bush to get around to issuing an executive order as required to implement UNSCR 1483 in the United States, and not until late 2004 was that implementing legislation passed, establishing a more permanent means of prohibiting import of stolen or illegally removed Iraqi artifacts.[36]

The British were more forceful on the legal front, in part because when the war began they happened to be in the midst of a legislative initiative dealing with the British art market's participation in the global illicit trade in antiquities. (Similar initiatives in the United States have long been stymied by collectors, dealers, and museums.) A ministerial committee had made a series of recommendations that the senior policy advisor in the Cultural Property Unit of the Department for Culture, Media and Sport (DCMS), David Gaimster, was transforming into legislative language. Gaimster had learned that Donny George was going to be brought to London for a British Museum event at the end of April. Accordingly, Gaimster prepared a briefing paper for the head of the department, Tessa Jowell, laying out how the government was going to react. At the British Museum meeting, based on this memo, Jowell announced that the Blair administration was calling for passing a bill to close the loophole that enabled (and in the United States still enables) unprovenanced artifacts to be legally purchased. Together with a statutory instrument implementing UNSCR 1483, the British measure, passed in June 2003, reversed the burden of proof for a criminal prosecution. From here on in, the purchaser would be required to show that the provenance of an item was solid or face charges. The effect of this move on Iraqi antiquities in particular would be negligible, however, since, as Jowell herself reminded the antiquities trade, it already was illegal to deal in Iraqi objects in Britain, just as in the United States.

Jowell's call for legislative action at the April 29 meeting did not placate the British archaeologists, still upset at DCMS for publicly defending the Ministry of Defence in the immediate aftermath of the sack of the museum.[37] At that time, Jowell had merely expressed a vague "hope" that "all the forces will see that protecting Iraq's treasures is not an optional extra. It is a duty they owe to the people they have come to set free." She had been equally vague about what exactly the department intended to do in this crisis. "We need to ensure that measures are put in place now both to protect immediately vulnerable sites and to begin the process of helping the Iraqi people to conserve and protect their heritage," a DCMS statement declared, but it was "local religious leaders" in Iraq and the director of the British Museum who were "taking a lead [sic]."[38]

The only measures the DCMS itself was prepared to undertake at that point were to tighten import controls and insist that officials from the ministry be brought into the Office of Reconstruction and Humanitarian Assistance. (Why DCMS had not thought of doing this before the war, when they must have been aware of the persistent warnings by archaeologist Colin Renfrew, aka Lord Renfrew of Kaimsthorn, and other parliamentarians that Iraq's cultural heritage would be put at risk of looting by an invasion, remains unexplained.) Two senior staffers were eventually posted to Iraq from an Iraq Response Team formed by the department. They provided operational support for the Coalition Provisional Authority's official charged with cultural heritage oversight at that point, Italian ambassador Mario Bondioli-Osio.

By the time of the meeting on April 29, 2003, archaeologists were hoping for something more concrete and immediate: a commitment of funds. On that score, they were bitterly disappointed. Jowell declared the UK government would offer no new monies, having already pledged $300 million in unrestricted funds to ORHA, which could if it so wished dip into its overall funding pot to help with cultural heritage.[39]

The United States was hardly more forthcoming. At the end of April, the State Department announced that the United States would contribute the munificent sum of $2 million (later supplemented by $500,000 from the National Endowment for the Humanities, all given to American institutions to preserve and document Iraq's cultural resources and provide professional development opportunities for Iraqi librarians). This sum is roughly equivalent to the amount spent every fifteen minutes on the overall Iraq war effort, and one-tenth of the funding provided to the Metropolitan Museum by the city of New York in 2005. The funds would be earmarked to reestablish an American overseas research center in Baghdad, to create a searchable online database of images from the National Museum, and to support the International Council of Museums' development of an "Emergency Red List of Iraqi

Antiquities at Risk," a list of categories of looted objects designed to assist customs officials in interdicting artifacts identified as having come from the museum.

What is most striking, in retrospect, about these earmarks is that they are all palliative in nature, aimed at helping an already looted museum recover its curatorial capacities and its holdings. No money was allocated to address an imminent disaster, in which the loss of antiquities would ultimately exceed twenty-fold or more what was stolen from the National Museum: the wholesale looting of Iraq's archaeological sites.

SEVEN

The Slow-Motion Disaster: Post-Combat Looting of Archaeological Sites

Even before the museum had been secured, McGuire Gibson of the Oriental Institute was already trying to get the Office of Reconstruction and Humanitarian Assistance (OHRA) and CENTCOM to recognize that the museum's looted holdings amounted to only a fraction of the archaeological treasure of Iraq, most of which still lay buried in the half million estimated sites in the country, of which only twenty-five thousand were registered.[1] In the immediate run-up to the war, there had been a surge in site looting, and with central authority now completely nonexistent, archaeologists feared that it would be open season for tomb robbers.

ORHA, however, already had its hands more than full in trying to administer a broken country after less than three months of preparation and with a skeleton staff. To get attention paid would be difficult, even with the museum's looting in the news. Gibson did his best, pointing out to ORHA's senior advisor on cultural affairs, Ambassador John Limbert, on April 13 that "a very important feature in stopping the looting atmosphere is to stop the ongoing digging on sites out in the countryside."[2]

How to do that efficiently was the problem. As he had done before, Gibson suggested putting Donny George in a helicopter for flyovers but got no response from Limbert.

Seeking other possible solutions, Gibson batted around ideas with Bonnie Magness-Gardiner, senior cultural property analyst from the State Department's Bureau of Educational and Cultural Affairs. They discussed the possibility of deploying soldiers on sites that already had guards—a waste of effort, and maybe even unwise, Gibson decided. A better idea, the two agreed, was to check to see that a guard or guards were in place at as many major sites as possible. By April 24 looting was known to have taken place at Umma, Umm al-Hafriyat, Umm al-Aqarib, Bismaya, Larsa, and Bad-tibira, all unguarded except for Umma and Umm al-Aqarib. In many cases, the looting was being led by workers who had been hired by the State Board of Antiquities and Heritage to assist in their digs and trained to recognize valuable artifacts.[3]

Some excavated cities, such as the World Heritage Site of Hatra, were being safeguarded by local tribes, but others were under active attack. At Nimrud looters engaged in a gun battle with guards before making off with two bas-reliefs and damaging at least three others.[4] Among the local population in Dhi Qar Province, a rumor was spreading that a fatwa had been issued allowing looting and selling of pre-Islamic antiquities if the proceeds were used to help fund the insurgency. The provincial inspector, Abdulamir al-Hamdani, managed to quash the rumors only by traveling to Najaf and persuading Grand Ayatollah Sistani to propagate a fatwa indicating that looting of archaeological sites was not permitted.[5]

By early May some help was on the way in the form of joint efforts by international groups. Unfortunately, most projects focused solely on mitigating the museum disaster rather than tackling the emerging problem of possible hemorrhaging at archaeological sites. Some hopeful steps were taken, however. The American Coordinating Committee for Iraqi Cultural Heritage, a steering committee of major academic organizations chaired by eminent Mesopotamian archaeologist and former Smithsonian director Robert McCormick Adams, was formed in New York to plan coordination of efforts.[6] The Archaeological Institute of America (AIA) established an internal Rapid Response to the Crisis Taskforce to assist the International Foundation for Art Research, the Oriental Institute, and others engaged in establishing online databases of items known to have been in the museum's collection. The Carabinieri assigned two officers to assist the National Museum in documenting what was missing and began to mobilize for deployment in July 2003 in the southwestern Iraqi province of Dhi Qar.[7] Teams from the British Museum, the Smithsonian, and the Getty were preparing to go, and others from Germany and France were awaiting permission to be allowed into the country. Gibson offered to send an Oriental Institute team to assess damage to the sites. The Global Heritage Fund announced it was applying to the U.S. Agency for International Development for funds to secure and manage nine sites, and the World Monuments Fund declared that it would focus first on Hatra, Iraq's only listed World Heritage Site.

For its part, UNESCO, with 400,000 euros provided by Italy, concentrated in the short run on assisting in efforts to locate, seize, and restore items stolen from the museum. The 1970 UNESCO Convention had established an Intergovernmental Committee for Promoting the Return of Cultural Property to Its Countries of Origin or Its Restitution in Case of Illicit Appropriation, which made it easy to reach out for help to Interpol, the World Customs Organization, and the International Confederation of Art and Antiques Dealer Associations. By early June, agreements were signed with these groups for UNESCO and Interpol to create and distribute a single shared list of stolen items, based on technical information prepared by UNESCO, experts from the National Museum in Baghdad, and the archaeological community. A few months later, UNESCO met in Tokyo to form an international committee to coordinate the flow of aid to the National Museum and the State Board of Antiquities and Heritage.

But none of these international efforts had an immediate direct impact on security on the sites themselves. What was needed was some coherent and robust action on the part of the U.S. military to deal with the problem. One possible source of assistance was Joris Kila, a reservist in the Dutch civil-military cultural protection unit attached to NATO's Civil-Military Co-operation group, from whom Gibson heard on May 2. He wished to be involved but needed an official request from the U.S. or UK side. None was to be forthcoming for months. The Italian Carabinieri were also possible recruits but were not to arrive for several months.

In the meantime, the U.S. military took some sporadic steps. The marines in Nāsirīyah set up base in the city's museum, and after some cajoling from antiquities inspector al-Hamdani, they conducted a raid in May on Umma, where hundreds of trenches had been dug, netting sixty looters. But, as had been the case every step of the way, the military had bigger problems than those of the looting of archaeological sites. The Office of Reconstruction and Humanitarian Assistance had been unable to establish security over the country as a whole, and on May 7 Bush replaced Gen. Jay Garner with L. Paul Bremer. Bremer was given much more power, reporting directly to Rumsfeld as head

of what in mid-June was renamed the Coalition Provisional Authority (CPA). Among Bremer's first acts were the banning of high-ranking
Ba'ath Party members from holding government jobs and the disband-
ing of what remained of the Iraqi army.

The disastrous effects of these moves on Iraqi society are too well
known to need repeating here, but it is worth noting their specific effect on Iraq's State Board of Antiquities. As noted above, the authority
of site guards under the Saddam regime had stemmed partly from their
ties to local elders, partly from the backing they received from the military. As the support of state power evaporated, guards—most of whom
had gone unpaid since the invasion because the State Board of Antiquities could not reach them—found themselves facing not casual looters
but teams of determined armed men, often from their own village. At
some sites, such as Ashur, local guards were forbidden by U.S. soldiers
to carry guns[8]—this despite the fact that before he and the rest of the
Office of Reconstruction and Humanitarian Assistance were dismissed,
Limbert had offered to provide sidearms to the Iraqis for security
not just on the sites but at ministry buildings as well. Limbert's well-
intentioned idea turned out to be impossible because the Iraq Ministry of Culture at this point was completely dysfunctional, incapable of
organizing the purchase of weapons, taking delivery, or distributing
them. But fear of reprisals against family members meant that even
guards who were armed with automatic weapons, as at Hatra, could not
be counted on to defend sites.[9]

An effective international police force might have been able to do
some good. Unfortunately, this was not part of the U.S. postwar plan,
which allocated a total of twenty-seven police advisors from the U.S.
Department of Justice's International Criminal Investigative Training
Assistance Program to the task of securing a country of 26 million people. (Several of these advisors were actually not police but corrections
officers, some of whom ended up in Abu Ghraib.) The military's Civil
Affairs Command, for its part, continued to give short shrift to the
problem of protecting cultural heritage: when John Malcolm Russell,
appointed senior advisor to the Coalition Provisional Authority, arrived in Baghdad in late September 2003, only one officer on the Civil
Affairs' Arts Monuments team possessed cultural expertise. Not until
January 2004 did the CPA get around to organizing a special archaeological protection service, committing to training 168 senior officers
and instructors. Cars, radios, and weapons for the new service were donated by the Carabinieri, which was by that point withdrawing from
Iraq after losing nineteen men in the bombing of their barracks.

Just how bad things were on the sites did not become clear until a team toured Iraq in the second half of May 2003, a trip sponsored by *National Geographic* magazine.[10] As originally planned before the war, this trip was supposed to provide a rapid assessment of cultural sites after the end of the conflict. In the wake of the museum's looting, the initial plan was augmented. Videographers were added to the two teams—one focusing on sites in the north, the other on those in the south—and arrangements made to include an Iraqi archaeologist on each team. Getting around the country was not easy. The leader of the expedition, Professor Henry Wright of the University of Michigan, asked Ambassador Limbert and the military for a helicopter for his team but was forced to find cars and travel on his own, a quite dangerous proposition even then. Because his team was not embedded with a military unit, he was refused gas from the U.S. Army in Dīwānīyah and nearly stranded. Toward the end of the trip, the team was finally provided an escort of three armored vehicles.

The northern team fared slightly better. Thanks to what Gibson was told was "White House interest" (though at least one unnamed source in the British Department for Culture, Media and Sport insists his ministry deserved credit for arranging it), a helicopter was provided for part of this period. Gibson traveled with Col. John Kessel of Civil Affairs and Italian ambassador Pietro Cordone, who had stepped into Limbert's job as senior cultural advisor as ORHA morphed into the CPA.

What they found was sobering. Most of the most famous locations— Hatra, Nimrud, Ur, Babylon—were now under U.S. military protection, even though the Defense Intelligence Agency had somehow failed to provide site coordinates to the soldiers tasked with guarding them. Less well-known but archaeologically significant sites remained unguarded when the National Geographic team arrived in mid-May. One frustrated Civil Affairs officer in Nāsirīyah greeted Wright by saying, "Boy, am I glad to see you. We are supposed to guard these sites and we need to know where they are!"[11] As a result, except for the 6,000-year-old site of Tell 'Ubaid that had been surrounded by a strong barbed-wire fence and remained untouched, every place the team visited had suffered some damage. "I don't think we saw any other site outside Baghdad that didn't have at least one looting hole," recalls archaeologist Elizabeth Stone, who accompanied Wright's team.[12] Heaped around the pits, Stone and Wright could see piles of dirt scattered with ancient animal bones, scraps of stone and bronze, and pottery shards, all deemed worthless on the antiquities market, and now all but worthless to archaeologists as well.

17   Looter holding up a piece of broken pottery. Photo courtesy of Joanne Farchakh Bajjaly, archaeologist-journalist.

Flying over various sites in the north, Gibson observed hundreds of men digging. Most ran when the helicopter landed, but at one site, Isin, dust-covered young men came up smiling by the dozen, thinking no one cared that they were looting. Told digging was forbidden, they left, returning the very next day to continue their dangerous, ill-paid work. At relatively undamaged Nippur, the religious center of ancient Mesopotamia and the most important archaeological site in Iraq to have been excavated by Americans (under the auspices of the Oriental Institute), Gibson paid the long-uncompensated guards employed by the Oriental Institute and received assurances from the local tribal leader that his site, at least, would be safeguarded.[13]

On his return, Gibson sent his assessment report to White House science advisor John Marburger and to Brig. Gen. John Kern. He reviewed

18   Soldiers surveying newly dug holes at Isin, with looters carrying shovels in the distance, May 2003. Photo courtesy of McGuire Gibson.

19   Looters at Isin, May 2003. Photo courtesy of McGuire Gibson.

the situation at the museum and within the State Board of Antiquities. Advisors named by the British and the United States, who should have already been helping the Iraqis recover, were still sitting in London and Washington, waiting for an invitation from the military, which seemed to be pursuing a "let the Iraqis do everything for themselves" policy. But, Gibson added, "the worst thing happening to antiquities is the continuing looting of sites, especially in the south. Maybe there is something that you can do to help stop this." Again, he urged helicopter overflights combined with announcements in local papers and on U.S.-sponsored TV and radio that looting was strictly prohibited.[14]

Gibson's broadside seems to have had some effect. The advisors were shaken free and arrived in Baghdad the following week. On the other more pressing issues involving site security, however, nothing happened. The archaeologist then tried another tack, e-mailing the targeters he had worked with, asking if they had been observing the looting remotely, and attaching a revision of the short list he had sent on April 10 of prioritized sites, now focused on where he believed looting was at its worst. He also suggested to Marburger that knowledgeable people on the Civil Affairs staff were not being used effectively. Corine Wegener, Chris Varhola, and William Sumner, all with either curatorial or archaeological expertise, could be combined with the newly arrived American and British experts to form an effective task force that could be used to help the museum while also securing sites, something that needed to be done fast. "Can you influence the process?" Gibson asked.[15] He got no reply.

All of Gibson's worst fears were realized in early July, when he learned from a UNESCO assessment team that until the last week of June, looting had still been going on at his own dig at Nippur. The American commander of the area where Nippur is situated had recently been quoted saying there was no looting of sites in his area. Infuriated (and perhaps somewhat abashed, since in his May visit with National Geographic he had paid the guards, talked to the local elder, and thought he had secured the site from further damage), Gibson appealed to Gen. Kern for help. Asking for American forces or even helicopter overflights would be useless, Gibson realized by now, so he tried instead to sell Kern on the international option. The Japanese government, which had guarded sites effectively in Cambodia, had already offered to send troops to do the same in Iraq, Gibson told Kern, and he reminded the general that the Dutch Civil-Military Co-operation/Cultural Affairs (CIMIC/CA) unit had also indicated willingness to participate, though neither the Japanese nor the Dutch had yet been invited.[16] Kern turned over the information about CIMIC/CA to the Coalition Affairs section working with U.S. Central Command but cautioned Gibson not to expect much fast, given the administrative hurdles.

On July 14 the State Department announced the formation of an interagency working group to assist in rebuilding Iraq's cultural heritage infrastructure, with the State Department helping to channel private donations. The range of actions listed as planned by U.S. federal government agencies included none directed at site security.[17] This is a remarkable lacuna, given that by this point, in addition to Gibson's complaints and the appalling conditions noted by the National Geographic team, journalist Micah Garen had presented the U.S. Army with photos documenting industrial-scale looting on important sites such as Umma (one of the world's oldest cities), where electrical generators were being brought onto sites to facilitate nighttime digs and cigarettes were being hawked to the hundreds of diggers.[18] None of this seems to have had any impact on U.S. policy. Admittedly, the State Department had no troops to send itself, but had it been thinking more broadly, it could have considered other indirect mechanisms for addressing the looting epidemic in the countryside. At the very least, it might have associated itself with the initiative announced six days earlier by Gen. John Abizaid to create two new security institutions in Iraq. A "militia-like defense force" of ten battalions, more heavily armed than police, was supposed to work with specified U.S. military units, while a new security-guard force, the Iraqi Facility Protection Service (FPS), would take up posts at public buildings and vital sites, "protecting Iraq's strategic infrastructure, government buildings and cultural and educational assets" while freeing up U.S. soldiers for more serious duties.[19]

Security guards were exactly what Gibson needed. He wrote, this time to his old acquaintance Ryan Crocker, who had been appointed interim envoy to the new Afghan government, asking for guards to be deployed to Iraq's sites. The reply, from an unnamed CPA official, did not satisfy Gibson's need but did describe a pilot project with a three-pronged strategy that might serve as a model for site-protection efforts. In cooperation with the local marine unit in Babil Province and the province's interim governor, a 200-man special guard force from the FPS was supposedly being trained to protect the province's archaeological sites (including Babylon). But the initiative also involved convincing local governors that protecting antiquities was in their economic interest, and it called for U.S. commanders to pay for reconstruction projects. One of these projects, on the museum at Babylon, was being undertaken at the request of Ambassador Bremer, the officer added.

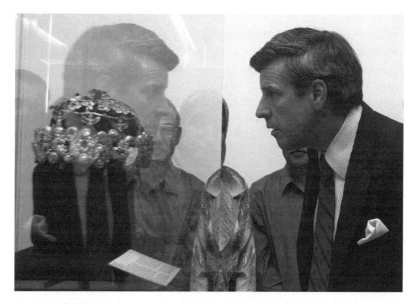

20   CPA chief Paul Bremer views the golden crown from Nimrud in the National Museum of Iraq on July 3, 2003. Photo courtesy of Marwan Naamani/AFP/Getty Images.

Bremer's involvement suggested to Gibson that the whole initiative was little more than a public-relations gimmick that was unlikely to be replicated any time soon for Nippur or any other site not immediately recognizable by the viewers of Fox News. By August the archaeologist had more or less given up on the hope of getting help from the CPA and decided to take direct action. He hired Wathiq Hindo (the businessman who had bought a rifle for a site guard just before the onset of the war, and who now was running a major Iraqi security firm) to try to deal with the plague of looting at Nippur. Guards there were reporting continued and expanded looting despite their presence, and over a much greater area even than before. Other sites in the province were being decimated as well by hordes of looters acting with total impunity. In May 2003, at ancient Girsu, seat of the queens of the Lagash kingdom around 2400 B.C., four guards had been able to drive off looters by firing their rifles over their heads.[20] Now, overmatched and not permitted by the CPA to carry weapons, there was little the guards could do, especially since the local authorities had also been disarmed. Gibson instructed Hindo to hire at least three more guards and to request permission from the CPA for them to carry weapons.

For this privilege, Gibson appealed directly to Col. Kessel, commander of the Special Functions Team of the U.S. Army 352nd Civil

Affairs Command. "If the local elder Abid Firhan is also allowed to arm his own family," the archaeologist added, "I think we can stop the destruction at Nippur." If this was not possible, he continued, could Kessel at least detail a small contingent to Afak, the nearest village? Gibson made certain that Kessel understood that Nippur had been excavated by Americans since 1900, and in all that time there had been no illegal digging on the site. "It is ironic," he noted, "that only after U.S. troops take the country can the site be looted." Because Nippur had been well guarded for years, and its cuneiform tablets are extremely sought after by collectors, Gibson considered it likely that the looters of Nippur had been sent on the order of antiquities dealers' agents. An American presence in the town of Afak would be an efficient way to put a damper on the illegal trade, saving not just Nippur but also Isin, capital of a century-long dynasty some four millennia ago.

What was not made clear in this appeal was why the military should care whether the illegal trade in antiquities was reduced. One good reason, which had not yet become evident in the summer of 2003 but should have been deducible, is that the same routes—and in some documented cases, the same individuals—involved in smuggling antiquities were also engaged in smuggling arms. Terrorists had a long history of using stolen valuables to finance their operations, including the IRA's 1974 theft of an entire art collection worth $32 million, and the looting of Beirut's museums in the 1980s by both Muslim and Christian factions. Certainly at least some in the military already knew what the German newspaper *Der Spiegel* reported in July 2005: that 9/11 ringleader Mohamed Atta had approached a professor at the University of Göttingen in Germany and asked about selling artifacts Atta said he could procure in Afghanistan. When asked why he wanted the money, Atta reportedly said he wanted to buy a plane.[21] And the military may also have been aware already that some of the looting crews were under at least the partial control of Muqtada al-Sadr, who the following year was able to command the release of journalist Micah Garen after Garen was kidnapped while collecting more information for a report and documentary on the looting of archaeological sites.[22]

None of this was known to Gibson at the time, however, and probably not known to Kessel either. In any case, the Civil Affairs commander was not in the mood to respond positively to an appeal to his sense of shame at the failure of the military to protect sites since the invasion. A number of his soldiers detailed to battling the antiquities looting and trading problem had been killed, most recently in Baghdad, as Gibson knew. It is perhaps not surprising, then, that in his reply to Gibson, Kessel ignored the pleas for U.S. troops. But he did say that the military was working to get Iraq's State Board of Antiquities and Heritage "equipped, trained and provided with satellite communications equipment, weapons and vehicles," adding that "any donors that are willing to step forward are welcome."

Frustrated, Gibson asked the White House Science Advisor's Office for help. The CPA was moving so slowly to put guards at some of the prominent sites that by the time they arrived there would be little to guard, the archaeologist fumed, and at the same time he was being refused permission to enable guards hired by the Oriental Institute to carry weapons. Noting none too subtly that he had not been saying much publicly about the continued looting, Gibson asked if the White House could simply alert the relevant military units that the administration was interested in this matter.

By the end of August, Gibson still had gotten no help, even after he nudged Crocker at the State Department, telling him he had received an e-mail from a soldier describing antiquities for sale on military bases. Gibson's last contact with the military reveals his utter exasperation. On September 11, 2003, he heard from Steven Hunter, one of the military geographers with whom Gibson had worked in the run-up to the war. Hunter forwarded an article about ethical guidelines for loans of Iraqi antiquities by collectors to museums. Gibson shot back a terse reply, to which there was no response: "The continuing destruction of sites all over southern Iraq and the theft of thousands of artifacts every week, with no visible effort on the part of U.S. authorities, makes the question of ethical behavior by museums pointless. Your unit of the Pentagon is capable of demonstrating the location and expansion of illegal digging. Are you at least doing that much?"[23]

EIGHT

Deathwatch for Iraqi Antiquities

Despite McGuire Gibson's urging, the idea of using satellite photographs to monitor illegal digging on Mesopotamian archaeological sites has never been taken up by the Defense Department, at least not publicly. While the Pentagon is almost certainly regularly photographing at least some sites so as to be able to respond to possible accusations that military operations are damaging them, they have shared no images with the archaeological community. As a result, there is no way to track the ongoing decimation of tells across the country over the years since the 2003 invasion. The rate of destruction of Iraq's archaeological patrimony could have served as an indicator of progress (or lack thereof) in the cultural sector, just as the rate of oil production does for the energy sector. And since once the oil runs out, Iraq's Mesopotamian past will be the country's most valuable national asset, it makes sense to pay attention to the sites now, before they all are completely plundered. But so little attention is being paid that, at least as of 2004, the maps being used by U.S. forces did not identify any archaeological sites.

Thanks to the work of archaeologist Elizabeth Stone, however, we have at least a partial view of what has occurred since the invasion. With funding cobbled together from the National Endowment for the Humanities, the State Department, the National Science Foundation, the National Geographic Society, and other nongovernmental donors—but none from the Pentagon—Stone purchased satellite images of seven thousand square kilometers in which there are known to be numerous sites. She then counted the holes at 1,837 separate sites, comparing photos from the 2001–2002 period with others taken at points in 2003. The results were sobering. Earlier observers flying by helicopter over Dhi Qar Province had noted massive looting there. Now even heavier looting was taking place farther south in southern Dīwānīyah Governate. Diggers were being very discriminating, focusing on sites likely to contain the items most in demand by collectors—cuneiform tablets and Parthian coins—while leaving mostly untouched the earliest settlements and Islamic-era sites. Stone also found that, surprisingly, looting slowed in early summer 2003, leading her to conclude that "if security had been established, the looting problem may have abated."[1]

Stone's project provided valuable objective data supplementing the reporting courageously attempted by freelance journalists Joanne Farchakh Bajjaly and Micah Garen as well as archaeologist Susanne Osthoff (the last two of whom were kidnapped in the course of their efforts to document the fate of archaeological sites). Unfortunately, there is no funding in place to repeat Stone's labor-intensive study on an annual basis. Simply to purchase commercial images would cost roughly $300,000 per set, and while UNESCO suggested early on that it might be able to cover the purchase costs, no monies have been forthcoming. Of course, the military could provide the needed images for little or no cost—if not satellite photos from the Defense Intelligence Agency, then more easily declassified images from the National Geospatial-Intelligence Agency (NGA). But leadership from above would be needed to make this happen.

Whatever the specific number of pillaged sites, there is no doubt that losses have been massive. Archaeologist John Malcolm Russell, who served as senior cultural advisor to the Coalition Provisional Authority in Iraq, estimates the number of artifacts ripped from the ground between 2003 and 2005 alone at 400,000 to 600,000, based on the average yield per site.[2] This is an astounding figure, three to four times the number of artifacts gathered from excavations since the 1920s by the National Museum of Iraq (some 170,000—though some of these are not single pieces but sets of shards), and thirty to forty times the 15,000 or so items ultimately determined to have been stolen from the museum.

Some two thousand antiquities confiscated abroad were returned to the museum between 2003 and 2006, including thirteen of the forty display pieces stolen from the public galleries. One of these thirteen priceless artifacts was recovered in New York; another was confiscated in Beirut after having been spotted by an Italian archaeologist involved in having excavated it. The archaeologist happened to be watching a show on Al Jazeera television about a Lebanese interior decorator when the camera panning around the apartment revealed a small stone head of King Sanatruq I of second-century B.C. Hatra mounted on the decorator's mantelpiece.[3]

The vast majority of the National Museum's pieces, however, have not surfaced, either because they are considered to be too hot to handle, or because they were stolen on commission and so do not need to be hawked. It took a decade for a Sumerian figurine stolen from a regional museum in Kirkuk in 1991 to surface at Christie's, and the museum's far more well-known lost artifacts are likely to remain underground for at least that long.[4]

As the rampant looting of artifacts from archaeological sites shows, however, there remains a robust market demand for Mesopotamian antiquities despite sanctions, so much so that in a country coming apart at the seams, looting is now one of the few roads to riches.[5] One report describes a former shoe repairman who hired three friends to help him dig at Ur, a venture that netted him enough to buy a new BMW after he discovered a gold statuette of a cow and calves worth $50,000 to the middleman. The usual yield was cylinder seals worth $50 on site, $700 in Jordan, and thousands of dollars on the black market in Europe or Japan.[6] The underground market, in fact, seems to be saturated, so much so that, according to illicit antiquities researcher Neil Brodie, "large numbers of artifacts are being openly traded on the Internet."[7] Prices being asked are low by historical standards, implying an oversupply from the looting in Iraq, according to Karl-Heinz Kind, one of only four Interpol officers at the Lyons headquarters assigned to deal with the global traffic in all illicit art.[8]

The number of artifacts actually circulating can only be guessed at, but the magnitude must be enormous if, as Donny George reports, "some 17,000 items stolen from unregistered archeological sites were returned," with no measurable effect on prices for items remaining on the market.[9] All antiquities are not created equal, of course, making it somewhat difficult to determine how large the market is in monetary terms. Overall, the revenue to looters generated by the trade in looted antiquities is estimated by the governing board of the Archaeological Institute of America as $10 to $20 million annually.[10] That may well be on the low side, however, given that a single Mesopotamian artifact, a tiny 5,000-year-old limestone figure of a lioness, was sold in 2007 for $57.2 million—the highest price ever paid for a sculpture or an antiquity.

How looted antiquities make their way from remote archaeological sites to the living rooms of wealthy collectors is not terribly well understood, though it is clear that the network involves middlemen who come to the sites, purchasing pieces for as little as ten to twenty dollars—and, when necessary, inciting flagging diggers by purchasing a single piece for several hundred dollars. Figurines, cylinder seals, cuneiform tablets, and Parthian and Sassanian coins by the thousands then make their way to antiquities bazaars in villages such as al-Fajr and Rifaʻi, where smugglers and dealers scoop them up.[11] From there, they are being smuggled abroad. According to Col. Matthew Bogdanos, by the end of 2003 approximately 1,900 Iraqi antiquities had been confiscated in neighboring countries: 1,450 in Jordan, 360 in Syria, 38 in Kuwait, and 18 in Saudi Arabia. Bogdanos notes that "no antiquities have been seized (or, to be more precise, acknowledged to have been seized) by the other two border nations, Turkey and Iran"—even though there is much evidence that smugglers are moving items toward those borders.[12] Nor have any items been returned from Kuwait or from the United Arab Emirates, countries where, according to a British Museum expert, royal family members have amassed private collections of thousands of artifacts.[13]

Cracking down on the illicit trade within Iraq itself would require going after the middlemen and smugglers spoken about by provincial antiquities inspector Abdulamir al-Hamdani, but so far is the U.S. military from doing so that it tolerates illicit antiquities sales on its own bases. Marine Corps reservist Matthew Boulay discovered this when stationed in Dīwānīyah, southwest of Baghdad, in the summer of 2003. Boulay was no archaeologist himself, but in tours of nearby Babylon given to marines by unemployed Iraqi archaeologists, he became sensitized to the cultural riches of Mesopotamia and learned about the Iraqis' resentment even of the legal removal of antiquities by Westerners: "One archaeologist read cuneiform and talked about how Germans and English had negotiated rights that in their eyes had unfairly taken a lot of their national treasures out of their country," the soldier recalls.[14] The sites around the country, Boulay also learned from the Iraqi archaeologist at Babylon, were not secured.

Back at the base, Boulay was shocked to discover that in a flea market authorized by the camp commander—where soda, junk food, rugs, trinkets, and bootleg music and movies were being hawked—"there was one little booth with guys who had laid out artifacts. They were selling them for $20, $40, $100 each." Lots of people on base were buying them, Boulay recalls, despite standing orders declaring it illegal to purchase or possess or bring back antiquities (as well as other contraband or spoils of war). Uncertain what to do, the marine first went online, Googled "Iraqi artifacts," and located McGuire Gibson, whom he e-mailed. Gibson was surprised and none too pleased, having visited the base earlier himself and spoken with several officers about the need to secure sites in his sector. The archaeologist suggested going straight to the base commander, but as Boulay remarked, "Corporals don't saunter up to colonels and make complaints." He went instead to his platoon commander, who ran the concern up the chain of command to the company commander. The response? Boulay received a "cease and desist" order to stop e-mailing about this to anyone.

By this point Boulay's unit was preparing to deploy home. He decided that the only way he could prove that antiquities were being openly sold on base to servicemen was to buy a few pieces himself and smuggle them back. Boulay went to the flea market stall, where the dealer had a coffee-table book filled with photos of cylinders and other artifacts, and other servicemen were haggling over prices:

I purchased eight cylinders over the course of several transactions. They cost anywhere from $20 to $80, based on haggling. I kept asking if there was anything else better he could show me. There was one piece that the dealer refused to sell, saying it was too valuable. It was kept in an empty cigarette box in his pocket. He said he was going to bring it to the U.S. and sell it.

"This was done openly, not in a back alley," Boulay adds. The dealer was happy to pose smiling with his buddy and the artifacts, and even gave the marine a receipt, the address of a jeweler in Dīwānīyah. To smuggle the pieces back home, Boulay simply packed them in a box with other belongings, wrapped in socks. The marines in the base post office cursorily inspected the package with him before he was allowed to tape it up and send it to his parents. Once back in New York, Boulay e-mailed Gibson, who thought it too risky to mail the artifacts to Chicago and recommended showing them to Zainab Bahrani, a Columbia University archaeologist. She instantly recognized them as authentic, dated them, and estimated their value at several thousand dollars apiece. What to do at this point was a touchy question: Boulay did not want the blame to fall only on lower-level marine corps officers, nor to be charged himself for having violated the law in trying to be a whistle-blower. With Bahrani as his intermediary, Boulay eventually turned the pieces over to the FBI, who arranged to hand them back to Iraqi authorities at a ceremony at the University of Pennsylvania.

There is no doubt that illicit trafficking of antiquities to coalition forces posted to bases near archaeological sites is a real problem. In addition to Boulay's story, we know that nearly fifty pieces were either turned in or confiscated from Polish soldiers at Babylon in 2003–2004 alone.[15] But this figure pales against the massive looting of artifacts by civilians from other archaeological sites, something that Babylon itself at least has largely been spared thanks to the efforts of the Poles. Thanks to a deal arranged between the Polish Ministry of Culture and Poland's Ministries of National Defence and Foreign Affairs, Polish Civil-Military Co-operation (CIMIC) archaeologists were embedded in the military at Babylon until the end of 2004, when responsibility for the Babylon site was turned over to the Iraqi archaeological police. With $680,000 from the Commander's Emergency Response Program provided by the U.S. military, the Polish forces protected Babylon and reconstructed its trashed museum infrastructure.[16]

The work on Babylon cost a half million dollars, leaving approximately $200,000 to be spent on a wide range of projects designed to help Iraq's archaeological police in al-Qādisīyah Province, where the Polish CIMIC team moved next. Aerial reconnaissance there in March 2005 noted "continuous and methodical illicit digging that neither the Coalition troops entering Iraq nor the local antiquity service have been able to prevent."[17] The Poles supplied some basic equipment to the Iraqis—bulletproof vests, metal detectors, walkie-talkies, and two cars. The team also worked with the State Board of Antiquities and Heritage to identify twenty-eight high-value sites in two other provinces, and barbed-wire fences, warning boards, guard posts, and observation towers were erected on some of these locations.[18]

Unfortunately, despite the Poles' efforts, looting was still being reported in fall 2006 at the putative birthplace of Abraham, Ur, whose tells are visible from the base on Babylon.[19] And while locating a coalition forces headquarters directly atop Babylon itself—described by John Curtis of the British Museum as "tantamount to establishing a military camp around the Great Pyramid in Egypt or around Stonehenge in Britain"—may have prevented looters from hacking away at its ruins, unconstrained construction activities by coalition forces have caused substantial damage to the site. Gravel brought in from elsewhere will contaminate the archaeological deposits, fuel is seeping from storage tanks into the strata below, trenches have been dug exposing unexcavated materials (including a complete vase), and the camp's perimeter is lined with sandbags and containers filled with potsherd-rich earth scooped up from the site.[20] The need to investigate and monitor the damage done to Babylon by American construction activities diverted Polish archaeologists from focusing greater attention on the problem of site looting.

The U.S. military has not disregarded completely the devastation of archaeological sites going on around it. It helped pay for 350 guards to protect 432 sites in Babil Province (though it is not clear how much funding was provided for this), and guards have also been assigned to Nippur, the Oriental Institute's site. Another site that has been excavated by American archaeologists for more than a hundred years, Tell Nuffar, has also been well taken care of (unlike all but one other of the five hundred registered sites in the province where it is located). Seven kilometers of barbed wire were placed around the site by Spanish forces in charge of the province until April 2004, and as of March 2005 twenty-four policemen stationed at a new headquarters built near the American Mission excavation house were patrolling Tell Nuffar around the clock, supplemented by helicopter overflights.[21] Nineveh, a third legendary site with links to American archaeologists (in this case, to John Malcolm Russell, who served in the Coalition Provisional Authority until June 2004 as the deputy senior advisor to the Iraq Ministry of Culture), has been less lavishly protected but did garner a $22,000 project funded by the Commander's Emergency Response Program. With the money, a Civil Affairs team working with the local director of antiquities and UNESCO built roofs, erected temporary fencing, and added security guards.

The Coalition Provisional Authority did make one effort to create a more fully developed site-protection project. In January 2004 Italian ambassador Mario Bondioli-Osio, senior advisor to the minister of culture, announced that an Archaeological Sites Protection Project would be put into effect. Beginning in Dhi Qar Province, Italian Carabinieri would train and transform Iraq's ragtag site guards into a "strong security force" in radio communication with local police and with the authority to carry weapons and detain suspects. The CPA's South Central Regional coordinator, foreign service officer Mike Gfoeller, committed $1 million in additional funding for the project to pay for vehicles, radios, and other matériel; UNESCO contributed $90,000 to help the Italians cover the costs of training. Once the kinks had been worked out in Dhi Qar, the project was to be extended to the entire Iraqi territory, ultimately employing a total of two thousand men. Within months the project was already in deep disarray, with an Iraqi official complaining to UNESCO that "1,200 guards in Diwaniyah, Wasit, Nasiriyah were not able to prevent the looting [in their sector] because of the lack of cooperation between the CPA and the guards."[22] With the turnover of sovereignty to the Iraqi government at the end of June 2004, the American funding of civil guards ended, and the guards were soon laid off.

After five long years of conflict, with conditions on the sites so grim and no likelihood of a stronger central government imposing order anytime in the foreseeable future, one might think that the military would be developing some new, tightly focused projects aimed at securing a few remote sites from looters. This does not appear to be happening, however. Instead, the Department of Defense is spending $200,000 from its Legacy Program (an obscure program usually devoted to stewardship of the 25 million acres of American land owned by the DoD) to increase "cultural awareness" among deploying personnel. Working in partnership with Saving Antiquities for Everyone (SAFE), an NGO formed in the wake of the looting of the National Museum of Iraq, Department of Defense cultural resources manager Dr. Laurie Rush produced 100,000 packs of playing cards to be distributed to troops. Each card carries images and information about Mesopotamian and Afghan artifacts and sites, as well as other instructional materials to help soldiers "recognize and protect historically sensitive areas."[23] While the motives of those involved in this effort are entirely laudable, the project's emphasis seems misplaced. "Our initiative is more geared toward awareness and teaching U.S. personnel the skills they need not to do damage themselves," Rush acknowledges, rather than toward preventing damage from being done by looters.[24]

More hopeful in preventing such damage is Rush's new interest in developing a partnership between the Defense Department and the Archaeological Institute of America to create a "reach back" capacity to subject-matter experts who could be consulted when American personnel encounter archaeological concerns overseas.[25] It is not clear, however, how this effort would mesh—or whether in fact it might interfere with—a parallel endeavor now under way by the recently established American branch of the Blue Shield, with support from the American Institute for Conservation. Corine Wegener, a curator and former Civil Affairs officer posted to Iraq, established the American Blue Shield committee to offer "training for [army] Civil Affairs units on how to give first aid to cultural property—how to recognize what is art and how to deal with it in an emergency situation and do the best to stabilize the situation until they can get a professional. The hope is that in the future, it will also be easier to deploy cultural heritage professionals in areas where sites are threatened."[26]

While the Blue Shield has a narrow focus on Civil Affairs, the Archaeological Institute of America (AIA) has launched a program of lectures aimed more broadly at troops awaiting deployment to Iraq or Afghanistan. "Since the soldiers had become the primary security agents at both archaeological sites and museums," reasoned the program's organizer, AIA president C. Brian Rose, "such briefings seemed essential in order to promote a greater comprehension of and respect for the cultural heritage of the areas in conflict." Securing the military's approval was no easy matter, since, as Rose noted, "no existing cooperative framework could be tapped,"[27] but with help from Col. Bogdanos, he managed to secure permission from Gen. John Abizaid, then head of the U.S. Central Command.

Unfortunately, like Rush's playing card program, the AIA's focus on comprehension and respect does not tackle the problem of looting head-on. Although the AIA's outgoing president, Jane Waldbaum, described the lectures as at least in part focused on "how to protect sites against looters," Rose's letter to Abizaid does not allude to site protection, and his objective seems to have been limited to trying to make soldiers "regard the ground and its antiquities with the same kind of reverence held by archaeologists." Beyond a general appeal to soldiers to be vigilant, the talks given have offered no concrete suggestions on how best to go about securing sites and museums. While Rose reports e-mails from soldiers in Iraq chronicling their attempts to hinder looting, it is doubtful that these attempts are as effective as they might have been had the AIA supplemented its exhortations to respect cultural heritage with specific, easy-to-take steps that would help prevent civilian plundering of sites. This seems a wasted opportunity.

Wegener's Blue Shield initiative seems more likely to have an impact, since it is both more practically oriented than the AIA's or Rush's and more focused on a particular pressure point within the military: Civil Affairs. Yet even Wegener's emphasis is more on providing first aid to artifacts than on protecting them. Palliative measures that mitigate damage are necessary but not sufficient. In addition, archaeologists and the military should be developing a set of recommended preventative measures that can be inserted into all relevant future operational orders.

The steps to be taken would of course need to be thought through carefully—and not by conservation experts or archaeologists, who know much about artifacts but very little about how to keep individuals from breaking into buildings or trespassing on remote sites. Rather, advice is needed from experts in non-lethal site protection, who could be asked to suggest innovative, cheap, but relatively effective technologies to deter looters from urban buildings such as museums, on the one hand, and remote sites, on the other.

There are many such possibilities beyond the obvious one of stringing barbed wire. One is suggested by Gertrude Bell, who reported in 1909 about a dig she was visiting at Babylon, where the upper layers of the tell consisted of garbage heaps: "When the workmen cut down through them to reach the temple gate the stench, combined with the stifling heat of the pit, was so intolerable that the work had to be discontinued for several days till a breeze arose and made it possible to proceed with it."[28] Modern chemistry has improved on nature's stench, and the Defense Department was already working on the ultimate stink bomb back in 2001.[29] It is not beyond the realm of possibility, then, to imagine a program to seed sites with stink mines (a tactic used to keep vagrants out of empty churches in some U.S. cities). If the aim were to identify looters, other mines could be designed to spray indelible ink or invisible dyes—concocted in such a way as not to ruin the artifacts they are intended to protect.

The laws of war discourage the use of mines, however, and might make such a program untenable. Other technological options for remote site protection have been suggested, such as seeding the roads to sites with tire-puncturing tacks or other devices to disable vehicles. Artifacts could be equipped with tracking devices and planted on promising sites so that the pathway from site to collector could be traced. It might even be possible to use insect pheromones to attract large numbers of scorpions or snakes onto sites.[30] But it is unlikely that any of these measures are contemplated at present in military circles.

Nor is any sustained effort toward securing sites and museums being undertaken by international and nongovernmental organizations, so far as can be determined. And this is the case even though the looting of Iraq's cultural heritage supposedly forced these organizations to face what the chair of the Committee for Conservation at the International Council of Museums (ICOM) described as "our political impotence" in 2003.[31] In response to this *crise de conscience*, a few tentative steps were taken to deal with the problem of looting. ICOM made contact with representatives from the U.S. armed forces in Iraq, while UNESCO contributed to the ill-fated Carabinieri-run guard-training project and also worked with Interpol on operations at Doha, Dubai, and elsewhere that netted around 190 artifacts by May 2004.

For the most part, as was the case immediately after the museum's looting, international and nongovernmental efforts have continued to focus not on site protection but on restoring the National Museum of Iraq and training Iraqi archaeologists in methods of inventorying and mapping. Of the thirty-six experts invited to a UNESCO meeting on Iraqi Cultural Heritage held in August 2003, not one was from the military, police, customs, or a site-security firm. UNESCO's own projected budget for culture-sector projects in Iraq in 2004, $7.3 million, allocated only $300,000 to be spent on security for archaeological sites and museums.[32]

Beyond this, UNESCO and other international organizations have done little, probably because a hoped-for outpouring of international aid has failed to materialize. An international coordination committee was created in September 2003 to distribute the expected largesse from the Madrid International Donors' Conference for Iraqi Reconstruction the following month. The World Bank's president, James Wolfensohn, opened the meeting on a hopeful note from UNESCO's point of view: "I start with culture. . . . Culture must be preserved and strengthened."[33] But the expected flood of donations did not materialize. The World Bank itself provided only around $60,000 to enable the Global Heritage Fund to conduct a ten-day workshop in Petra, Jordan, for Iraqi site inspectors in June 2004. The response from other countries has also been underwhelming, to say the least.

In the United States, the picture is similar. Funding for nongovernmental professional and academic organizations is in short supply, and what funding there is has gone to programs that emphasize conservation and archaeological training over site protection. In October 2003, for example, the U.S. Agency for International Development (USAID) awarded $4 million to SUNY Stony Brook, part of which was to be used to develop an academic program in archaeology for Iraqi archaeologists. One year into what was to have been a three-year program, USAID pulled the plug. Luckily, the Mellon Foundation stepped in to cover the remaining two years' costs. But it seems questionable, to say the least, to invest scarce funding in bringing archaeologists from Iraq to the United States for training. Working with Americans is likely to expose them to grave dangers when they return to Iraq. Meanwhile, the sites they are being taught to painstakingly excavate and conserve are being decimated.

Like the U.S. Agency for International Development and the Mellon Foundation, the Getty Conservation Institute's Iraq Cultural Heritage Conservation Initiative established a training program for Iraqi archaeologists, but the Getty's initiative also included grants for site protection. As of December 2006, however, the program had awarded only two grants: the Massachusetts College of Art and Design was given money to replace the protective roofing over the Palace of Sennacherib in the archaeological site at Nineveh, which was looted again during the 2003 war, and the American Association for Research in Baghdad received money (through the conduit of the World Monuments Fund) to help place guards at several archaeological sites that had already been looted.[34]

The Getty's stated aim is "to develop long-term tools and professional capacities to support the role of the Iraq State Board of Antiquities and Heritage [SBAH] in the stewardship of Iraq's archaeological and architectural sites."[35] That is certainly a good strategic objective. But stewardship, in the lawless climate of postwar Iraq, means more than conservation and site management. Devoting funds to training archaeologists in these specialties makes no sense when the SBAH lacks the resources to secure the sites that the archaeologists are supposedly going to manage.

It is not that the Iraqis have not tried to address the problem. Donny George, who was appointed director of museums in 2004, worked with a colleague to persuade the first elected Iraqi government to provide $3.4 million annually for a program to create a specialized, armed antiquities police force, the Facility Protection Service (FPS), comparable to those for railroads and oil installations. Getting this program up and running took far longer than it would have with additional funding from the international community or private donors (so far as can be determined, only the Carr Foundation has provided any money for civil guards), but by the summer of 2006, a force of fourteen hundred was finally in place, each earning about $200 a month. Only one-fourth of the guards are armed, however, and the small number of SBAH vehicles available to patrol sites sit mostly idle because since 2006 the government has not seen fit to provide the FPS with gasoline.[36]

The total number of archaeological police, in any case, is far too low to cover the areas they are supposed to patrol. In al-Qādisīyah, for example, 4 officers and 93 guards are expected to patrol 350 sites (out of 500 registered ones).[37] Not much help is to be had from Iraqi or other security forces, either: as Micah Garen reported in 2004 (and there is little reason to think matters have improved since then), local police feared reprisals from the looters' tribes, the Iraqi National Guard claimed it lacked weaponry, the Carabinieri insisted they were only on a humanitarian mission, the Iraqi government saw the problem as one for coalition forces, and the Americans saw it as the responsibility of the Iraqis.[38]

One sticking point in garnering international support may have been concern that much of whatever would be given might be wasted because of rampant corruption. This may explain why the United States contributed no money to this effort, but instead donated some four-wheel-drive vehicles, as did Japan, working through UNESCO. If the purpose behind providing equipment rather than money was indeed to prevent losses from corruption, it did not succeed. "What we got," recalls George,

was fifteen four-wheel-drive cars—and they arrived at the airport and five of them just disappeared. We got only ten of those. Then we started working with UNESCO. Forty-five cars were donated, again through UNESCO with money coming from Japan, but eight of those forty-five also disappeared on the road between Amman and Baghdad.

By 2006, in any case, graft was the least of the SBAH's problems. In the elections of December 2005 that installed a Shiite-dominated government, radical Shiite cleric Muqtada al-Sadr's party had done extremely well. One of its electoral spoils was control of the Ministry of Tourism and Antiquities. As the name implied, this ministry now controlled the State Board of Antiquities and Heritage, which had previously been under the wing of the Ministry of Culture. Even before the official turnover of power to al-Sadr's appointees, the Iraqi government had permitted al-Sadr loyalists to monitor and control Donny George's activities as director of museums. "They interfered in every single thing and changed things without our knowledge," George recalls. "They encouraged the staff of the department to go directly to the ministry, rather than through us. They removed people not connected to the party and put people in who were not qualified. It is worse than under Saddam."[39] Far from championing Iraq's antiquities, the SBAH now allowed other government agencies to profit from looting them. One government-sponsored plan proposed to sell land adjacent to Sumerian sites for a so-called "brick-making factory" that was really a front for digging up and selling ancient bricks from the sites. When a provincial antiquities director refused to go along with the scheme, he was himself charged with corruption and thrown in jail for three months.

It was bad enough that the professionals on the staff found themselves without support from their own ministers, subordinated to or purged by unqualified party hacks like the dentist appointed in 2006 to head the Ministry of Tourism and Antiquities because he was related through marriage to al-Sadr. Much more ominous was the tilt toward a fundamentalist attitude toward antiquities that went along with the takeover of the Ministry of Tourism and Antiquities. One might think that tourism has no more to do with religion than do antiquities, but in Iraq tourism means religious pilgrimages. Managing (and profiting from) the massive numbers of visitors to holy shrines has been the central concern of al-Sadr's ministry. As journalist Sumedha Senanayake notes, "The ministry is only focusing on protecting Islamic sites and artifacts and turning a blind eye to pre-Islamic ones."[40]

If officially al-Sadr's followers have turned a blind eye to Mesopotamia, unofficially they have tended to give it the evil eye. In May 2004 al-Sadr's followers in Nāsirīyah rampaged through the city, smashing Sumerian-inspired sculptures, particularly those of women with their legs exposed.[41] They then burned and looted the museum at Nāsirīyah, telling the museum's guards to warn the local inspector that "we will do to your antiquities exactly what the Taliban did!"[42]

There is no doubt that for devout Muslims, whether Shiite or Sunni, pre-Islamic artifacts are "idols" (as a note attached to two pre-Islamic statues returned to the National Museum described them). Iconoclasm is nonetheless very rare, even among fundamentalists—and even rarer when it is deemed better to put pre-Islamic antiquities to some good use. According to Donny George, worshippers in al-Sadr's stronghold of Najaf were told that looting artifacts is ethical so long as the money goes for building mosques—or buying guns. Given such encouragement, it is hardly surprising that in October 2005 multinational forces working with police in Nāsirīyah arrested two men for terrorist acts who had in their possession seven Sumerian artifacts. As Col. Bogdanos notes, "When tracking down terrorists, we now find antiquities." And this is as much the case for Sunni as for Shiite insurgents. Bogdanos revealed that a series of raids in June 2005 in northwest Iraq had netted "five terrorists in underground bunkers filled with automatic weapons, ammunition stockpiles, black uniforms, ski masks, night-vision goggles and 30 vases, cylinder seals and statuettes that had been stolen from the Iraq Museum."[43]

One might think that the surfacing of evidence tying looted antiquities to terrorism would be enough to persuade the American military to finally take some robust action against the networks fueling the illicit international trade in Mesopotamian artifacts. But the United States was already well aware that terrorists and antiquities traffickers ran in the same circles. As FBI director Robert Mueller noted in a November

2004 speech, the United Kingdom's National Criminal Intelligence Service had already concluded in 2003 that "there is a link between the removal and transport of cultural objects and the funding of terrorism."[44] Yet three years after Mueller's speech, there is no indication, beyond the one arrest cited by Bogdanos, that this link is being pursued.

Certainly, the chance of any cooperative ventures between the U.S. military and Iraq's State Board of Antiquities and Heritage in pursuit of terrorist-connected antiquities crime is now nil. Relations have soured, in part because of the backlash against the building of military bases on historic sites, in part because the Ministry of Tourism and Antiquities is in the hands of Sadrists. By spring 2007 the SBAH had become so vehemently anti-American that a friendly visit by American forces to the offices of the Department of Antiquities (adjacent to the museum), intended by the Americans to signal their commitment to protecting the building, was denounced by the director as a violation of Iraq's ancient heritage.[45]

It is not the Americans, however, who threaten the SBAH and the heritage it is charged to protect. The true threat comes from other Iraqis. In May 2007, for example, a political faction took over and held for ransom the Basra Museum, which had been looted during the invasion of 1991 and (like the Mosul Museum) occupied since spring 2003 by families of squatters. The Basra incident was peaceful in comparison with what happened in Samarra three months later. In a scene eerily reminiscent of Baghdad in April 2003, the SBAH building in Samarra was attacked by armed men who reportedly stole everything there was to take, including cars, furniture, and all the archaeological equipment.[46] And soon after that, the SBAH representative in Basra was assassinated.[47]

Even more ominous, a new phenomenon emerged in 2007 of Muslim shrines being targeted by Salafist radical groups opposed to all shrines. The February 2006 Al Qaeda bombing of the golden dome at Samarra set this trend in motion, and by June 2007 at least eighteen other holy sites had been attacked.

Donny George, who over the years since the invasion had risen to become director of the National Museum of Iraq and president of the State Board of Antiquities and Heritage, himself fled the country with his family in August 2006 after his son received a death threat—a letter accusing his father of cooperating with foreign elements, with a bullet enclosed in the envelope.[48] The archaeologist had already applied for retirement, after being told officially that he was being forced out on the orders of al-Sadr's party because he was a Christian rather than a Shiite Muslim.

As for the National Museum of Iraq, as 2007 came to a close, it remained under siege in one of the most dangerous neighborhoods in Baghdad. In 2005 a Katyusha missile had landed in the museum garden. That might just have been an accident, albeit a frightening one. But there could be no mistaking the intentions of the violence that occurred in spring 2007, when fifty people were kidnapped from the street outside the museum by armed, uniformed men in official cars. George feared the same men might force their way into the museum itself eventually, or that civil order might break down again. In a little-noted incident in October 2003, the museum had nearly been breached by hundreds of rioting former soldiers who ultimately satisfied themselves with stoning the employees' cars before going on to trash the nearby School of Music and Dance.[49] Taking all possible measures to prevent a repeat of the museum's looting after this close call, George and his staff removed the antiquities from registration rooms and labs to the storeroom and then welded shut all the doors leading to it. For good measure, they also sealed the museum entrance by building an additional concrete-and-brick wall half a meter thick—all this supplementing the three-meter-high fence topped with sharp blades that had been erected several years earlier.[50]

In the summer of 2002, warning the president that the United States would be held responsible for damage done to Iraq if the United States invaded the country, Secretary of State Colin Powell invoked what he privately called the "Pottery Barn rule: You break it, you own it."[51] Powell's point was that a long occupation would be required to put the shattered country together again. But in a land that is itself literally one gigantic Pottery Barn, whose sites and museums held some of the earliest and most beautifully crafted pottery known to man, the "You break it, you own it" rule now reads with a bitter irony. Five years into the occupation, the barn door knocked in by the Americans remains wide open, and Iraq's cultural heritage is being broken day by day into fragments, site by site. That the loss is not just to Iraq but to us all—because, in a sense, Iraq's cultural patrimony is also the patrimony of humankind, in which we all share ownership—only makes the irony the more bitter.

Coda

As of spring 2008, the future of Iraq's past looks bleak indeed. The museum has been reduced from a repository into a prison for antiquities, with little prospect to reopen for years to come. A new program put in place offering rewards for the return of missing pieces has netted several thousand items, but the costs of paying ransom have sapped the museum's budget, leaving it without the funds to take action to retrieve artifacts that turn up at foreign auctions.[1] Out on the sites, prospects are even more dire. Most will be ruined within the next decade, absent some effort by those with the wherewithal to stop the looting.

Neither the U.S. military, nor Iraq's own government, nor international cultural heritage organizations, nor foundations, nor the collectors of antiquities show much sign of wishing to devote the resources needed to help Iraq salvage what remains of its archaeological heritage before it is entirely broken up and its jumbled remnants disappear altogether into warehouses, dealers' galleries, and the living rooms of the well-to-do. By the end of 2007, the museum was turning to help from Ahmad Chalabi, the former exile leader who played a major role in persuading the United States that Saddam could be toppled without concern for the aftermath. In misleading administration officials into believing we would be greeted with flowers rather than with crowds of looters, Chalabi is arguably among those most responsible for what happened to the National Museum of Iraq. Having ruined the museum in 2003, Chalabi four years later was able to use the museum to stage a media event in which he presented the museum's director with some four hundred missing artifacts that, it was reported without comment, "he had procured through a friend."[2]

As this book went to press, the Bush administration at long last announced a new initiative to assist Iraq in conserving and preserving its cultural heritage, the Iraq Cultural Heritage Project. Unfortunately, the $13 million program focuses solely on professional development for conservators and other museum professionals without providing any funding to improve site security; reliable anonymous sources report that several proposals for joint U.S.-Iraqi site policing programs were turned down by the State Department. No help is needed on that score, supposedly, because, as Laura Bush put it in her remarks announcing the project, "Recent security gains and increased stability have set the stage now for a more vigorous effort to promote Iraq's cultural history."[3] The talking game now—for both the United States and the Iraqi government—is that order has been restored, the Iraqis are fully capable of running their own affairs, and the Americans are seeking to reduce their footprint in the country.

Given that objective, it is hardly surprising that beginning in July 2008 a flurry of stories appeared in the press suggesting that post-invasion looting of archaeological sites was either no longer a problem ("Iraq's Top Archaeologists Says Looting of Sites Is Over"; "'Cultural Heritage Sites Safe,' According to State Board of Antiquities Inspector Qais Rashid") or that site looting had never really been a problem to begin with ("So Much for the 'Looted Sites'").[4] The public relations campaign was abetted inadvertently by a British Museum team that was permitted to visit eight major sites in southern Iraq and found little evidence of post-2003 looting. Unreported, for the most part, was the reason for this surprisingly happy situation: unlike most of the ten thousand or so other sites in Iraq, these eight were either close to (and in one case within!) coalition bases, were under the long-standing control of local sheikdoms paid to guard them, or had received special protection after media reported on their looting in 2003.[5]

The reality about how much looting is now occurring on Iraq's sites will remain murky until and unless the military begins to share satellite or aerial imagery. But if looting rates are tied to security gains and increased stability, then there is some reason for worry, since civilian casualty rates in summer 2008 were down to the levels seen in 2004, a year that we know saw much looting of sites.

Meanwhile, the Bush administration continues rattling its saber

None of these obstacles is insuperable, and some have already be-
un to be dismantled. Only time will tell whether the bitter lessons
arned in Iraq will translate into new and better institutional struc-
res and practices, or whether they will be gradually forgotten until
e cause yet another inadvertent cultural disaster and lose still more of
r common past.

toward two other adjacent antiquities-rich countries, Syria and Iran.[6]
Obviously, the war-fighting scenarios being crafted in the Pentagon
will differ from those that were developed for Iraq in 2002–2003, but
whatever the scenario, archaeological heritage will once again be at
risk. While the United Kingdom has announced that it would ratify the
1954 Hague Convention for the Protection of Cultural Property in the
Event of Armed Conflict—based on a new understanding of the danger
to the United Kingdom's reputation if its military became "involved
in occupation of territory with significant risk of damage to/unlaw-
ful removal of cultural assets in that territory"—as of August 2008 the
United States had taken no such steps.[7]

And it is far from clear whether war planners have made the structural adjustments necessary to keep cultural heritage protection from
falling through the cracks again. Some small steps have been taken
to avoid the stove-piping of information within offices and agencies.
In Great Britain, the Ministry of Defence has developed a new series
of networking arrangements to link with other departments, including the Department for Culture, Media and Sport. Civil servants from
DCMS are now invited to relevant high-level Ministry of Defence planning meetings, something that never happened before 2003. One senior DCMS official who prefers to remain anonymous comments, "We
felt very exposed by the war because we had absolutely no influence
in it, nothing to do with its planning. By the beginning of this year
[2005], there was a lot more communication taking place."

Some slight improvements in information sharing seem to have been
made within the United States military as well. Lt. Gen. Michael D.
Maples, director of the Defense Intelligence Agency, insists that the
"DIA has applied lessons learned from Operation Iraqi Freedom and
continues to work closely with the national intelligence community,
military planners, and policy makers to safeguard all known cultural
sites." Maples notes that the DIA's targeting information "supports a
full range of planning requirements from major military to stability
operations."[8] There is no way of knowing, however, whether those
planning requirements go beyond avoiding damaging sites to actively
securing and protecting them from looting.

Some hope that securing sites may now be on the military's radar
screen is, however, to be gleaned from the revised field manual on stability operations released by the military just as this book goes to press.
Among the "Essential Stability Tasks" identified by the manual is the
requirement that forces "protect and secure places of religious worship

and cultural sites," and that they "protect and secure strategically important institutions (such as government buildings; medical and public health infrastructure; the central bank, national treasury, and integral commercial banks; museums; and religious sites)."[9] Although it is a bare mention, the insertion of this language is potentially far more consequential than the ratification of the 1954 Hague Convention. It means that cultural heritage protection is now embedded in the task matrix that operational planners will take as the starting point for future war planning. That is a step forward.

The executive branch has taken a small step to improve its post-conflict reconstruction planning, with a key new agency, the Office of the Coordinator for Reconstruction and Stabilization (S/CRS), now in place. There is no reference to cultural protection in the only article posted on S/CRS's "Lessons Learned" Web page, and the "Essential Tasks" matrix developed by S/CRS did not originally include securing of museums and cultural sites.[10] That lacuna has been addressed, however. Unfortunately, funding for this office has been inconsistent and inadequate for it to function effectively, and its future remains uncertain.[11]

Cultural heritage organizations, which Archaeological Institute of America president C. Brian Rose admits "ran around like chickens with our heads cut off" in 2002–2003, may also be somewhat more prepared to work together now. "We watched what the other did in response to the emergency, saw each others' strength and weaknesses, and the leadership of organizations met and saw who was effective at doing what," he notes. "We would be better able to move forward as a more coordinated unit." Yet the same "jockeying for power and prestige, a kind of 'learned society competition'"[12] that Rose says hampered archaeological associations from working together will continue to be a problem in the future, since no new interorganizational entity has emerged to unify the cultural heritage sector.

Even with interagency coordination having been improved slightly, reconstruction planning beginning to take into account the need to protect cultural heritage, and archaeological groups establishing some tenuous lines of communication among themselves, there still remains a real and serious likelihood that military and civilian postwar planners will be unable to muster from the archaeologists themselves the cooperation and expertise needed to protect museums and archaeological sites, at least if Iraq is any indication. Jobs posted in June 2007 by the State Department for senior cultural heritage advisors to be posted

to Iraq as members of provincial reconstruction [...] filled five months later.

The underwhelming response from archaeolo[...] partment job opportunity might be chalked up [...] straightforward recognition that archaeological t[...] vation is of little use when the challenge is how [...] looters. The lack of interest in the position proba[...] from a built-in disciplinary aversion to collabor[...] A similar program assigning teams of anthropo[...] gades has been denounced by some as "mercena[...] could inadvertently cause all anthropologists t[...] as tools of the U.S. military, and archaeologists [...] concerns.[13] But even archaeologists who overca[...] aid the United States in 2003 have turned thei[...] the disaster in Iraq. In 2005 the military cont[...] cal Institute of America seeking archaeologists [...] coordinate information for archaeological sites i[...] for such information would be Columbia Univ[...] who went to Iraq independently in 2003 to t[...] ally served as senior consultant for the Coalitio[...] "When that news [of the military's request for [...] via colleagues, recalls Bahrani, "I said, 'Leave [...] you a single site.'"[14]

For an effective policy protecting archaeol[...] termath of armed conflict to ever take shape[...] ment will have to be overcome, along with th[...] that this history has revealed: general indiffe[...] protection in the foreign policy and defense [...] ing agendas between military planners and [...] the scope of the military's responsibilities fo[...] tage; international legal conventions that do [...] relatively new problem of looting by civilian[...] formation within pockets of the bureaucracy [...] ologists who fail to see the difference betw[...] securing it from looters; a paucity of ongoi[...] as formal, between cultural heritage organi[...] on the one hand, and defense policy maker[...] planners, on the other; and a community [...] museum officials that for the most part has [...] service to a problem that its own appetite fo[...]

Appendix: Interviews

Zainab Bahrani, interviewed by the author, March 14, 2005.

Matthew Boulay, interviewed by the author, July 24, 2007.

Bonnie Burnham, interviewed by the author, March 14, 2005.

Joseph Collins (former deputy assistant secretary of defense for stability operations), interviewed by the author, October 5, 2005.

Harriet Crawford, interviewed by the author, December 22, 2004.

John Curtis, interviewed by the author, December 21, 2004.

James Fitzpatrick, interviewed by the author, March 3, 2005.

Sharon Flescher, interviewed by the author, March 14, 2005.

McGuire Gibson, interviewed by the author, February 9, 2006.

Ashton Hawkins, interviewed by the author, March 14, 2005.

Lt. Col. Chris Herndon, interviewed by the author, April 15, 2005.

Arthur Houghton, interviewed by the author, March 3, 2005.

Maria Kouroupas, C. Miller Crouch et al. (Educational and Cultural Affairs, State Department), interviewed by the author, April 15, 2005.

Ambassador John M. Limbert (former civil administrator for Iraqi Cultural Heritage in the Office of Reconstruction and Humanitarian Assistance), interviewed by the author, March 3, 2005.

David Mack (director, Middle East Institute), interviewed by the author, April 15, 2005.

William R. Polk, interviewed by the author, June 28, 2007.

Nicholas Postage, interviewed by the author, December 21, 2004.

Colin Renfrew, interviewed by the author, December 21, 2004.

C. Brian Rose (president, Archaeological Institute of America), interviewed by the author, December 18, 2007.

Dr. Laurie Rush, interviewed by the author, April 11, 2008.

Lt. Col. Eric Schwartz, interviewed by the author, August 15, 2007.

Elizabeth Stone (archaeologist), interviewed by the author, February 19, 2007.

Capt. William Sumner, interviewed by the author, August 30, 2006.

Maj. Christopher Varhola (Civil Affairs officer), interviewed by the author, April 15, 2005.

Rasool Vatandoust (director, Research Centre for Conservation of Cultural Relics, Tehran, Iran; and head, Department of International and Cultural Relations, Iran), interviewed by author, November 28, 2006.

Jane Waldbaum, interviewed by the author, December 19, 2007.

Donny George Youkhanna (former director of museums, State Board of Antiquities and Heritage, Iraq), interviewed by the author, February 19, 2007.

Lt. Col. Peter Zarcone, interviewed by the author, July 24, 2007.

Notes

INTRODUCTION

1. Matthew Arnold, "Doing as One Likes," in *Culture and Anarchy: An Essay in Political and Social Criticism* (London: Smith, Elder & Co., 1869), 52.

2. Rasool Vatandoust (director, Research Centre for Conservation of Cultural Relics, Tehran, Iran; and head of the Department of International and Cultural Relations, Iran), interviewed by the author, November 28, 2006. The ancient Persian capital of Persepolis was also saved during the revolution, not from looters, but from a mob led by a mullah, which was convinced to disperse by the brave intervention of the provincial governor of Shiraz. See Andrew Lawler, "International Collaboration: Iran Reopens Its Past," *Science* 302, no. 5647 (November 2003): 970–73.

3. Kirsty Norman, "The Invasion of Kuwait, and the Subsequent Recovery of Its National Museum: A Conservator's View," *Museum Management and Curatorship* 16, no. 2 (1997): 180–91.

4. Fred Iklé, preface to *Every War Must End,* 2nd rev. ed. (New York: Columbia University Press, 2005); quoted in Thomas E. Ricks, *Fiasco: The American Military Adventure in Iraq* (New York: Penguin, 2006), 106.

CHAPTER ONE

1. The stele was rediscovered in 1901 by French archaeologists and removed to the Louvre, under a special treaty that had been negotiated in 1900 with the shah granting France all antiquities that might be discovered in their expeditions in Susiana. See *Encyclopedia Iranica,* s.v. "Delegations

Archéologiques" (by François Tissot), http://www.iranica.com/newsite/
search/index.isc/ (accessed August 7, 2007); and Jean Bottéro, "The 'Code'
of Hammurabi," in *Mesopotamia: Writing, Reasoning, and the Gods,* trans.
Zainab Bahrani and Marc van de Mieroop (Chicago: University of Chicago
Press, 1992), 156–84. When the French prime minister visited Baghdad in
1979, Saddam Hussein demanded, to no avail, that the Louvre return the
Hammurabi stele.

2. Comte de Choiseul-Gouffier, quoted in Wendy K. Shaw, *Possessors and
Possessed: Museums, Archaeology, and the Visualization of History in the Late
Ottoman Empire* (Berkeley: University of California Press, 203), 70.

3. Karl E. Meyer, *The Plundered Past* (New York: Atheneum, 1973), 133.

4. Claudius Rich, quoted in Magnus Bernhardsson, *Reclaiming a Plundered
Past: Archaeology and Nation Building in Modern Iraq* (Austin: University of
Texas Press, 2005), 9.

5. See Shaw, *Possessors,* 73.

6. See Christopher E. Woods, "The Sun-God Tablet of Nabû-Apla-Iddina
Revisited," *Journal of Cuneiform Studies* 56 (2004): 82; and Irene J. Winter,
"Babylonian Archaeologists of The(ir) Mesopotamian Past," in *Proceedings
of the First International Congress on the Archaeology of the Ancient Near East,*
ed. P. Matthiae et al. (Rome: Dipartimento di scienze storiche, archeologiche e antropologiche dell'antichità, 2000), 2:1785–1800.

7. A. H. Layard, *Autobiography and Letters from His Childhood until His Appointment as H.M. Ambassador at Madrid* (London: John Murray, 1903), 306–7;
quoted in Mogens Trolle Larsen, *The Conquest of Assyria: Excavations in an
Antique Land, 1840–1860* (New York: Routledge, 1996), 6.

8. See Claudius Rich, *Narrative of a Residence in Koordistan, and on the Site
of Ancient Nineveh* (London: James Duncan, 1836), 39; quoted in Larsen,
Conquest of Assyria, 9.

9. On the digging of bricks at Hillah, see Claudius Rich, *Narrative of a
Journey to the Site of Babylon* (London: Duncan and Malcolm, 1839), 9.
British officers after World War I found the owner of the land containing
the site of Nimrud removing blocks for use in building his own house.
See Henry Breasted, "The Oriental Institute—a Beginning and a Program,"
American Journal of Semitic Languages and Literatures 38, no. 4 (July
1922): 255.

10. A. H. Layard, *Nineveh and Its Remains: With an Account of a Visit to the
Chaldean Christians of Kurdistan, and the Yezidis, or Devil-Worshippers; and
an Enquiry into the Manners and Arts of the Ancient Assyrians,* 2 vols.
(London: John Murray, 1849), 1:66–67; quoted in Larsen, *Conquest of
Assyria,* 92.

11. [Gertrude Bell], "The First Capital of Assyria," *Times* (London), August 23,
1910.

12. See Roger Matthews, *The Archaeology of Mesopotamia: Theories and
Approaches* (London: Routledge, 2003), 9.

13. Quoted in Shaw, *Possessors,* 112.
14. The French excavators in Persia were granted exclusive rights to remove anything they wished, so long as the Persian government was compensated for gold or silver objects only. See F. Bagherzadeh, "Jean Perrot, un ami de l'Iran," in *Contribution à l'histoire de l'Iran: Mélanges offerts à Jean Perrot,* ed. F. Vallat (Paris: Editions Recherche sur les civilisations, 1990), xv. The Germans, too, concluded a secret agreement entitling them to export antiquities despite the Ottoman Antiquities Law of 1884, which had declared all objects excavated in Ottoman dominions to be state property and required them to stay on the spot or be transported to the Imperial Museum in Istanbul.
15. Quoted in Suzanne Marchand, *Down from Olympus: Archaeology and Philhellenism in Germany, 1750–1970* (Princeton, NJ: Princeton University Press, 1996), 204.
16. Shaw, *Possessors,* 73, 75.
17. See Matthews, *Archaeology of Mesopotamia,* 11.
18. See Patty Gerstenblith, "From Bamiyan to Baghdad: Warfare and the Preservation of Cultural Heritage at the Beginning of the 21st Century," *Georgetown Journal of International Law* 37, no. 2 (Winter 2006): 256; James Nafziger, "Protection of Cultural Heritage in Time of War and Its Aftermath," *IFAR Journal* 6 (2003): 56–61; and Sharon A. Williams, *The International and National Protection of Cultural Property* (Dobbs Ferry, NY: Oceana Publications, 1977), 17–19.
19. See Bernhardsson, *Reclaiming a Plundered Past,* 74.
20. The Germans had been excavating under a secret agreement with the Ottoman government allowing them to export artifacts.
21. R. H. Hall, quoted in Bernhardsson, *Reclaiming a Plundered Past,* 80.
22. On Lawrence's archaeological-*cum*-espionage exploits, see Stephen E. Tabachnik, "Lawrence of Arabia as Archaeologist," *Biblical Archaeology Review* 23 (1997): 45.
23. Bernhardsson, *Reclaiming a Plundered Past,* 89.
24. Ibid., 92.
25. Breasted, "Oriental Institute," 241, 255.
26. Bernhardsson, *Reclaiming a Plundered Past,* 126.
27. See Amatzia Baram, "A Case of Imported Identity: The Modernizing Secular Ruling Elites of Iraq and the Concept of Mesopotamian-Inspired Territorial Nationalism, 1922–1992," *Poetics Today* 15 (1994): 280.
28. Quoted in ibid., 283.
29. See Bernhardsson, *Reclaiming a Plundered Past,* 122.
30. Gertrude Bell, "Report on Kish, Warka, Sunkara, and Ur," British Museum Central Archives, WY1/2/83, January 19 [no year given—probably 1925]; quoted in Bernhardsson, *Reclaiming a Plundered Past,* 156.
31. Quoted in Bernhardsson, *Reclaiming a Plundered Past,* 157.
32. Ibid., 160.

33. Quoted in Roger Atwood, "In the North of Iraq," *Archaeology,* June 4, 2003, http://www.archaeology.org/online/features/iraq/mosul.html.

34. See Eric Davis, *Memories of State: Politics, History, and Collective Identity in Modern Iraq* (Berkeley: University of California Press, 2005), 157.

35. Amatzia Baram, *Culture, History, and Ideology in the Formation of Ba'thist Iraq, 1968–89* (New York: St. Martin's Press, 1991), 41. On the progressive "Mesopotamization" of Iraq under Saddam, see Frederick Mario Fales, *Saccheggio in Mesopotamia: Il museo di Baghdad dalla nascita dell'Iraq à oggi* (Udine: Forum, 2006), 161ff.

36. See Baram, *Culture,* 49, 108.

37. Quoted in William Honan, "Attacks on Iraq Worry and Divide Archeologists," *New York Times,* February 9, 1991, sec. 1.

38. Baram, *Culture,* 158. On Saddam's use of Babylonian imagery for political purposes, see also Muhsin al-Musawi, *Reading Iraq: Culture and Power in Conflict* (London: I. B. Tauris, 2006), 80.

39. Rose George, "Going for an Iraqi Dig? Don't Forget the AK-47," *Financial Times,* August 4, 2001, 3.

40. Neil MacFarquhar, "Hussein's Babylon: A Beloved Atrocity," *New York Times,* August 19, 2003, A11.

41. Davis, *Memories of State,* 169.

42. Elizabeth Stone, interviewed by the author, February 19, 2007.

43. Donny George Youkhanna (former director of museums, State Board of Antiquities and Heritage, Iraq), interviewed by the author, February 19, 2007.

44. Jonathan M. Bloom and Lark Ellen Gould, "Patient Restoration: The Kuwait National Museum," *Saudi Aramco World,* September/October 2000, http://www.saudiaramcoworld.com/issue/200005/patient.restoration-the .kuwait.national.museum.htm.

45. McGuire Gibson, interviewed by the author, February 9, 2006. For more on the handling of artifacts from the Kuwait National Museum, see Kirsty Norman, "The Invasion of Kuwait, and the Subsequent Recovery of Its National Museum: A Conservator's View," *Museum Management and Curatorship* 16, no. 2 (1997): 180–91; Selma Al-Radi, "War and Cultural Heritage: Lessons from Lebanon, Kuwait and Iraq" (lecture, Cultural Emergency Response, Prinsenhof Museum, Delft, the Netherlands, September 26, 2003), *Der Kracht van Cultuur,* October 2003, cached text of Web site retrieved by Google, July 25, 2007, http://64.233.167.104/ search?q=cache:U9M2HK2MjlYJ:www.powerofculture.nl/nl/artikelen/ war_and_cultural_heritage.html (accessed September 21, 2007); and, authoritatively, McGuire Gibson and Augusta McMahon, *Lost Heritage: Antiquities Stolen from Iraq's Regional Museums,* fasc. 1 (Chicago: American Association for Research in Baghdad, 1992).

46. The popular association of cultural professionals with the Ba'ath Party remained a problem in the aftermath of the fall of Saddam, when a crowd

of residents guarding a cache of ancient manuscripts nearly rioted when asked to turn them over to the Ba'athist head of the manuscript museum. See Matthew Bogdanos, "The Casualties of War: The Truth about the Iraq Museum," *American Journal of Archaeology* 109, no. 3 (July 2005): 500.

47. See Gibson and McMahon, *Lost Heritage,* fasc. 1; H. D. Baker, Roger Matthews, and Nicholas Postgate, *Lost Heritage: Antiquities Stolen from Iraq's Regional Museums,* fasc. 2 (London: British School of Archaeology in Iraq, 1993); and Hideo Fujii and Kazumi Oguchi, *Lost Heritage: Antiquities Stolen from Iraq's Regional Museums,* fasc. 3 (Tokyo: Institute for Cultural Studies of Ancient Iraq, Kokushikan University, 1996).

48. Friedrich Schipper, "Iraq: Its Cultural Heritage—a Post-Gulf-War Front," in *Protection of Cultural Property in the Event of Armed Conflict—a Challenge in Peace Support Operations,* ed. Edwin Micewski and Gerhard Sladek (Vienna: Austrian Military Printing Press, 2002), 109–16.

49. On cylinder seals, see Dominique Collon, *Near Eastern Seals* (Berkeley: University of California Press, 1990).

50. Andrew Lawler, "Mayhem in Mesopotamia," *Science* 301, no. 5633 (August 1, 2003): 582.

51. On the fate of the Sennacherib reliefs, see John M. Russell, *The Final Sack of Nineveh: The Discovery, Documentation, and Destruction of King Sennacherib's Throne Room at Nineveh, Iraq* (New Haven, CT: Yale University Press, 1998), 48–50.

52. Erica Hunter, e-mail message to McGuire Gibson, April 15, 2003.

53. Martin Gottlieb with Barry Meier, "Of 2,000 Treasures Stolen in Gulf War of 1991, Only 12 Have Been Recovered," *New York Times,* May 1, 2003, East Coast late edition, A16, Banking Information Source database, document ID #331083461.

54. Robert M. Perito, *Where Is the Lone Ranger When We Need Him? America's Search for a Post-Conflict Stability Force* (Washington, DC: U.S. Institute of Peace, 2004), 303.

55. See George, "Going for an Iraqi Dig?"

56. Hussein Ali al-Yasiri, "Plundering the Past," *ICR* 82 (September 6, 2004), posted on IraqCrisis listhost, September, 18, 2004, https://listhost .uchicago.edu/pipermail/iraqcrisis/2004-September/000858.html.

57. See Douglas Birch, "In North Iraq, an Ancient Past Falls Victim to a Modern War," *Baltimore Sun,* April 18, 2003, www.baltimoresun.com/ news/nationworld/iraq/bal-te.north18apr18,0,532697.story?coll=bal-home-headlines (accessed July 19, 2007).

58. George Youkhanna interview.

59. George, "Going for an Iraqi Dig?" 3.

60. George Youkhanna interview.

61. On the Kurdish smuggling operations, see John E. Conklin, *Art Crime* (Westport, CT: Praeger, 1994), 204.

62. Zainab Bahrani, interviewed by the author, March 14, 2005.

63. George Youkhanna interview.

64. On the Baghdad meeting, see Hugh Dellios, "Birth of Writing Explored in Baghdad Conference," *National Geographic News,* March 26, 2001, http://news.nationalgeographic.com/news/2001/03/0326_writing.html. The British Museum meeting is described in Fales, *Saccheggio in Mesopotamia,* 326, 172n.

CHAPTER TWO

1. As James Fallows points out, postwar planning in previous conflicts took substantial time and effort: "Before the United States entered World War II, teams at the Army War College were studying what went right and wrong when American doughboys occupied Germany after World War I. Within months of the attack on Pearl Harbor, a School of Military Government had been created at the University of Virginia to plan for the occupation of both Germany and Japan." James Fallows, "Blind into Baghdad," *Atlantic Monthly,* January/February 2004, http://www.theatlantic.com/doc/200401/fallows.

2. The Clinton administration's response to the debacle in Somalia—firing or ruining several good officers to shift blame away from its failure to adequately back up those sent in to do the policing—led many officers to conclude that Civil Affairs was a bad career choice, with little chance for glory, but high probability of disaster and scapegoating.

3. Robert M. Perito, *Where Is the Lone Ranger When We Need Him? America's Search for a Post-Conflict Stability Force* (Washington, DC: U.S. Institute of Peace, 2004), 320.

4. Scott Feil, e-mail message to the author, August 17, 2006.

5. On the role of CIMIC, see Joris D. Kila, "The Role of NATO and Civil Military Affairs," in *Antiquities under Siege: Cultural Heritage Protection after the Iraq War,* ed. Lawrence Rothfield (Lanham, MD: AltaMira Press, 2008), 175–92.

6. According to Rasool Vatandoust, director of the Research Centre for Conservation of Cultural Relics and head of Iran's Department of International and Cultural Relations, Iran's Cultural Heritage Organization includes "a special department that is called 'Cultural Heritage Guards,' and they are part of the military, in fact. Anyone going to military service (which is mandatory for a two-year term) can choose whether they want to be in the cultural heritage division or not." Rasool Vatandoust, interviewed by the author, November 28, 2006.

7. Louise Haxthausen and Jim Williams, "International Cooperation in Afghanistan: Strategies, Funding and Modalities of Action," *Museum International* 55 (2003): 84–90.

8. James Astill, "Plunder Goes on Across Afghanistan as Looters Grow Ever Bolder: Trade in Antiquities Worth Up to £18bn as Thieves Excavate Sites,"

Guardian, December 13, 2003, 21, ProQuest Newsstand database, document ID #490249441.

9. See Christina Lamb, "Looted Afghan Art Smuggled into UK," *Sunday Times,* March 12, 2006, http://www.timesonline.co.uk/article/0,2089-2081457_1,00.html.

10. For the story of how the kouros came to be recognized as fake, see Malcolm Gladwell, *Blink: The Power of Thinking without Thinking* (New York: Little, Brown, 2005), 3–8.

11. Located bureaucratically in the State Department's Bureau of Educational and Cultural Affairs, CPAC recommends approval or denial of requests made by countries, under the 1970 UNESCO Convention on the Means of Prohibiting and Preventing the Illicit Import, Export and Transfer of Ownership of Cultural Property, to impose U.S. import restrictions on categories of archaeological or ethnological material being pillaged.

12. Arthur Houghton, interviewed by the author, March 3, 2005.

13. Lynn Nicholas, *The Rape of Europa: The Fate of Europe's Treasures in the Third Reich and the Second World War* (New York: Vintage, 1994), 211–12.

14. There was, however, something like an old-boy network in the ties between neoconservative political scientists trained at the University of Chicago: Wolfowitz, Ph.D. '72; Ahmad Chalabi, Ph.D. '69 (the CIA's Iraqi puppet); Abram Shulsky, A.M. '68, Ph.D. '72 (head of the Pentagon's special intelligence unit); Zalmay Khalilzad, Ph.D. '79; Gary Edson, J.D. '82 (deputy national security advisor to Bush). It is tantalizing to think what might have happened had McGuire Gibson crossed the street separating the Oriental Institute from the political science department or used university ties to make contact with Wolfowitz. But ideological networks are not the same as collegial ones, and this may just be wishful thinking.

15. David Mack (director, Middle East Institute), interviewed by the author, April 15, 2005.

16. On Chalabi's relation to the Future of Iraq Project, see David Rieff, "Blueprint for a Mess," *Foreign Service Journal,* March 2004, 22–28.

17. Houghton interview.

18. Mack interview.

19. Ibid.

20. Vatandoust interview.

21. Pew Charitable Trusts, "The Pew Charitable Trusts Announce Landmark Cultural Policy Initiative for American Arts and Culture," news release, August 2, 1999, http://www.pewtrusts.com/ideas/ (accessed July 13, 2007). For an exemplary conservative response, see Alice Goldfarb Marquis, "Culture Has No Infrastructure," *New York Times,* August 9, 1999, A15.

22. Joseph Collins (former deputy assistant secretary of defense for stability operations), interviewed by the author, October 5, 2005.

23. Cultural heritage organizations seem not to have evolved to meet changes in the international environment during the 1990s, a period when "the

general movement away from UN-led missions and the greater reliance on lead states, ad hoc coalitions, and regional bodies to lead military and civilian functions gave rise to a growing number of [war-oriented] NGOs and private military companies." Roland Paris, "International Machinery for Postwar Peace-Building: The Dilemmas of Coordination" (paper presented at PIPES Seminar, University of Chicago, May 2006).

24. See John W. Betlyon, "Afghan Archaeology on the Road to Recovery," *Daily Star,* October 12, 2004, 12.

25. Andrew Maykuth, "A Plea to Save Afghan Antiquities," *Philadelphia Inquirer,* May 3, 2006, http://www.philly.com/mld/philly/entertainment/14485199.htm.

26. Unwillingness to put one's life at risk was of course not limited to cultural heritage NGOs; according to Michael R. Gordon and Gen. Bernard E. Trainor, "The State Department disaster relief team did not want to venture into areas of Iraq that were still contested by Saddam's support-ers." See Gordon and Trainor, *Cobra II: The Inside Story of the Invasion and Occupation of Iraq* (New York: Pantheon, 2006), 154.

27. For a discussion of the history of UNESCO's cultural heritage protec-tion efforts, see Mounir Bouchenaki, "UNESCO and the Safeguarding of Cultural Heritage in Postconflict Situations," in *Antiquities under Siege,* ed. Rothfield, 207–18.

CHAPTER THREE

1. James Fallows, "Blind into Baghdad," *Atlantic Monthly,* January/February 2004, 58, http://www.theatlantic.com/doc/200401/fallows.

2. See Michael R. Gordon and Gen. Bernard E. Trainor, *Cobra II: The Inside Story of the Invasion and Occupation of Iraq* (New York: Pantheon, 2006), 106.

3. See ibid.

4. Ibid., 108.

5. Ibid., 107.

6. See Thomas E. Ricks, *Fiasco: The American Military Adventure in Iraq* (New York: Penguin, 2006), 79–80.

7. Gordon and Trainor, *Cobra II,* 205.

8. For more on the Civil Affairs mission, see www.armyreserve.army.mil/ARMYDRU/USACAPOC/Overview.htm.

9. Maj. Christopher Varhola (Civil Affairs officer), interviewed by the author, April 15, 2005.

10. McGuire Gibson, interviewed by the author, February 9, 2006.

11. Varhola interview.

12. Ibid.

13. George Packer, "War after the War," *New Yorker,* November 24, 2003, 62.

14. The humanitarian group was one of four set up by Rice following a con-tentious Senate Committee on Foreign Relations hearing in August, where

the lack of post-conflict planning came in for heavy criticism. What is striking is the lack of a sense of urgency, even after this hearing, with the meeting being put off weeks until after summer vacation (an echo of what happened in August 2001).

15. Elliott Abrams, "Briefing on Humanitarian Reconstruction Issues," White House news release, February 24, 2003, http://www.whitehouse.gov/news/releases/2003/02/20030224-11.html. For more on DART, see Joseph Collins, "Briefing on Humanitarian Relief Planning for Iraq," Federal News Service, February 25, 2003, http://www.defenselink.mil/transcripts/2003/t02262003_t0225col.html. Like some archaeologists, some humanitarian NGOs were unwilling to associate themselves with the military; see William Bole, "Relief Groups, Bush Administration at Odds on Iraq Aid," Religion News Service, (undated) 2003, http://nns.wieck.com/forms/text/.

16. The Bush administration's distaste for nation building and peacekeeping, it is worth noting, is grounded in a deep ideological view of humanitarian affairs that worries about creating a "culture of dependence" and seeks instead to create "self-reliant" countries. See Donald Rumsfeld, "Beyond Nation-Building" (speech delivered at 11th Annual Salute to Freedom, Intrepid Sea-Air-Space Museum, New York, NY, February 14, 2003), http://www.defenselink.mil/speeches/2003/sp20030214-secdef0024.html.

17. Collins, quoted in Casie Vinall, "Profile of Joseph Collins," *Defend America: U.S. Department of Defense News about the War on Terrorism,* June 23, 2003, http://www.defendamerica.mil/profiles/june2003/pr062403a.html.

18. Joseph Collins, e-mail message to author, July 27, 2006.

19. A few sites, however, did sustain damage due to U.S. military action—bulldozers creating rocket positions badly scarred Tell al-Lahm, and a thirteenth-century mosque in Basra was damaged.

20. The United States and Britain did not formally accept the status of occupying powers until May 22, 2003, when the UN Security Council passed Resolution 1483. On arguments about the status of the United States in Iraq, see Jordan J. Paust, "The US as Occupying Power over Portions of Iraq and Relevant Responsibilities under the Laws of War," *American Society of International Law Insights* (April 2003), http://www.asil.org/insights/insigh102.htm.

21. Ratification of the 1954 Hague Convention was blocked during the Cold War by the Pentagon's worry that the Kremlin, a recognized cultural heritage site as well as the seat of the Soviet government, would be protected, and that bombing it would open Americans to charges of war crimes. See Patrick J. Boylan, *Review of the Convention for the Protection of Cultural Property in the Event of Armed Conflict* (Paris: UNESCO, 1993), 104. On the question of whether the convention imposes on states an obligation to prevent theft, pillaging, or vandalism carried out by civilians, see Kevin Chamberlain, *War and Cultural Heritage: An Analysis of the 1954 Hague Convention for the Protection of Cultural Property in the Event of Armed*

Conflict and the Two Protocols (London: Institute of Art and Law, 2004); Sasha P. Paroff, "Comment: Another Victim of the War in Iraq: The Looting of the National Museum in Baghdad and the Inadequacies of International Protection of Cultural Property," *Emory Law Journal* 53, no. 4 (Fall 2004): 2021–54; and Wayne Sandholtz, "The Iraqi National Museum and International Law: A Duty to Protect," *Columbia Journal of Transnational Law* 44 (2005): 185–240.

22. Paul Wolfowitz, "Wolfowitz Says U.S. Warred on Saddam's Regime, Not Iraqi People," interview on Egyptian TV, April 16, 2003, http://www.america.gov/st/washfile-english/2003/April/20030419181303ynnedd0.3930475.html.

23. Joseph Collins, interviewed by the author, October 5, 2005.

24. On the problem of interagency coordination, see, inter alia, Roland Paris, "International Machinery for Postwar Peace-Building: The Dilemmas of Coordination" (paper presented at PIPES Seminar, University of Chicago, May 2006); Scott Feil et al., *Play to Win: The Final Report of the Bi-Partisan Commission on Post-Conflict Reconstruction* (Arlington, VA, and Washington, DC: AUSA and CSIS, 2003); and Matthew Bogdanos, "Transforming Joint Interagency Coordination: The Missing Link between National Strategy and Operational Success," *Case Studies in National Security Transformation* 9 (n.d.), http://www.ndu.edu/CTNSP/pubs/Case%209%20-%20TransformingJointInteragencyCoordination.pdf.

25. Collins interview.

26. Arthur Houghton, interviewed by the author, March 3, 2005.

27. David Mack (director, Middle East Institute), interviewed by the author, April 15, 2005.

28. Arthur Houghton, e-mail message to McGuire Gibson, October 2, 2002.

29. The critique of retentionism is made most forcefully in the classic paper by John Merryman, "Two Ways of Thinking about Cultural Property," *American Journal of International Law* 80, no. 4 (October 1986): 831–53.

30. Kwame Anthony Appiah, "Whose Culture Is It?" *New York Review of Books* 53, no. 2 (February 9, 2006), http://www.nybooks.com/articles/article-preview?article_id=18682. Appiah's expanded version of this argument, within which aesthetic appreciation is more fully tied to a cosmopolitan ethics, is developed in *Cosmopolitanism* (New York: Norton, 2006), 115–36.

31. Gary Vikan, quoted in Alexi Shannon Baker, "Pt. II: Collectors and Protectors," in "Selling the Past: *United States v. Frederick Schultz*," *Archaeology*, April 22, 2002, http://www.archaeology.org/online/features/schultz.

32. Gary Vikan, "An Obscure State Department Committee . . . " Director's Blog, Walters Art Museum, April 16, 2007, http://www.thewalters.org/blog/comments.aspx?b=19.

33. The spurious linkage between iconoclasm and retentionism is made by James Cuno, director of the Art Institute of Chicago. See Cuno, "Beyond

Bamiyan: Will the World Be Ready Next Time?" in *Art and Cultural Heritage: Law, Policy, and Practice,* ed. Barbara T. Hoffman (New York: Cambridge University Press, 2006), 43.

34. David D'Arcy, "Legal Group to Fight 'Retentionist' Policies," *Art Newspaper,* October 24, 2002.

35. On the difficulty of determining with any accuracy the size of the antiquities market, see Neil Brodie, "Smoke and Mirrors," in *Who Owns Objects? The Ethics and Politics of Collecting Cultural Artefacts,* ed. Eleanor Robson, Luke Treadwell, and Chris Gosden (Oxford: Oxbow Books, 2007), 1–14.

36. Morag Kersel, who has studied the Israeli market in detail, concludes that "the current licensed trade in antiquities in Israel has too many illegal elements to be considered a successful legal market, essentially it is legal in name only. . . . Inconsistencies in IAA oversight of the dealer registers, forgery of export certificates, and legislative loopholes in the current state laws (AL 1978 and AL 1989, Antiquities Law Amendments 2002) all combine to create illegal elements in an allegedly legal market." See Kersel, "License to Sell: The Legal Antiquities Trade in Israel," (Ph.D. diss., Cambridge University, 2006); and Kersel, "From the Ground to the Buyer: A Market Analysis of the Trade in Illegal Antiquities," in *Archaeology, Cultural Heritage, and the Antiquities Trade,* ed. Neil Brodie, Morag Kersel, Christina Luke, and Kathryn Walker Tubb (Gainesville: University Press of Florida, 2006), 188–205.

37. Christopher Chippindale and David W. J. Gill, "Material Consequences of Contemporary Classical Collecting," *American Journal of Archaeology* 104, no. 3 (July 2000): 463–511.

38. Houghton interview.

39. Arthur Houghton, e-mail message to McGuire Gibson, October 23, 2002.

40. The other organizations included the Asia Society, the Association of Art Museum Directors, and the American Schools of Oriental Research.

41. Ashton Hawkins and Maxwell L. Anderson, "Preserving Iraq's Past," *Washington Post,* November 29, 2002, A43.

42. McGuire Gibson, e-mail message to Arthur Houghton, October 30, 2002.

43. McGuire Gibson, letter to Ryan Crocker, November 21, 2002.

44. Archaeological Institute of America, "AIA Urges Governments to Respect Hague Convention When Confronting Iraq," AIA Web site, n.d., http://www.archaeological.org/webinfo.php?page=10174.

45. Maria Kouroupas, C. Miller Crouch et al. (ECA, State Department), interviewed by author, April 15, 2005. It seems likely that both the ECA and the NEA were goaded into action by Ryan Crocker at the NEA after Gibson alerted Crocker in late November 2002.

46. Ironically, after having been spared by targeters during the invasion, many of these listed sites were eventually used for military purposes: as U.S. military bases, including Babylon and Kish; for a landing strip (the legendary city of Ur); and as munitions demolition areas (Sippar, the

city of the sun god Shamash), in spite of persistent warnings by Bahrani and others that this violated international conventions. "They just don't listen," Bahrani ultimately concluded despairingly; "they know that this is against international law." Zainab Bahrani, interviewed by the author, March 14, 2005.

47. Ibid.

48. One reason for the AIA's relative poverty despite its 8,000-strong membership is that it does not allow active collectors or dealers to serve on its board, pursuant to its general ethics policy.

49. Gibson interview.

50. McGuire Gibson, e-mail message to Arthur Houghton, January 15, 2003. A more serious concern about publicity would emerge later: While working with the military's targeting team on site coordinates, Gibson had to ask the targeters not to write to his student assistants on the project directly or to use their names publicly, because their helping the Pentagon with location information might lay them open to charges of spying by other academics or Near Eastern countries.

51. Arthur Houghton, e-mail message to McGuire Gibson, January 16, 2002.

52. Gordon and Trainor, *Cobra II,* 106.

53. Houghton interview.

54. Commons Hansard, Bound Volume Hansard—Debate, March 19, 2003, Column 940, http://www.publications.parliament.uk/pa/cm200203/cmhansrd/vo030319/debtext/30319-03.htm.

55. "Iraq: Protection of Cultural Property," Lord Hansard text for April 28, 2003: Column WA64, http://www.publications.parliament.uk/pa/ld200203/ldhansrd/vo030428/text/30428w02.htm#30428w02_wqn10.

56. "Letter from Lord Renfrew of Kairmsthorn to the Rt Hon Tessa Jowell MP, the Secretary of State for Culture, Media and Sport, dated 12 May 2003," Select Committee on Culture, Media and Sport, House of Commons Written Evidence, First Report, Annex 6, 2003, http://www.publications.parliament.uk/pa/cm200304/cmselect/cmcumeds/59/59we08.htm.

57. Harriet Crawford, interviewed by the author, December 22, 2004.

CHAPTER FOUR

1. The Memorandum of Conversation is no longer available directly from the ACCP, which is now defunct, but it has been posted on https://listhost.uchicago.edu/pipermail/iraqcrisis/2005-November/001396.html (accessed August 24, 2007).

2. Arthur Houghton, interviewed by the author, March 3, 2005.

3. McGuire Gibson, private communication, August 4, 2006.

4. Ibid.

5. Andrew Lawler, "Impending War Stokes Battle over Fate of Iraqi Antiquities," *Science* 299, no. 5607 (January 31, 2003): 643.

6. Lt. Col. Chris Herndon, interviewed by the author, April 15, 2005. This is not to say, of course, that ACCP, or at least some members, did not view the organization's efforts as linked to the broader objective of liberalizing Iraq's export laws. It is difficult to read otherwise William Pearlstein's comments that "a sensible post-Saddam cultural administration" would include laws to allow "some objects [to be] certified for export. If we can get the Defense Department to listen when it comes to targeting [bombs], and influence conservation of cultural heritage [with the State Department], then that's a pretty good start." Quoted in Lawler, "Impending War," 643.

7. McGuire Gibson, interviewed by the author, February 9, 2006.

8. Squeamishness about collaborating with the military was not limited to academic archaeologists. One senior official at the United Kingdom's Department for Culture, Media and Sport admits privately that he "wouldn't have been comfortable with actually participating in the planning of the invasion. . . . It would be very compromising to even have been involved in those discussions."

9. In the midst of heavy fighting within a mile or so of the museum, the tank unit commander, Capt. Jason Conroy, called his tactical operations command several times asking for smart bombs to be dropped on buildings, only to be told that some were protected sites and could not be bombed. See Jason Conroy, *Heavy Metal: A Tank Company's Battle to Baghdad* (Washington, DC: Potomac Books, 2005), 200.

10. Donny George Youkhanna (former director of museums, State Board of Antiquities and Heritage, Iraq), interviewed by the author, February 19, 2007.

11. Harrison was a public relations professional and political operative who had co-chaired the Republican National Committee for four years before being appointed to run the BECA in 2001. She was later to be named acting under secretary of state for public diplomacy, in which capacity her biggest achievement was collaborating with the Kennedy Center to bring the Iraqi National Symphony Orchestra to Washington. In June 2005 she was appointed president and CEO of the Corporation for Public Broadcasting in an effort by the CPB's then-chairman, Kenneth Tomlinson, to "restore balance." Tomlinson resigned from the CPB in November 2005 following an inspector general's finding that Tomlinson had improperly applied political tests when seeking a CEO for the CPB.

12. Houghton interview.

13. Arthur Houghton, e-mail message to McGuire Gibson, October 3, 2002.

14. A member of one of the ruling families of Iraq before 1958, Istrabadi needed to be convinced to support this position, since it would mean giving up on his family's claim to historical houses on agricultural lands confiscated (and later paid for) by the Iraq government.

15. Zainab Bahrani, interviewed by the author, March 14, 2005.

16. Houghton interview.

17. Joseph Collins, interviewed by the author, October 5, 2005.

18. Andrew Rathmell, "Planning Post-Conflict Reconstruction in Iraq: What Can We Learn?" *International Affairs* 81, no. 5 (October 2005): 1021. See also, and more definitively, Donald L. Dreschler, "Reconstructing the Interagency Process after Iraq," *Journal of Strategic Studies* 28, no. 1 (February 2005): 3–30; and Michael R. Gordon and Gen. Bernard E. Trainor, *Cobra II: The Inside Story of the Invasion and Occupation of Iraq* (New York: Pantheon, 2006), 159.

19. L. Paul Bremer III, *My Year in Iraq* (New York: Simon & Schuster, 2006), 25.

20. The absence of continued congressional pressure on the issue of postwar planning, in the interim between the red flags raised in the August 2002 Senate Committee on Foreign Relations hearings and the February hearings, is notable.

21. Robert Perito, *Establishing the Rule of Law in Iraq,* Special Report no. 104 (Washington, DC: U.S. Institute of Peace, April 2003), 10. On Hungary's role, see Stefan Bos, "Hungary Agrees to Allow Military Training for Iraqi Exiles," *Palestine Chronicle,* December 18, 2002, http://palestinechronicle .com/story-20021218191133578.htm.

22. Gordon and Trainor, *Cobra II,* 107.

23. Perito, *Establishing the Rule,* 12.

24. Donald Rumsfeld, "Rumsfeld Says Iraqis Celebrate Freedom from Fear of Regime," transcript of Defense Department Briefing, April 11, 2003, http://www.america.gov/st/washfile-english/2003/April/20030412135241a ttocnich0.1897852.html.

25. Ambassador John M. Limbert (former civil administrator for Iraqi Cultural Heritage in the Office of Reconstruction and Humanitarian Assistance), interviewed by the author, March 3, 2005.

26. Lt. Col. John Moran, e-mail message to Patty Gerstenblith, February 5, 2003.

27. McGuire Gibson, e-mail message to Larry Hanauer, March 18, 2003.

28. International Council of Museums Executive Council, *The Minutes of the 103rd Session of the Executive Council of ICOM,* June 1, 2003, http://icom .museum/download/103/2003ex04_eng.doc.

29. Ibid.

30. Mounir Bouchenaki, e-mail message to the author, June 21, 2007. See also Mounir Bouchenaki, "UNESCO and the Safeguarding of Cultural Heritage in Postconflict Situations," in *Antiquities under Siege: Cultural Heritage Protection after the Iraq War,* ed. Lawrence Rothfield (Lanham, MD: AltaMira Press, 2008), 212.

31. Society for American Archaeology, "Letter to Secretary of Defense on Protection of Antiquities in Iraq," February 27, 2003, http://www.saa .org/goverment/Iraq.html.

32. Letter from William J. Haynes III (military assistant to the General Coun-
    sel, DoD) to Robert Kelly (president of the Society for American Archaeol-
    ogy), March 18, 2003, Society for American Archaeology Web site, http://
    www.saa.org/goverment/DODresponse.html.

33. McGuire Gibson, "Fate of Iraqi Archaeology," *Science* 99, no. 5614
    (March 21, 2003): 1848.

34. "Statement by the International Committee of the Blue Shield on the
    impact of a war on cultural heritage in Iraq," March 19, 2003, http://www
    .ica.org/en/node/579 (accessed June 20, 2008).

35. Gen. Richard Myers, "Department of Defense News Briefing—Secretary
    Rumsfeld and General Myers," Federal News Service, April 15, 2003, http://
    www.defenselink.mil/transcripts/transcript.aspx?transcriptid=2413.

36. McGuire Gibson, private communication, January 25, 2008.

37. Henry Wright, private communication, April 2, 2008.

38. As Dreschler notes, sending the task force to Kuwait meant that "Phase IV
    was being planned at the CFLCC headquarters at least two levels removed
    from the State Department, with no State Department representation, and
    with little direction even from CENTCOM due to geographic separation."
    Dreschler, "Reconstructing," 19.

39. "En cas d'offensive américaine, le pillage des sites sera infiniment plus
    puissant qu'en 1991. (. . .) Les pilleurs ont eu le temps d'organiser leur
    trafic et de se créer une clientèle internationale. Ils sont puissants et
    armés." Donny George Youkhanna, quoted in Philippe Baqué, "Un trafic
    particulièrement lucrative: Enquête sur le pillage des objets d'art," *Le
    Monde diplomatique*, February 2005, http://cpprot.te.verweg.com/2005-
    March/000913.html.

40. George Youkhanna interview.

41. Muriel Mirak-Weissbach and Ortrun Cramer, "World Robbed of Iraq's
    Museums, Antiquities: An Interview with Donny George," in *Executive
    Intelligence Review*, July 25, 2003, http://www.larouchepub.com/other/
    interviews/2003/3029donny_george.html.

42. George Youkhanna interview.

43. See Andrew Lawler, "Mayhem in Mesopotamia," *Science* 301, no. 5633
    (August, 1, 2003): 582–88.

44. George Youkhanna interview.

45. Ibid.

46. See Bouchenaki, "UNESCO and the Safeguarding of Cultural Heritage,"
    213.

47. See Elizabeth Stone, "Patterns of Looting in Southern Iraq," *Antiquity* 82
    (2008): 125–38.

48. To a reporter's question on March 17 about the military's postwar policy,
    Gibson declared, "If firm control of the countryside is not established
    fairly soon after the war, the looting will continue. But the US govern-
    ment is aware of the problem and will, I presume, take responsibility for

protecting the sites from further pillaging and smuggling out of antiquities." Gibson, e-mail message to Melinda Liu, March 17, 2003.

49. McGuire Gibson, interviewed by the author, February 9, 2006.

50. Joseph Collins, "Rear Area Forces Gap" memo, quoted in Gordon and
Trainor, *Cobra II*, 116–17.

51. Maj. Christopher Varhola (Civil Affairs officer), interviewed by the author,
April 15, 2005.

52. McGuire Gibson, e-mail message to Arthur Houghton, March 3, 2003.

53. William Polk to former Jordanian prime minister Zaid Rifai, February 27,
2003 (personal communication).

54. William R. Polk, interviewed by the author, June 28, 2007. See also Wil-
liam R. Polk, introduction to *The Looting of the Iraq Museum, Baghdad: The
Lost Legacy of Ancient Mesopotamia*, ed. Milbry Polk and Angela Schuster
(New York: Harry Abrams, 2005), 5–9.

55. Bill Glauber, "$300 and a Prewar Promise Save Famed Archaeological
Sites," Knight-Ridder/Tribune News Service, May 1, 2003, posted on
IraqCrisis listhost, May 1, 2003, https://listhost.uchicago.edu/pipermail/
iraqcrisis/2003-May/000027.html.

56. This anecdote is described by Jeff Spurr, who attributes it to *New York
Times* reporter Dexter Filkins. See Jeff Spurr, "Iraqi Libraries and Archives
in Peril: Survival in a Time of Invasion, Chaos, and Civil Conflict, A
Report," Oriental Institute Web site, April 11, 2007, http://oi.uchicago.edu/
OI/IRAQ/mela/update_2007.htm. It is worth noting that Filkins's report-
age from the opening days of the war does not mention this incident.

57. See Ryan Dilley, "Law and Disorder in Iraq," BBC News Online, April 11,
2003, http://news.bbc.co.uk/1/low/world/middle_east/2939573.stm.

58. The ORHA memo, titled "Guidance for CFLCC's Priorities for Securing Key
Baghdad Institutions," is quoted from in Paul Martin, "Troops Were Told
to Guard Treasures; Two Weeks after the Memo Was Sent, U.S. Forces Took
Baghdad and Iraqi Looters Hit Museum," *Washington Times*, April 20, 2003,
http://www.proquest.com.proxy.uchicago.edu/ (accessed June 25, 2008).

59. Paul Martin, Ed Vulliamy, and Gaby Hinsliff, "US Army Was Told to Protect Looted Museum," *Observer*, April 20, 2003, 4.

60. Brig. Gen. Vincent Brooks, "Central Command Briefing," Office of International Information Programs, U.S. Department of State, March 26,
2003, posted on the Information Warfare Site, http://www.iwar.org.uk/
news-archive/2003/03-26-4.htm. The quote from an unnamed official
is from Karen Mazurkewich, "Ancient Treasures in Peril—Archeologists
Warn Fighting in Iraq May Destroy Trove of Mesopotamian Antiquities,"
Wall Street Journal, March 27, 2003, Eastern Edition, B1.

61. Karen Mazurkewich "Ancient Treasures in Peril—Archeologists Warn
Fighting in Iraq May Destroy Trove of Mesopotamian Antiquities," *Wall
Street Journal*, March 27, 2003, Eastern edition, http://www.proquest.com
.proxy.uchicago.edu/ (accessed June 29, 2008).

62. See David Perlman, "Protecting Iraq's Treasures," *San Francisco Chronicle,* March 31, 2003, W-5.

63. The rumor, which remains unsubstantiated, was published a few days later in an article, which Gibson forwarded to Collins. The rumor may have originated in the exchange between Hawkins and Luti in early January 2003, discussed above in chap. 3, p. 51. Both Houghton and Hawkins vigorously deny having met with Luti.

64. McGuire Gibson, e-mail message to Joseph Collins, April 4, 2003.

65. Ibid.

66. Frank Romano, e-mail message to McGuire Gibson, April 4, 2003.

CHAPTER FIVE

1. Brig. Gen. Vincent Brooks, "Central Command Briefing," CNN.com, April 8, 2003, http://transcripts.cnn.com/TRANSCRIPTS/0304/08/se.05 .html.

2. Ibid.

3. William Sumner, interviewed by the author, August 30, 2006.

4. Ibid.

5. Peter Zarcone, interviewed by the author, July 24, 2007.

6. Sumner interview.

7. McGuire Gibson, e-mail message to Lt. Col. Kraig Kenworthy, April 10, 2003.

8. Open letter from Jane Waldbaum, President, Archaeological Institute of America, and McGuire Gibson, President, American Association for Research in Baghdad, April 9, 2003.

9. McGuire Gibson, e-mail message to Chris Varhola et al., April 9, 2003.

10. McGuire Gibson, e-mail message to Kraig Kenworthy et al., April 10, 2003.

11. John Limbert, e-mail message to McGuire Gibson et al., April 10, 2003.

12. Henry Wright to John Limbert, e-mail communication, April 11, 2003.

13. McGuire Gibson, e-mail message to John Limbert, April 10, 2003.

14. See Matthew Bogdanos, "Casualties of War: The Truth about the Iraq Museum," *American Journal of Archaeology* 109, no. 3 (July 2005): 501–6.

15. Donny George, e-mail message to the author, July 21, 2007.

16. Ibid.

17. The National Iraqi News Agency and the central telecommunications building both had been badly damaged by car bombs in 2000 or 2001, according to Donny George. George decided to urge building the blast wall at the museum after seeing a similar wall erected in front of the telecommunications building after it was rebuilt. The museum wall was supposed to have eventually been extended to cover all sides of the complex, but, George says, funding ran out. Donny George, e-mail message to the author, July 22, 2007.

18. Quoted in Eric Westervelt, "Baghdad Museum," NPR's *Weekend Edition*, April 20, 2003, http://www.npr.org/templates/story/story .php?storyId=1237927.

19. Jason Conroy, *Heavy Metal: A Tank Company's Battle to Baghdad* (Washington, DC: Potomac Books, 2005), 222.

20. Andrew Lawler, "Mayhem in Mesopotamia," *Science* 301, no. 5633 (August 1, 2003): 582–88.

21. Lt. Col. Eric Schwartz, interviewed by the author, August 15, 2007.

22. The legal instruments laying out this logic include: Protocol Additional to the 1949 Geneva Conventions (Protocol I); the Protocol Additional to the Geneva Conventions of 12 August 1949 (Protocol II); the 1954 Hague Convention for the Protection of Cultural Property in the Event of Armed Conflict; Protocol for the Protection of Cultural Property in the Event of Armed Conflict (Protocol I), The Hague, 14 May 1954; Second Protocol to the Hague Convention of 1954 for the Protection of Cultural Property in the Event of Armed Conflict (Protocol II), 1999.

23. Schwartz interview.

24. Conroy, *Heavy Metal*, 224. I have been unable to determine whether the order to not interfere with looting came before or after Schwartz heard reports of looting at the museum and sent the tank crew out to investigate.

25. Ibid., 224. For Perkins's use of the analogy of the parade grounds to the Washington Mall, see Michael R. Gordon and Gen. Bernard E. Trainor, *Cobra II: The Inside Story of the Invasion and Occupation of Iraq* (New York: Pantheon, 2006), 393.

26. Matthew Bogdanos argues that securing the museum with less than a full-scale assault would have been highly hazardous to the troops, but this would only have been the case if Iraqi forces had remained in force at the museum. Conroy's unit cleared a number of buildings that were on the no-strike list (including a school with an anti-aircraft weapon on its roof) without casualties. Bogdanos also argues that posting a stationary tank in front of the museum "would have required a willingness to forfeit the lives of that tank's four-man crew. A stationary tank inside a city during active combat (such as was the situation in April in that section of Baghdad) is a guaranteed death trap. In urban combat, a tank's survivability is directly linked to its mobility and ability to return fire, both of which would have been nullified by placing it on sentry duty in front of the museum. There would be no survivors of a direct hit from an antitank weapon." But RPGs were fired numerous times at Conroy's tanks, often at point-blank range, with little success, and tanks obviously did not stay in perpetual motion. This is not to say that there were not risks involved, only that they were not as extreme as suggested by Bogdanos. See Bogdanos, "Casualties of War," 504; and Conroy, *Heavy Metal*, 200.

27. By 2005 the security situation in Iraq had worsened so much that the rules of engagement were changed to permit warning shots in general, and

CENTCOM authorized using deadly force if needed to protect property—including museums—designated as vital to the execution of the mission. See "Annex E (Consolidated ROE) to 3-187 FRAGO 02, OPORDER 02-005," http://wikileaks.la/wiki/US_Rules_of_Engagement_for_Iraq.

28. Schwartz interview.
29. See John Alexander, "Technology for the Protection of Cultural Theft," in *Antiquities under Siege: Cultural Heritage Protection after the Iraq War,* ed. Lawrence Rothfield (Lanham, MD: AltaMira Press, 2008), 141–50.
30. Zarcone interview.
31. Col. Gregory Fontenot (ret.), Lt. Col. E. J. Degen, and Lt. Col. David Tohn, *"On Point": The United States Army in Operation Iraqi Freedom,* GlobalSecurity.org, n.d. http://www.globalsecurity.org/military/library/report/2004/onpoint/ch-6.htm.
32. Faisal Istrabadi, an Iraqi American lawyer who worked on the Future of Iraq Project, argues that the Americans could easily have found their way to the museum: "It can't be that U.S. troops didn't know where the National Museum was. All you have to do is follow the signs—they're in English!—to Museum Square." But even if soldiers were proceeding on foot rather than inside their tanks, they would be very unlikely to trust signs posted by Iraqis. See David Rieff, "Blueprint for a Mess," *Foreign Service Journal,* March 2004, 22–28.
33. Joseph Collins (former deputy assistant secretary of defense for stability operations), interviewed by the author, October 5, 2005.
34. Quoted in Westervelt, "Baghdad Museum."
35. Joseph Collins, personal communication, July 5, 2006.
36. Quoted in Paul McGeough, "Rich Past Stripped as Future in Tatters," *Sydney Morning Herald,* April 14, 2003, http://www.smh.com.au/articles/2003/04/13/1050172478179.html.
37. McGuire Gibson, e-mail message to Kraig Kenworthy, April 11, 2003.
38. John Limbert, e-mail message to McGuire Gibson, April 12, 2003.
39. John Limbert, interviewed by the author, March 3, 2005.

CHAPTER SIX

1. James Fitzpatrick, interviewed by the author, March 3, 2005.
2. John Limbert, interviewed by the author, March 3, 2005.
3. Maj. Christopher Varhola (Civil Affairs officer), interviewed by the author, April 15, 2005.
4. McGuire Gibson, e-mail message to Kraig Kenworthy, April 12, 2003.
5. On the role of the hawza in stemming looting, see David Rieff, "Blueprint for a Mess," *Foreign Service Journal,* March 2004, 22–28.
6. Neal Ascherson, "Iraq and Ruin," *Guardian,* May 2, 2003, http://arts.guardian.co.uk/features/story/0,947799,00.html.
7. Kraig Kenworthy, e-mail message to McGuire Gibson, April 12, 2003.

8. Arthur Houghton, interviewed by the author, March 3, 2005.

9. Jane Waldbaum and Patty Gerstenblith, "Tracing Iraq's Lost Treasures," *Washington Post,* April 27, 2003, B7.

10. Several years later, in March 2005, Mellon would be even more generous, stepping in with $117,000 when USAID reneged after one year on an agreement with Stone to provide three years of funding to train Iraqi archaeologists.

11. McGuire Gibson, e-mail message to Kraig Kenworthy, April 13, 2003.

12. Peter Zarcone, interviewed by the author, July 24, 2007.

13. Donny George Youkhanna (former director of museums, State Board of Antiquities and Heritage, Iraq), interviewed by the author, February 19, 2007.

14. See Gregory Elich, "Spoils of War: The Antiquities Trade and the Looting of Iraq," Centre for Research on Globalisation, http://globalresearch.ca/articles/ELI401A.html; Matthew Bogdanos, "Casualties of War: The Truth about the Iraq Museum," *American Journal of Archaeology* 109, no. 3 (July 2005): 505; and Donny George Youkhanna and McGuire Gibson, "Preparations at the Iraq Museum in the Lead-Up to War," in *Antiquities under Siege: Cultural Heritage Protection after the Iraq War,* ed. Lawrence Rothfield (Lanham, MD: AltaMira Press, 2008), 31.

15. See Robert Fisk, "Library Books, Letters and Priceless Documents Are Set Ablaze in Final Chapter of the Sacking of Baghdad," *Independent,* April 15, 2003, http://news.independent.co.uk/fisk/article115214.ece.

16. Donald Rumsfeld and Richard Myers, "DoD News Briefing," April 11, 2003, http://www.defenselink.mil/transcripts/2003/tr20030411-secdef0090.html.

17. Donald Rumsfeld interview with Tim Russert, NBC *Meet the Press,* http://www.defenselink.mil/transcripts/transcript.aspx?transcriptid=2383 (accessed December 4, 2007).

18. Ironically, half the collection of the Mosul Museum had been sent to the National Museum of Iraq for safety. On the looting of the Mosul Museum, see Douglas Birch, "In North Iraq, an Ancient Past Falls Victim to a Modern War," *Baltimore Sun,* April 18, 2003, www.baltimoresun.com/news/nationworld/iraq/bal-te.north18apr18,0,532697.story?coll=bal-home-headlines (accessed July 19, 2007); and Roger Atwood, "In the North of Iraq," *Archaeology,* June 4, 2003, http://www.archaeology.org/online/features/iraq/mosul.html.

19. Secretary of State Colin Powell, "Cooperation for the Safeguarding of Iraqi Antiquities and Cultural Property," April 14, 2003, http://www.globalsecurity.org/wmd/library/news/iraq/2003/iraq-030414-dos-19628pf.htm.

20. George Youkhanna interview.

21. John Curtis, interviewed by the author, December 21, 2004.

22. Brig. Gen. Vincent Brooks, "Central Command Operation Iraqi Freedom News Briefing," Gulf Investigations news service, April 15, 2003, www .gulfinvestigations.net/document615.html.

23. Donald Rumsfeld and Richard Myers, "DoD News Briefing," April 15, 2003, http://www.defenselink.mil/transcripts/transcript .aspx?transcriptid=2413.

24. Pres. George W. Bush, "Remarks by the President on Operation Iraqi Freedom," Ford Community and Performing Arts Center, Dearborn, MI, April 28, 2003, White House news release, http://www.whitehouse.gov/ news/releases/2003/04/print/20030428-3.html.

25. Lt. Gen. William "Scott" Wallace, who led the Battle of Baghdad, crowed that, according to a report he had read (Bogdanos's, almost certainly), "of the artifacts that were allegedly taken from the main museum downtown, all but 38 of them have been accounted for [sic]." Lt. Gen. William Wallace, "News Briefing," May 7, 2003, http://www.defenselink.mil/transcripts/transcript.aspx?transcriptid=2573. As the general surely must have known, the number 38 referred only to artifacts taken from the main display cases, not the vastly greater number stolen from the museum's back rooms. For a detailed though somewhat skewed critique of the early reportage on the events at the museum, see Jeffrey Schuster, "Iraqi Antiquities Revisited (with Endnotes)," Gutenblog Castle, http://gutenblogcastle .blogspot.com/2005/02/iraq-antiquities-revisited-with.html.

26. Donald Rumsfeld, "Rumsfeld, Myers Pentagon Briefing," May 20, 2003, http://www.america.gov/st/washfile-english/2003/May/20030521075931n osnhojb4.883975e-02.html.

27. Donald Rumsfeld, "Rumsfeld, Franks Pentagon Briefing," May 9, 2003, http://www.america.gov/st/washfile-english/2003/May/ 20030509172225ifas0.7209436.html.

28. Charles Krauthammer, "Hoaxes, Hype and Humiliation," *Washington Post,* June 13, 2003, A29.

29. George Youkhanna interview.

30. Chris Varhola, e-mail message to McGuire Gibson, April 16, 2003.

31. Zainab Bahrani, interviewed by the author, March 14, 2005.

32. William Jeffrey, e-mail message to McGuire Gibson, April 15, 2003.

33. McGuire Gibson, e-mail message to John Limbert, April 15, 2003.

34. As late as August 6, 2003, cuneiform tablets from the museum were recovered in a Baghdad bazaar.

35. A team from the Library of Congress worked with the State Department's Cultural Property Office and the Coalition Provisional Authority for months to organize a mission to assist the National Library. The success of this initiative owes much to the leadership of James Billington, Librarian of Congress, whose personal engagement stands in marked contrast to the passivity of his counterparts in most other federal cultural agencies.

36. This legislation also closed a loophole in the Cultural Property Implementation Act, authorizing the president to exercise his authority under the CPIA to prohibit import of designated archaeological and ethnological materials from Iraq without need for Iraq to bring a request under the CPIA. The loophole remains open, however, for other countries, including Afghanistan. See Patty Gerstenblith, "From Bamiyan to Baghdad: Warfare and the Preservation of Cultural Heritage at the Beginning of the 21st Century," *Georgetown Journal of International Law* 37, no. 2 (Winter 2006): 245–352.

37. In a statement released on April 15, DCMS declared: "The Ministry of Defence have throughout the conflict been alert to the need to protect sensitive cultural and archaeological sites in Iraq. More recently they have been working hard to ensure that such sites are secured from the risk of looting." Department for Culture, Media and Sport, "Statement from the DCMS Regarding Iraq's Cultural Heritage," Museum Security Network Web site, April 15, 2003, http://www.museum-security.org/03/052.html#2.

38. Tessa Jowell, "Excerpts from Tessa Jowell, Secretary of State for Culture's Speech at the British Museum on 15 April 2003," DCMS media release, under "Archive 2003," http://www.culture.gov.uk/Reference_library/Press_notices/archive_2003/statement_iraq.htm.

39. Renfrew notes that it was the British Museum, not the DCMS, which set up the meeting at which Jowell spoke. "She clearly saw the opportunity to suggest that she and her ministry were doing something . . . but it has not been followed up by any actions." Colin Renfrew, interviewed by the author, December 21, 2004. A senior official in the department who prefers to remain unnamed insists that DCMS ministers pushed hard in top-level one-to-one ministerial meetings to persuade other departments to reallocate some humanitarian assistance funding to DCMS to improve cultural heritage protection, but these requests were invariably dismissed.

CHAPTER SEVEN

1. These figures are from an undated prewar memo sent by Jeremy Black, an archaeologist at Oxford University, to the British foreign secretary Jack Straw. The same information is included in Harriet Crawford, John Baines, Jeremy Black et al., "Letter: Bombing Could Devastate Rich Remains of Ancient Cities," *Independent* (London), March 5, 2003, http://findarticles.com/p/articles/mi_qn4158/is_20030305/ai_n12679517.

2. McGuire Gibson, e-mail message to John Limbert, April 13, 2003.

3. Andrew Lawler, "Archaeology: On Iraq's Front Lines," *Science* 321, no. 5885 (July 4, 2008): 29; DOI: 10.1126/science.321.5885.29, http://www.sciencemag.org/cgi/content/full/321/5885/29 (accessed July 6, 2008).

4. See Samuel Paley, "Nimrud, the War, and the Antiquities Markets," *IFAR Journal* 6, nos. 1 and 2, http://www.ifar.org/nimrud.htm.

5. Al-Hamdani, private communication.

6. Piotr Michalowski, "U.S. Scholarly Organizations Unite to Protect Iraqi Cultural Heritage," University of Michigan news release, May 9, 2003, http://www.umich.edu/news/Releases/2003/May03/r050903c.html. Despite its organizational heft, this group appears to have failed to raise any funds whatsoever.

7. Carabinieri Unit for the Protection and Safeguarding of Italian Cultural Heritage, "Italian Carabinieri and the Protection of Iraq's Cultural Heritage," in *Antiquities under Siege: Cultural Heritage Protection after the Iraq War*, ed. Lawrence Rothfield (Lanham, MD: AltaMira Press, 2008), 136, 138.

8. Elizabeth Stone, "Cultural Assessment of Iraq: The State of Sites and Museums in Southern Iraq," *National Geographic*, May 2003, http://news.nationalgeographic.com/news/2003/06/0611_030611_iraqlootingreport3.html.

9. On the problem at Hatra, see Roger Atwood, "In the North of Iraq," *Archaeology*, June 4, 2003, http://www.archaeology.org/online/features/iraq/mosul.html.

10. UNESCO had also arrived at almost the same time but was restricted from traveling around the country. See the UNESCO survey, http://portal.unesco.org/culture/en/ev.php-URL_ID=14658&URL_DO=DO_TOPIC&URL_SECTION=201.html.

11. Henry Wright, personal communication, April 7, 2008.

12. Quoted in Mary Wiltenburg, "A Fertile Crescent for Looting," *Christian Science Monitor*, June 12, 2003, http://www.csmonitor.com/2003/0612/p03s01-woiq.html.

13. For the results of the National Geographic survey, see http://news.nationalgeographic.com/news/2003/06/0611_030611_iraqlootingreport.html.

14. McGuire Gibson, e-mail message to John Marburger, May 31, 2003.

15. McGuire Gibson, e-mail message to John Marburger, June 12, 2003.

16. On the successful efforts by the Dutch CIMIC/CA in securing the important southern Iraq site of Uruk, see Joris D. Kila, "The Role of NATO and Civil Military Affairs," in *Antiquities under Siege*, 179–80.

17. U.S. Department of State, "Iraq Cultural Heritage Update," July 14, 2003, http://www.state.gov/r/pa/prs/ps/2003/22388.htm.

18. Micah Garen, interviewed by C. Brian Rose, March 14, 2008, http://www.salon.com/news/feature/2008/03/20/iraq_roundtable/index1.html.

19. On the Facility Protection Service, see GlobalSecurity.org, "Facility Protection Service (FPS)—Facilities Protection Forces," under "Intelligence," n.d., http://www.globalsecurity.org/intell/world/iraq/fps.htm.

20. Wright, personal communication.

21. See the somewhat suspect piece by Joel Leyden, "Swift-Find: Terrorism Funded by Stolen Property," Israel News Agency, October 16, 2005, http://

www.israelnewsagency.com/terrorismstolenpropertyswiftfindregistry881016
.html; and, more authoritatively, Laura De la Torre, "Terrorists Raise Cash
by Selling Antiquities," *Government Security News,* February 20, 2006, http://
www.gsnmagazine.com/pdfs/38_Feb_06.pdf (Web page now invalid).

22. See Micah Garen and Marie-Hélène Carleton, *American Hostage: A Memoir
of a Journalist Kidnapped in Iraq and the Remarkable Battle to Win His Release*
(New York: Simon & Schuster, 2005).

23. McGuire Gibson, e-mail message to Steven Hunter, September 11, 2003.

CHAPTER EIGHT

1. Elizabeth Stone, "Patterns of Looting in Southern Iraq" (PowerPoint pre-
sentation, American Schools of Oriental Research meeting, Washington,
DC, November 16, 2006); see also Stone, "Patterns of Looting in Southern
Iraq," *Antiquity* 82 (2008): 125–38.

2. David Johnston, "Marine's Mementos Turn Out to Be 5,000 Years Old,"
New York Times, February 15, 2005, http://www.iht.com/articles/2005/
02/14/news/artifacts.php.

3. For an assessment of the losses to the museum, see Martin Bailey, "After
the Looting Was Over: One Year after the Iraq War, the Damage to the
Country's National Museum Is Still Being Assessed," *Apollo,* May 1, 2004,
http://findarticles.com/p/articles/mi_m0PAL/is_507_159/ai_n6157843.

4. See Guy Gugliotta, "Treasure Trove of Antiquities May Prove Difficult to
Recover," *Washington Post,* May 2, 2003, A3.

5. For a discussion of Iraq's grave robbers, see Joanne Farchakh Bajjaly, "Who
Are the Looters?" in *Antiquities under Siege: Cultural Heritage Protection after
the Iraq War,* ed. Lawrence Rothfield (Lanham, MD: AltaMira Press, 2008),
49–56.

6. Hussein Ali al-Yasiri, "Plundering the Past," *ICR* 82 (September 6, 2004),
posted on IraqCrisis listhost, September 18, 2004, https://listhost.uchicago
.edu/pipermail/iraqcrisis/2004-September/000858.html.

7. Neil Brodie, "The Western Market in Iraqi Antiquities," in *Antiquities under
Siege,* ed. Rothfield, 69.

8. Christoph Plate, "Sumerischer Terracotta-Löwenkopf im Angebot:
Interpol und die irakischen Behörden arbeiten gegen den Handel mit
Artefakten im Internet," *Neue Zürcher Zeitung,* July 3, 2005, posted on
IraqCrisis listhost, July 14, 2007, https://listhost.uchicago.edu/pipermail/
iraqcrisis/2005-July/001284.html.

9. George is quoted in "Iraq Archaeologist Flees to Syria," *Middle East News,*
August 28, 2006, http://monstersandcritics.com/news/middleeast/news/
article_1195508.php.

10. The figure is quoted in "Resolution by the Governing Board of the Archaeological Institute of America to Support the U.S. Funding Proposal
for Archaeological Site Protection in Iraq," in *Archaeological Institute of*

America, online, January 6, 2005, http://www.archaeological.org/pdfs/archaeologywatch/Iraq/AIA_Iraq_Resolution0501.pdf?page=10248.

11. National Iraqi News Agency, "Thieves Threaten the Elimination of the Sumerian Civilization in Dhi-Qar," wna-news.com, December 6, 2006, posted on IraqCrisis listhost, December 7, 2006, https://listhost.uchicago.edu/pipermail/iraqcrisis/2006-December/001665.html.

12. Fifty-one objects stolen from the aboveground storage rooms were recovered in a raid at a location approximately ten kilometers from the Turkish border. See Matthew Bogdanos, *Thieves of Baghdad* (New York: Bloomsbury, 2005), 295, 232n, 298, 270n.

13. Nidhal al-Laithi, "Iraqi Officials Implicated in Smuggling of Antiquities, British Museum Expert Says," Azzaman.com, May 13, 2008, http://www.azzaman.com/english/index.asp?fname=news%5C2008-05-13%5Ckurd.htm.

14. Matthew Boulay, interviewed by the author, July 24, 2007.

15. See Miroslaw Olbrys, "The Polish Contribution to the Protection of the Archaeological Heritage in Central South Iraq, November 2003 to April 2005," *Conservation and Management of Archaeological Sites* 8 (2007): 94.

16. See T. Burda, "Specification of Projects Realized by Specialists in Archaeology and Protection of Cultural Heritage in Polish Military Contingent in Iraq in Period from November 2003 to February 2005," http://www.mk.gov.pl/website/index.jsp.catId=340.

17. Ibid., 95.

18. Ibid., 96–97.

19. Roger Matthews, "By the Waters of Babylon," *British Archaeology* 90 (September/October 2006), http://www.britarch.ac.uk/BA/ba90/feat3.shtml. See also al-Yasiri, "Plundering the Past."

20. See John Curtis, "Report on Meeting at Babylon 11–13 December 2004," British Museum Web site, n.d., http://www.thebritishmuseum.ac.uk/the_museum/news_and_debate/news/meeting_at_babylon.aspx.

21. Olbrys, "Polish Contribution," 96; Miroslaw Olbrys, "The Possibilities and Restrictions of the Archeologist's Work during Open Armed Conflict— Experiences from Iraq 2004/2005," in *Cultural Heritage in the 21st Century: Opportunities and Challenges,* ed. Monika Murzyn and Jacek Purchla (Krakow: International Cultural Centre, 2007), 241.

22. This is a paraphrased summary of comments by Kamel Shiyah (director of cultural relations, the Ministry of Culture), "Final Report," first plenary session, UNESCO's International Coordination Committee for the Safeguarding of the Cultural Heritage of Iraq, Paris, May 24, 2004, 6.

23. E. Mattingly, "Prof. to Train Soldiers to Preserve Sites," *The Dartmouth* (NH), April 26, 2006, https://listhost.uchicago.edu/pipermail/iraqcrisis/2006-April/001524.html.

24. Dr. Laurie Rush, personal communication, August 15, 2007.

25. Dr. Laurie Rush, personal communication, August 7, 2007.

26. U.S. Committee of the Blue Shield, "ICOM-US Announces 2007 International Service Citation," news release, May 22, 2004, http://uscbs.org/news/?p=8.

27. C. Brian Rose, "Talking to the Troops about the Archaeology of Iraq and Afghanistan," in *The Acquisition and Exhibition of Classical Antiquities: Professional, Legal, and Ethical Perspectives,* ed. Robin Rhodes (Notre Dame, IN: University of Notre Dame Press, 2007), 141, 142.

28. An Occasional Correspondent [Gertrude Bell], "The Excavations at Babylon," *Times,* June 4, 1909, no. 38977, 6, col. B.

29. Bijal Trivedi, "U.S. Military Working on Ultimate 'Stink Bomb,'" *National Geographic Today,* January 7, 2002, http://news.nationalgeographic.com/news/2002/01/0107_020107TVstinkbomb.html.

30. For a discussion of these and other technological options for protecting remote archaeological sites, see John Alexander, "Technology for the Prevention of Cultural Theft," in *Antiquities under Siege,* ed. Rothfield, 141–50.

31. Jørgen Wadum, "ICOM-CC Chair Report, May 2003–January 2004" (The Hague, January 2004), http://www.icom-cc.org/index.php?page_id=50.

32. See UNESCO, "Republic of Iraq UN/WB Joint Needs Assessment: Culture Sector," UNESCO Web site (under "Iraq," within the "Culture" sector), October 1, 2003, http://portal.unesco.org/culture/en/ev.php-URL_ID=17322&URL_DO=DO_TOPIC&URL_SECTION=201.html.

33. Ibid.

34. See the description of Getty's initiative at the J. Paul Getty Trust, "Iraq Cultural Heritage Conservation Initiative," Getty Conservation Institute, December 2006, http://www.getty.edu/conservation/field_projects/iraq/index.html.

35. Ibid.

36. See National Iraqi News Agency, "Thieves Threaten the Elimination."

37. Olbrys, "Polish Contribution," 96.

38. See Micah Garen and Marie-Hélène Carleton, *American Hostage: A Memoir of a Journalist Kidnapped in Iraq and the Remarkable Battle to Win His Release* (New York: Simon & Schuster, 2005), 32–33.

39. Andrew Lawler, "Interview with Donny George," *Discover,* August 3, 2007, http://discovermagazine.com/2007/aug/discover-interview-director-iraqi-national-museum/article_print.

40. Sumedha Senanayake, "Iraq: Antiquities Continue to Be Pillaged, Destroyed," *Radio Free Europe,* October 12, 2006, http://www.rferl.org/featuresarticle/2006/10/6f5f571b-f0f8-4ff9-899f-b8341676574b.html.

41. Garen and Carleton, *American Hostage,* 12.

42. Lawler, "Interview with Donny George."

43. Matthew Bogdanos, "The Terrorist in the Art Gallery," *New York Times,* December 10, 2005, A15.

44. Robert S. Mueller, "Remarks Prepared for Director Robert S. Mueller III"

BIBLIOGRAPHY

as Thieves Excavate Sites." *Guardian*, December 13, 2003. ProQuest
Newsstand database, document ID #490249441.

Atwood, Roger. "In the North of Iraq." *Archaeology*, June 4, 2003. http://www
.archaeology.org/online/features/iraq/mosul.html.

Bagherzadeh, F. "Jean Perrot, un ami de l'Iran." In *Contribution à l'histoire de
l'Iran. Mélanges offerts à Jean Perrot*, edited by F. Vallat. Paris: Editions
Recherche sur les civilisations, 1990.

Bailey, Martin. "After the Looting Was Over: One Year after the Iraq War, the
Damage to the Country's National Museum Is Still Being Assessed." *Apollo*,
May 1, 2004. http://findarticles.com/p/articles/mi_m0PAL/is_507_159/
ai_n6157843.

———. "Iraq's Top Archaeologists Says Looting of Sites Is Over." *Art Newspaper*,
August 28, 2008. http://www.theartnewspaper.com/article.asp?id=16008.

Bajjaly, Joanne Farchakh. "Who Are the Looters?" In *Antiquities under Siege:
Cultural Heritage Protection after the Iraq War*, edited by Lawrence Rothfield,
49–56. Lanham, MD: AltaMira Press, 2008.

[B]aker, Alexi Shannon. "Selling the Past: *United States v. Frederick Schultz*."
Archaeology, April 22, 2002.

[B]aker, H. D., Roger Matthews, and Nicholas Postgate. *Lost Heritage: Antiquities
Stolen from Iraq's Regional Museums*. Fasc. 2. London: British School of
Archaeology in Iraq, 1993.

[Ba]qué, Philippe. "Un trafic particulièrement lucrative: Enquête sur le pillage
des objets d'art." *Le Monde diplomatique*, February 2005. http://cpprot
.te.verweg.com/2005-March/000913.html.

[Bar]am, Amatzia. "A Case of Imported Identity: The Modernizing Secular
Ruling Elites of Iraq and the Concept of Mesopotamian-Inspired
Territorial Nationalism, 1922–1992." *Poetics Today* 15 (1994): 279–319.

———. *Culture, History, and Ideology in the Formation of Ba'thist Iraq, 1968–89*.
New York: St. Martin's Press, 1991.

[Bell], Gertrude, as the "Occasional Correspondent"]. "The Excavations at
Babylon." *Times* (London), June 4, 1909, no. 38977.

———. "The First Capital of Assyria." *Times* (London), August 23, 1910.

———. "Report on Kish, Warka, Sunkara, and Ur." British Museum Central
Archives, WY1/2/83, January 19 [no year given—probably 1925].

[Bern]hardsson, Magnus. *Reclaiming a Plundered Past: Archaeology and Nation
Building in Modern Iraq*. Austin: University of Texas Press, 2005.

[Bix]on, John W. "Afghan Archaeology on the Road to Recovery." *Daily Star*,
October 12, 2004, 12.

[Birch], Douglas. "In North Iraq, an Ancient Past Falls Victim to a Modern War."
Baltimore Sun, April 18, 2003. www.baltimoresun.com/news/nationworld/
iraq/bal-te.north18apr18,0,532697.story?coll=bal-home-headlines
(accessed July 19, 2007).

[Bloom], Jonathan M., and Lark Ellen Gould. "Patient Restoration: The Kuwait
[N]ational Museum." *Saudi Aramco World*, September/October 2000. http://

speech, Town Hall Los Angeles, Los Angeles, CA, November 15, 2004,
http://www.fbi.gov/pressrel/speeches/mueller111504.htm.

45. See Amar Imad, "U.S. Troops Storm Antiquities Department," Azzaman.
com, May 19, 2007, http://www.azzaman.com/english/index
.asp?fname=news%5C2007-05-19%5Cmos.htm.

46. See Alastair Northedge, "SBAH in Samarra Attacked and Looted,"
IraqCrisis listhost, July 10, 2007, https://listhost.uchicago.edu/pipermail/
iraqcrisis/2007-July/001821.html.

47. See Charles Jones, "SBAH Representative in Basra Killed," IraqCrisis
listhost, July 11, 2007, https://listhost.uchicago.edu/pipermail/
iraqcrisis/2007-July/001822.html.

48. Lucian Harris, "Iraq's Top Cultural Official Resigns," *Art Newspaper*,
August 26, 2006.

49. Corine Wegener, personal communication, June 7, 2007.

50. David D'Arcy, "Archaeologists Say Iraq Antiquities Still Unprotected,"
NPR's *Morning Edition*, broadcast on January 11, 2005, http://www.npr.org/
templates/story/story.php?storyId=4277978.

51. Powell is quoted in Bob Woodward, *Plan of Attack* (New York: Simon &
Schuster, 2004), 150.

CODA

1. Cara Buckley, "A Peek Inside before the Museum Doors Close Again," *New
York Times*, December 12, 2007, A15.

2. Ibid.

3. Laura Bush, "Mrs. Bush's Remarks at the Launch of the 'Iraq Cultural
Heritage Project,'" October 16, 2008, http://www.whitehouse.gov/news/
releases/2008/10/20081016-1.html (accessed October 24, 2008). The State
Department's fact sheet on the new project touts its having spent several
million dollars since 2003 in support of "numerous activities relating
to the protection and preservation of Iraq's cultural heritage," including
"emergency response to the looting of the Iraq National Museum, training
of Iraqi museum professionals, support for archaeological site protection,
and instituting legal measures to mitigate illicit trafficking in Iraq's looted
cultural property." The results, it is claimed, include "improved archaeological site security in Iraq." No details are provided on how much has
actually been spent on what measures. See U.S. Department of State Office
of the Spokesman, "Iraq Cultural Heritage Project (ICHP) Fact Sheet,"
October 16, 2008, http://www.state.gov/r/pa/prs/ps/2008/oct/111017.htm
(accessed October 24, 2008).

4. Martin Bailey, "Iraq's Top Archaeologists Says Looting of Sites Is Over,"
Art Newspaper, August 28, 2008, http://www.theartnewspaper.com/article
.asp?id=16008; Department of State Ninewa Provincial Reconstruction
Team, "'Cultural Heritage Sites Safe,' According to State Board of Antiquities Inspector Qais Rashid," *Ninewa Province Bulletin*, http://iraq.usembassy

.gov/root/pdfs/ninewa-prt-story.pdf (accessed October 24, 2008); Melik Kaylan, "So Much for the 'Looted Sites,'" *Wall Street Journal,* July 15, 2008, http://online.wsj.com/article/SB121607917797452675.html#printMode (accessed October 24, 2008).

5. John M. Curtis et al., "An Assessment of Archaeological Sites in June 2008: An Iraqi-British Project," http://www.britishmuseum.org/the_museum/ museum_in_the_world/middle_east_programme/iraq_project/overview_ of_site_surveys.aspx (accessed October 24, 2008). For a critique of this report and others, see Lawrence Rothfield, "Assessment Report on 8 Southern Sites Released at Last," The Punching Bag, http://larryrothfield .blogspot.com (accessed October 24, 1008). For an overview of the issues, see Hugh Eakin, "The Devastation of Iraq's Past," *New York Review of Books,* August 14, 2008, http://www.nybooks.com/articles/21671 (accessed October 24, 2008).

6. In the case of Syria, the saber rattling has had an unintended positive side effect. On the day the United States released photos intended to show the Syrians had been constructing a nuclear reactor with help from North Korea, Syrian officials handed over to the Iraqis some seven hundred Mesopotamian artifacts seized since 2003. See Albert Aji, "Syria Hands Over 700 Looted Artifacts to Iraqi Authorities," World-Wire, April 23, 2008, http://www.kansascity.com/451/story/588707.html.

7. On September 25, 2008, as this book was going to press, the 1954 Hague Convention was ratified by the Senate. On the British ratification, see UK Department for Culture, Media and Sport, "Consultation Paper on the 1954 Hague Convention on the Protection of Cultural Property in the Event of Armed Conflict and Its Two Protocols of 1954 and 1999" (London: Department for Culture, Media and Sport, 2005), 63. See also Matthew D. Thurlow, "Protecting Cultural Property in Iraq: How American Military Policy Comports with International Law," *Yale Human Rights and Development Law Journal* 8 (2005): 153–87.

8. Lt. Gen. Michael D. Maples, personal communication to author, November 1, 2007.

9. Department of the Army, *FM 3-07: Stability Operations,* October 2008, 3–5, http://usacac.army.mil/CAC2/Repository/FM307/FM3-07.pdf (accessed October 24, 2008).

10. Andrew Rathmell, "Planning Post-Conflict Reconstruction in Iraq: What Can We Learn?" *International Affairs* 81, no. 5 (October 2005): 1013–38.

11. See Scott R. Feil, "Engaging Interagency Processes to Protect Cultural Sites," in *Antiquities under Siege: Cultural Heritage Protection after the Iraq War,* ed. Lawrence Rothfield (Lanham, MD: AltaMira Press, 2008), 219–34.

12. C. Brian Rose, interviewed by the author, December 18, 2007.

13. David Rohde, "Army Enlists Anthropology in War Zones," *New York Times,* October 5, 2007, A1.

14. Zainab Bahrani, interviewed by the author, March 14, 2005.

Bibliography

Abrams, Elliott. "Briefing on Humanitarian Issues." White House news release, Feb http://www.whitehouse.gov/news/rele 20030224-11.html.

Aji, Albert. "Syria Hands Over 700 Looted Authorities." World-Wire, April 23, 2 .kansascity.com/451/story/588707.ht

Alexander, John. "Technology for the Pr Theft." In *Antiquities under Siege: Cu after the Iraq War,* edited by Lawren Lanham, MD: AltaMira Press, 200

"Annex E (Consolidated ROE) to 3-187 02-005." http://wikileaks.la/wiki/ _Engagement_for_Iraq.

Appiah, Kwame Anthony. *Cosmopolita* 2006.

———. "Whose Culture Is It?" *New Y* no. 2 (February 9, 2006). http:// article-preview?article_id=1868

Archaeological Institute of America Respect Hague Convention W] Web site, n.d. http://www.arch .php?page=10174.

Armstead, James H. "The Chain of under Siege: Cultural Heritage I ited by Lawrence Rothfield,] Press, 2008.

Ascherson, Neal. "Iraq and Ruin arts.guardian.co.uk/feature

Astill, James. "Plunder Goes on Grow Ever Bolder: Trade in

www.saudiaramcoworld.com/issue/200005/patient.restoration-the.kuwait
.national.museum.htm.

Bogdanos, Matthew. "The Casualties of War: The Truth about the Iraq
Museum." *American Journal of Archaeology* 109, no. 3 (July 2005).

———. "The Terrorist in the Art Gallery." *New York Times,* December 10,
2005, A15.

———. "Transforming Joint Interagency Coordination: The Missing Link
between National Strategy and Operational Success." *Case Studies
in National Security Transformation* 9 (n.d.). http://www.ndu.edu/CTNSP/
pubs/Case%209%20-%20TransformingJointInteragencyCoordination
.pdf.

———. *Thieves of Baghdad.* New York: Bloomsbury, 2005.

Bole, William. "Relief Groups, Bush Administration at Odds on Iraq Aid."
Religion News Service, 2003. http://nns.wieck.com/forms/text/.

Bos, Stefan. "Hungary Agrees to Allow Military Training for Iraqi Exiles." *Palestine Chronicle,* December 18, 2002. http://palestinechronicle.com/story-
20021218191133578.htm.

Bottéro, Jean. "The 'Code' of Hammurabi." In *Mesopotamia: Writing, Reasoning,
and the Gods,* trans. Zainab Bahrani and Marc van de Mieroop, 156–84.
Chicago: University of Chicago Press, 1992.

Bouchenaki, Mounir. "UNESCO and the Safeguarding of Cultural Heritage in
Postconflict Situations." In *Antiquities under Siege: Cultural Heritage Protec-
tion after the Iraq War,* edited by Lawrence Rothfield, 207–18. Lanham,
MD: AltaMira Press, 2008.

Boylan, Patrick J. *Review of the Convention for the Protection of Cultural Property
in the Event of Armed Conflict.* Paris: UNESCO, 1993.

Breasted, Henry. "The Oriental Institute—A Beginning and a Program."
American Journal of Semitic Languages and Literatures 38 (1922): 233–328.

Bremer, L. Paul., III. *My Year in Iraq.* New York: Simon & Schuster, 2006.

Brodie, Neil. "Smoke and Mirrors." In *Who Owns Objects? The Ethics and Politics
of Collecting Cultural Artefacts,* edited by Eleanor Robson, Luke Treadwell,
and Chris Gosden, 1–14. Oxford: Oxbow Books, 2007.

———. "The Western Market in Iraqi Antiquities." In *Antiquities under Siege:
Cultural Heritage Protection after the Iraq War,* edited by Lawrence Rothfield,
207–18. Lanham, MD: AltaMira Press, 2008.

Brooks, Brig. Gen. Vincent. "Central Command Briefing." CNN.com, April 8,
2003. http://transcripts.cnn.com/TRANSCRIPTS/0304/08/se.05.html.

———. "Central Command Briefing," Office of International Information
Programs, U.S. Department of State, March 26, 2003. Posted on the Information Warfare Site. http://www.iwar.org.uk/news-archive/2003/03-26-4
.htm.

———. "Central Command Operation Iraqi Freedom News Briefing." Gulf
Investigations news service, April 15, 2003. www.gulfinvestigations.net/
document615.html.

Buckley, Cara. "A Peek Inside before the Museum Doors Close Again." *New York Times,* December 12, 2007.

Burda, T. "Specification of Projects Realized by Specialists in Archaeology and Protection of Cultural Heritage in Polish Military Contingent in Iraq in Period from November 2003 to February 2005." http://www.mk.gov.pl/website/index.jsp.catId=340.

Burnham, Bonnie, and Stephen K. Urice. "Preventing Looting after Armed Combat: The Way Forward for U.S. Nongovernmental Cultural Heritage Organizations." In *Antiquities under Siege: Cultural Heritage Protection after the Iraq War,* edited by Lawrence Rothfield, 257–71. Lanham, MD: AltaMira Press, 2008.

Bush, George W. "Remarks by the President on Operation Iraqi Freedom." Speech, Ford Community and Performing Arts Center, Dearborn, MI, April 28, 2003. White House news release. http://www.whitehouse.gov/news/releases/2003/04/print/20030428-3.html.

Bush, Laura. "Remarks at the Launch of the 'Iraq Cultural Heritage Project.'" October 16, 2008. http://www.whitehouse.gov/news/releases/2008/10/20081016-1.html (accessed October 24, 2008).

Carabinieri Unit for the Protection and Safeguarding of Italian Cultural Heritage. "Italian Carabinieri and the Protection of Iraq's Cultural Heritage." In *Antiquities under Siege: Cultural Heritage Protection after the Iraq War,* edited by Lawrence Rothfield, 135–40. Lanham, MD: AltaMira Press, 2008.

Chamberlain, Kevin. *War and Cultural Heritage: An Analysis of the 1954 Hague Convention for the Protection of Cultural Property in the Event of Armed Conflict and the Two Protocols.* London: Institute of Art and Law, 2004.

Chippindale, Christopher, and David W. J. Gill. "Material Consequences of Contemporary Classical Collecting." *American Journal of Archaeology* 104, no. 3 (July 2000): 463–511.

Collins, Joseph. "Briefing on Humanitarian Relief Planning for Iraq." Federal News Service, February 25, 2003. http://www.defenselink.mil/transcripts/2003/t02262003_t0225col.html.

Collon, Dominique. *Near Eastern Seals.* Berkeley: University of California Press, 1990.

Conklin, John E. *Art Crime.* Westport, CT: Praeger, 2004.

Conroy, Jason. *Heavy Metal: A Tank Company's Battle to Baghdad.* Washington, DC: Potomac Books, 2005.

Crawford, Harriet, John Baines, Jeremy Black et al. "Letter: Bombing Could Devastate Rich Remains of Ancient Cities." *Independent* (London), March 5, 2003. http://findarticles.com/p/articles/mi_qn4158/is_20030305/ai_n12679517.

Cuno, James. "Beyond Bamiyan: Will the World Be Ready Next Time?" In *Art and Cultural Heritage: Law, Policy, and Practice,* ed. Barbara T. Hoffman. New York: Cambridge University Press, 2006.

Curtis, John. "Report on Meeting at Babylon 11–13 December 2004." British Museum Web site, n.d. http://www.thebritishmuseum.ac.uk/the_museum/news_and_debate/news/meeting_at_babylon.aspx.

Curtis, John M., et al. "An Assessment of Archaeological Sites in June 2008: An Iraqi-British Project." http://www.britishmuseum.org/the_museum/museum_in_the_world/middle_east_programme/iraq_project/overview_of_site_surveys.aspx (accessed October 24, 2008).

Danner, Mark. "Iraq: The War of the Imagination." *New Yorker,* December 21, 2006. http://www.nybooks.com/articles/19720.

D'Arcy, David. "Archaeologists Say Iraq Antiquities Still Unprotected." NPR's *Morning Edition,* January 11, 2005. http://www.npr.org/templates/story/story.php?storyId=4277978.

———. "Legal Group to Fight 'Retentionist' Policies." *Art Newspaper,* October 24, 2002.

Davis, Eric. *Memories of State: Politics, History, and Collective Identity in Modern Iraq.* Berkeley: University of California Press, 2005.

Deblauwe, Francis. "Donny George's Exile and the State of the SBAH." *IW&A Documents* 10. http://iwa.univie.ac.at/georgesbah.html.

De la Torre, Laura. "Terrorists Raise Cash by Selling Antiquities." *Government Security News,* February 20, 2006. http://www.gsnmagazine.com/cms/lib/399.pdf (accessed July 8, 2008).

Dellios, Hugh. "Birth of Writing Explored in Baghdad Conference." *National Geographic News,* March 26, 2001. http://news.nationalgeographic.com/news/2001/03/0326_writing.html.

Department of the Army. *FM 3-07: Stability Operations.* October 2008, 3–5. http://usacac.army.mil/CAC2/Repository/FM307/FM3-07.pdf (accessed October 24, 2008).

Department for Culture, Media and Sport. "Statement from the DCMS Regarding Iraq's Cultural Heritage." Museum Security Network Web site, April 15, 2003. http://www.museum-security.org/03/052.html#2.

Department of State Ninewa Provincial Reconstruction Team. "'Cultural Heritage Sites Safe,' According to State Board of Antiquities Inspector Qais Rashid." *Ninewa Province Bulletin.* http://iraq.usembassy.gov/root/pdfs/ninewa-prt-story.pdf (accessed October 24, 2008).

Dilley, Ryan. "Law and Disorder in Iraq." BBC News Online, April 11, 2003. http://news.bbc.co.uk/1/low/world/middle_east/2939573.stm.

Dreschler, Donald L. "Reconstructing the Interagency Process after Iraq." *Journal of Strategic Studies* 28, no. 1 (February 2005): 3–30.

Dziedzic, Michael, and Christine Stark. "Bridging the Public Security Gap: Stability Police Units in Contemporary Peace Operations and the Center of Excellence for Stability Police Units." In *Antiquities under Siege: Cultural Heritage Protection after the Iraq War,* edited by Lawrence Rothfield, 127–34. Lanham, MD: AltaMira Press, 2008.

Eakin, Hugh. "The Devastation of Iraq's Past." *New York Review of Books,* August 14, 2008. http://www.nybooks.com/articles/21671 (accessed October 24, 2008).

Elich, Gregory. "Spoils of War: The Antiquities Trade and the Looting of Iraq." Centre for Research on Globalisation Web site. http://globalresearch.ca/articles/ELI401A.html.

Fales, Frederick Mario. *Saccheggio in Mesopotamia: Il museo di Baghdad dalla nascita dell'Iraq à oggi.* Udine: Forum, 2006.

Fallows, James. "Blind into Baghdad." *Atlantic Monthly,* January/February 2004. http://www.theatlantic.com/doc/200401/fallows.

Feil, Scott R. "Engaging Interagency Processes to Protect Cultural Sites: Communities, Authorities, and Capabilities." In *Antiquities under Siege: Cultural Heritage Protection after the Iraq War,* edited by Lawrence Rothfield, 219–34. Lanham, MD: AltaMira Press, 2008.

Feil, Scott R., Johanna Mendelson Forman, Robert Orr, and Michele Flournoy. *Play to Win: The Final Report of the Bi-Partisan Commission on Post-Conflict Reconstruction.* Arlington, VA, and Washington, DC: AUSA and CSIS, 2003.

Fisk, Robert. "Library Books, Letters and Priceless Documents Are Set Ablaze in Final Chapter of the Sacking of Baghdad." *Independent,* April 15, 2003. http://news.independent.co.uk/fisk/article115214.ece.

Fontenot, Col. Gregory, Lt. Col. E. J. Degen, and Lt. Col. David Tohn. *"On Point": The United States Army in Operation Iraqi Freedom.* GlobalSecurity.org, 2004. http://www.globalsecurity.org/military/library/report/2004/onpoint/ch-6.htm.

Fujii, Hideo, and Kazumi Oguchi. *Lost Heritage: Antiquities Stolen from Iraq's Regional Museums.* Fasc. 3. Tokyo: Institute for Cultural Studies of Ancient Iraq, Kokushikan University, 1996.

Garen, Micah. Interviewed by C. Brian Rose, March 14, 2008. http://www.salon.com/news/feature/2008/03/20/iraq_roundtable/index1.html.

Garen, Micah, and Marie-Hélène Carleton. *American Hostage: A Memoir of a Journalist Kidnapped in Iraq and the Remarkable Battle to Win His Release.* New York: Simon & Schuster, 2005.

George, Rose. "Going for an Iraqi Dig? Don't Forget the AK-47." *Financial Times,* August 4, 2001, 3.

Gerstenblith, Patty. "From Bamiyan to Baghdad: Warfare and the Preservation of Cultural Heritage at the Beginning of the 21st Century." *Georgetown Journal of International Law* 37, no. 2 (Winter 2006): 245–351.

Gibson, McGuire. "Fate of Iraqi Archaeology." *Science* 99, no. 5614 (March 21, 2003): 1848–49.

Gibson, McGuire, and Augusta McMahon. *Lost Heritage: Antiquities Stolen from Iraq's Regional Museums.* Fasc. 1. Chicago: American Association for Research in Baghdad, 1992.

Gibson, McGuire, and Donny George Youkhanna. "What Cultural Ministries and Heritage Sites Should Do to Prepare for Conflict." In *Antiquities under*

Siege: Cultural Heritage Protection after the Iraq War, edited by Lawrence Rothfield, 249–54. Lanham, MD: AltaMira Press, 2008.

Gladwell, Malcolm. *Blink: The Power of Thinking without Thinking.* New York: Little, Brown, 2005.

Glauber, Bill. "$300 and a Prewar Promise Save Famed Archaeological Sites." Knight-Ridder/Tribune News Service, May 1, 2003. Posted on IraqCrisis listhost, May 1, 2003. https://listhost.uchicago.edu/pipermail/ iraqcrisis/2003-May/000027.html.

GlobalSecurity.org. "Facility Protection Service (FPS)—Facilities Protection Forces." Under "Intelligence," n.d. http://www.globalsecurity.org/intell/ world/iraq/fps.htm.

Gordon, Michael R., and Gen. Bernard E. Trainor. *Cobra II: The Inside Story of the Invasion and Occupation of Iraq.* New York: Pantheon, 2006.

Gottlieb, Martin, with Barry Meier. "Of 2,000 Treasures Stolen in Gulf War of 1991, Only 12 Have Been Recovered." *New York Times,* May 1, 2003, eastern late edition. Banking Information Source database, document ID #33108346.

Gugliotta, Guy. "Treasure Trove of Antiquities May Prove Difficult to Recover." *Washington Post,* May 2, 2003, A3.

Harris, Lucian. "Iraq's Top Cultural Official Resigns." *Art Newspaper,* August 26, 2006.

Hawkins, Ashton, and Maxwell L. Anderson. "Preserving Iraq's Past." *Washington Post,* November 29, 2002, A43.

Haxthausen, Louise, and Jim Williams. "International Cooperation in Afghanistan: Strategies, Funding and Modalities of Action." *Museum International* 55 (2003): 84–90.

Hoh, Christopher. "Practical and Policy Considerations in Protecting Cultural Heritage and Preventing Looting during International Peace and Stability Operations." In *Antiquities under Siege: Cultural Heritage Protection after the Iraq War,* edited by Lawrence Rothfield, 195–206. Lanham, MD: AltaMira Press, 2008.

Honan, William. "Attacks on Iraq Worry and Divide Archeologists." *New York Times,* February 9, 1991, sec. 1.

Iklé, Fred. *Every War Must End.* 2nd rev. ed. New York: Columbia University Press, 2005.

Imad, Amar. "U.S. Troops Storm Antiquities Department." Azzaman.com, May 19, 2007. http://www.azzaman.com/english/index.asp?fname= news%5C2007-05-19%5Cmos.htm.

International Council of Museums Executive Council. *The Minutes of the 103rd Session of the Executive Council of ICOM,* June 1, 2003. http://icom.museum/ download/103/2003ex04_eng.doc.

"Iraq Archaeologist Flees to Syria." *Middle East News,* August 28, 2006. http://monstersandcritics.com/news/middleeast/news/article_1195508 .php.

J. Paul Getty Trust. "Iraq Cultural Heritage Conservation Initiative." Getty Conservation Institute, December 2006. http://www.getty.edu/conservation/field_projects/iraq/index.html.

Johnston, David. "Marine's Mementos Turn Out to Be 5,000 Years Old." *New York Times,* February 15, 2005. http://www.iht.com/articles/2005/02/14/news/artifacts.php.

Jones, Charles. "SBAH Representative in Basra Killed." IraqCrisis listhost, July 11, 2007. https://listhost.uchicago.edu/pipermail/iraqcrisis/2007-July/001822.html.

Jowell, Tessa. "Excerpts from Tessa Jowell, Secretary of State for Culture's Speech at the British Museum on 15 April 2003." DCMS media release, under "Archive 2003." http://www.culture.gov.uk/Reference_library/Press_notices/archive_2003/statement_iraq.htm.

Kaylan, Melik. "So Much for the 'Looted Sites.'" *Wall Street Journal,* July 15, 2008. http://online.wsj.com/article/SB121607917797452675.html#printMode (accessed October 24, 2008).

Kersel, Morag. "From the Ground to the Buyer: A Market Analysis of the Trade in Illegal Antiquities." In *Archaeology, Cultural Heritage, and the Antiquities Trade,* edited by Neil Brodie, Morag Kersel, Christina Luke, and Kathryn Walkter Tubb, 188–205. Gainesville: University Press of Florida, 2006.

———. "License to Sell: The Legal Antiquities Trade in Israel." Ph.D. diss., Cambridge University, 2006.

Kila, Joris D. "The Role of NATO and Civil Military Affairs." In *Antiquities under Siege: Cultural Heritage Protection after the Iraq War,* edited by Lawrence Rothfield, 175–92. Lanham, MD: AltaMira Press, 2008.

Krauthammer, Charles. "Hoaxes, Hype and Humiliation." *Washington Post,* June 13, 2003, A29.

Lamb, Christina. "Looted Afghan Art Smuggled into UK." *Sunday Times,* March 12, 2006. http://www.timesonline.co.uk/article/0,2089-2081457_1,00.html.

Larsen, Mogens Trolle. *The Conquest of Assyria: Excavations in an Antique Land, 1840–1860.* New York: Routledge, 1996.

Lawler, Andrew. "Archaeology: On Iraq's Front Lines." *Science* 321, no. 5885 (July 4, 2008): 29. DOI: 10.1126/science.321.5885.29. http://www.sciencemag.org/cgi/content/full/321/5885/29 (accessed July 6, 2008).

———. "Impending War Stokes Battle over Fate of Iraqi Antiquities." *Science* 299, no. 5607 (January 31, 2003): 643.

———. "International Collaboration: Iran Reopens Its Past." *Science* 302, no. 5647 (November 2003): 970–73.

———. "Interview with Donny George." *Discover,* August 3, 2007. http://discovermagazine.com/2007/aug/discover-interview-director-iraqi-national-museum/article_print.

———. "Mayhem in Mesopotamia." *Science* 301, no. 5633 (August, 1, 2003).

Layard, A. H. *Autobiography and Letters from His childhood until His Appointment as H.M. Ambassador at Madrid.* London: John Murray, 1903.

———. *Nineveh and Its Remains: With an Account of a Visit to the Chaldean Christians of Kurdistan, and the Yezidis, or Devil-Worshippers; and an Enquiry into the Manners and Arts of the Ancient Assyrians.* London: John Murray, 1849.

Leyden, Joel. "Swift-Find: Terrorism Funded by Stolen Property." Israel News Agency, October 16, 2005. http://www.israelnewsagency.com/ terrorismstolenpropertyswiftfindregistry881016.html.

MacFarquhar, Neil. "Hussein's Babylon: A Beloved Atrocity." *New York Times,* August 19, 2003, A11.

Marchand, Suzanne. *Down from Olympus: Archaeology and Philhellenism in Germany, 1750–1970.* Princeton, NJ: Princeton University Press, 1996.

Marquis, Alice Goldfarb. "Culture Has No Infrastructure." *New York Times,* August 9, 1999, A15.

Martin, Paul, Ed Vulliamy, and Gaby Hinsliff. "US Army Was Told to Protect Looted Museum." *Observer,* April 20, 2003, 4.

Mathews, Roger. *The Archaeology of Mesopotamia: Theories and Approaches.* London: Routledge, 2003.

———. "By the Waters of Babylon." *British Archaeology* 90 (September/October 2006). http://www.britarch.ac.uk/BA/ba90/feat3.shtml.

Mattingly, E. "Prof. to Train Soldiers to Preserve Sites." *Dartmouth* (NH), April 26, 2006. Posted on IraqCrisis listhost, April 26, 2006. https:// listhost.uchicago.edu/pipermail/iraqcrisis/2006-April/001524.html.

Maykuth, Andrew. "A Plea to Save Afghan Antiquities." *Philadelphia Inquirer,* May 3, 2006. http://www.philly.com/mld/philly/entertainment/ 14485199.htm.

Mazurkewich, Karen. "Ancient Treasures in Peril—Archeologists Warn Fighting in Iraq May Destroy Trove of Mesopotamian Antiquities." *Wall Street Journal,* March 27, 2003, eastern edition, sec. B.

McGeough, Paul. "Rich Past Stripped as Future in Tatters." *Sydney Morning Herald,* April 14, 2003. http://www.smh.com.au/articles/2003/04/13/ 1050172478179.html.

Merryman, John. "Two Ways of Thinking about Cultural Property." *American Journal of International Law* 80, no.4 (October 1986): 831–53.

Meyer, Karl E. *The Plundered Past.* New York: Atheneum, 1973.

Michalowski, Piotr. "U.S. Scholarly Organizations Unite to Protect Iraqi Cultural Heritage." University of Michigan news release, May 9, 2003. http://www.umich.edu/news/Releases/2003/May03/r050903c.html.

Mirak-Weissbach, Muriel, and Ortrun Cramer. "World Robbed of Iraq's Museums, Antiquities: An Interview with Donny George." In *Executive Intelligence Review,* July 25, 2003. http://www.larouchepub.com/other/ interviews/2003/3029donny_george.html.

Mueller, Robert S. "Remarks Prepared for Director Robert S. Mueller III."
Speech, Town Hall Los Angeles, Los Angeles, CA, November 15, 2004.
http://www.fbi.gov/pressrel/speeches/mueller111504.htm.

Musawi, Muhsin al-. *Reading Iraq: Culture and Power in Conflict.* London: I. B.
Tauris, 2006.

Myers, Gen. Richard. "Department of Defense News Briefing—Secretary Rumsfeld and General Myers." Federal News Service, April 15, 2003. http://
www.defenselink.mil/transcripts/transcript.aspx?transcriptid=2413.

Nafziger, James. "Protection of Cultural Heritage in Time of War and Its Aftermath," *IFAR Journal* 6 (2003): 56–61.

National Geographic Survey. http://news.nationalgeographic.com/news/2003/
06/0611_030611_iraqlootingreport.html.

National Iraqi News Agency. "Thieves Threaten the Elimination of the Sumerian Civilization in Dhi-Qar." Wna-news.com, December 6, 2006. Posted to
IraqCrisis listhost, December 7, 2006. https://listhost.uchicago.edu/
pipermail/iraqcrisis/2006-December/001665.html.

Nicholas, Lynn. *The Rape of Europa: The Fate of Europe's Treasures in the Third
Reich and the Second World War.* New York: Vintage, 1994.

Norman, Kirsty. "The Invasion of Kuwait, and the Subsequent Recovery of Its
National Museum: A Conservator's View." *Museum Management and Curatorship* 16 (1997): 180–91.

Northedge, Alastair. "SBAH in Samarra Attacked and Looted." IraqCrisis
listhost, July 10, 2007. https://listhost.uchicago.edu/pipermail/
iraqcrisis/2007-July/001821.html.

Olbrys, Miroslaw. "The Polish Contribution to the Protection of the Archaeological Heritage in Central South Iraq, November 2003 to April 2005."
Conservation and Management of Archaeological Sites 8 (2007): 94.

———. "The Possibilities and Restrictions of the Archeologist's Work during
Open Armed Conflict—Experiences from Iraq 2004/2005." In *Cultural
Heritage in the 21st Century: Opportunities and Challenges,* edited by Monika
Murzyn and Jacek Purchla, 233–42. Krakow: International Cultural
Centre, 2007.

Packer, George. "War after the War." *New Yorker,* November 24, 2003, 62.

Page, Laura. "A Failed Security Plan for Iraq." In *Antiquities under Siege: Cultural
Heritage Protection after the Iraq War,* edited by Lawrence Rothfield, 146–47.
Lanham, MD: AltaMira Press, 2008.

Paley, Samuel. "Nimrud, the War, and the Antiquities Markets." *IFAR Journal* 6,
nos. 1 and 2. http://www.ifar.org/nimrud.htm.

Paris, Roland. "International Machinery for Postwar Peace-Building: The
Dilemmas of Coordination." Paper presented at PIPES Seminar, University
of Chicago, May 2006.

Paroff, Sasha P. "Comment: Another Victim of the War in Iraq: The Looting of
the National Museum in Baghdad and the Inadequacies of International

Protection of Cultural Property." *Emory Law Journal* 53, no. 4 (Fall 2004): 2021–54.

Paust, Jordan J. "The US as Occupying Power over Portions of Iraq and Relevant Responsibilities under the Laws of War." *American Society of International Law Insights* (April 2003). http://www.asil.org/insights/insigh102.htm.

Perito, Robert M. *Establishing the Rule of Law in Iraq* (Special Report No. 104). Washington, DC: U.S. Institute of Peace, April 2003.

———. *Where Is the Lone Ranger When We Need Him? America's Search for a Post-Conflict Stability Force.* Washington, DC: U.S. Institute of Peace, 2004.

Perlman, David. "Protecting Iraq's Treasures." *San Francisco Chronicle,* March 31, 2003, W-5.

Pew Charitable Trusts. "The Pew Charitable Trusts Announce Landmark Cultural Policy Initiative for American Arts and Culture." News release, August 2, 1999. http://www.pewtrusts.com/ideas/ (accessed July 13, 2007).

Plate, Christoph. "Sumerischer Terracotta-Löwenkopf im Angebot. Interpol und die irakischen Behörden arbeiten gegen den Handel mit Artefakten im Internet." *Neue Zürcher Zeitung,* July 3, 2005. Posted to IraqCrisis listhost, July 14, 2007. https://listhost.uchicago.edu/pipermail/iraqcrisis/2005-July/001284.html.

Polk, William R. Introduction to *The Looting of the Iraq Museum, Baghdad: The Lost Legacy of Ancient Mesopotamia,* edited by Milbry Polk and Angela Schuster, 5–9. New York: Harry Abrams, 2005.

Powell, Colin. "Cooperation for the Safeguarding of Iraqi Antiquities and Cultural Property," April 14, 2003. http://www.globalsecurity.org/wmd/library/news/iraq/2003/iraq-030414-dos-19628pf.htm.

Radi, Selma al-. "War and Cultural Heritage: Lessons from Lebanon, Kuwait and Iraq." Lecture, Cultural Emergency Response, Prinsenhof Museum, Delft, the Netherlands, September 26, 2003. *Der Kracht van Cultuur,* October 2003. Cached text, retrieved by Google, July 25, 2007. http://64.233.167.104/search?q=cache:U9M2HK2MjlYJ:www.powerofculture.nl/nl/artikelen/war_and_cultural_heritage.html (accessed September 21, 2007).

Rathmell, Andrew. "Planning Post-Conflict Reconstruction in Iraq: What Can We Learn?" *International Affairs* 81, no. 5 (October 2005): 1021.

"Resolution by the Governing Board of the Archaeological Institute of America to Support." *Archaeological Institute of America,* online, January 6, 2005. http://www.archaeological.org/pdfs/archaeologywatch/Iraq/AIA_Iraq_Resolution0501.pdf?page=10248.

Rich, Claudius. *Narrative of a Journey to the Site of Babylon.* London: Duncan and Malcolm, 1839.

———. *Narrative of a Residence in Koordistan, and on the Site of Ancient Nineveh.* London: James Duncan, 1836.

Ricks, Thomas E. *Fiasco: The American Military Adventure in Iraq.* New York: Penguin, 2006.

Rieff, David. "Blueprint for a Mess." *Foreign Service Journal,* March 2004, 22–28.

Rohde, David. "Army Enlists Anthropology in War Zones." *New York Times,* October 5, 2007.

Rose, C. Brian. "Talking to the Troops about the Archaeology of Iraq and Afghanistan." In *The Acquisition and Exhibition of Classical Antiquities: Professional, Legal, and Ethical Perspectives,* ed. Robin Rhodes. Notre Dame, IN: University of Notre Dame Press, 2007).

Rothfield, Lawrence. "Assessment Report on 8 Southern Sites Released at Last." The Punching Bag, http://larryrothfield.blogspot.com (accessed October 24, 1008).

Rumsfeld, Donald. "Beyond Nation-Building." Speech, 11th Annual Salute to Freedom, New York, NY, February 14, 2003. http://www.defenselink.mil/speeches/2003/sp20030214-secdef0024.html.

———. Interview with Tim Russert, NBC *Meet the Press.* http://www.defenselink.mil/transcripts/transcript.aspx?transcriptid=2383 (accessed December 4, 2007).

———. "Rumsfeld, Franks Pentagon Briefing," May 9, 2003. http://www.america.gov/st/washfile-english/2003/May/20030509172225ifas0.7209436.html.

———. "Rumsfeld, Myers Pentagon Briefing," May 20, 2003. http://www.america.gov/st/washfile-english/2003/May/20030521075931nosnhojb4.883975e-02.html.

———. "Rumsfeld Says Iraqis Celebrate Freedom from Fear of Regime." Transcript of Defense Department Briefing, April 11, 2003. http://www.america.gov/st/washfile-english/2003/April/20030412135241attocnich0.1897852.html.

Rumsfeld, Donald and Richard Myers. "DoD News Briefing," April 11, 2003. http://www.defenselink.mil/transcripts/2003/tr20030411-secdef0090.html.

———. "DoD News Briefing," April 15, 2003. http://www.defenselink.mil/transcripts/transcript.aspx?transcriptid=2413.

Russell, John M. *The Final Sack of Nineveh: The Discovery, Documentation, and Destruction of King Sennacherib`s Throne Room at Nineveh, Iraq.* New Haven, CT: Yale University Press, 1998.

Sandholtz, Wayne. "The Iraqi National Museum and International Law: A Duty to Protect." *Columbia Journal of Transnational Law* 44 (2005): 185–240.

Schipper, Friedrich. "Iraq: Its Cultural Heritage—a Post-Gulf-War Front." In *Protection of Cultural Property in the Event of Armed Conflict—A Challenge in Peace Support Operations,* edited by Edwin Micewski and Gerhard Sladek, 109–16. Vienna: Austrian Military Printing Press, 2002.

Schuster, Jeffrey. "Iraqi Antiquities Revisited (with endnotes)." Gutenblog Castle, February 2005. http://gutenblogcastle.blogspot.com/2005/02/iraq-antiquities-revisited-with.html.

Senanayake, Sumedha. "Iraq: Antiquities Continue to Be Pillaged, Destroyed." *Radio Free Europe,* October 12, 2006. http://www.rferl.org/featuresarticle/2006/10/6f5f571b-f0f8-4ff9-899f-b8341676574b.html.

Shaw, Wendy K. *Possessors and Possessed: Museums, Archaeology, and the Visualization of History in the Late Ottoman Empire.* Berkeley: University of California Press, 2003.

Shiyah, Kamel. "Final Report." From the first plenary session, UNESCO's International Coordination Committee for the Safeguarding of the Cultural Heritage of Iraq, Paris, May 24, 2004.

Society for American Archaeology. "Letter to Secretary of Defense on Protection of Antiquities in Iraq," February 27, 2003. http://www.saa.org/goverment/Iraq.html.

Society for American Archaeology Web site. "Department of Defense Response to SAA Letter," March 18, 2003. http://www.saa.org/goverment/DODresponse.html.

Spurr, Jeff. "Iraqi Libraries and Archives in Peril: Survival in a Time of Invasion, Chaos, and Civil Conflict, a Report." Oriental Institute Web site, April 11, 2007. http://oi.uchicago.edu/OI/IRAQ/mela/update_2007.htm.

Stone, Elizabeth. "Cultural Assessment of Iraq: The State of Sites and Museums in Southern Iraq." *National Geographic,* May 2003. http://news.nationalgeographic.com/news/2003/06/0611_030611_iraqlootingreport3.html.

———. "Patterns of Looting of Archaeological Sites in Southern Iraq." PowerPoint presentation, American Society for Oriental Research meeting, Washington, DC, November 16, 2006.

———. "Patterns of Looting in Southern Iraq." *Antiquity* 82 (2008): 125–38.

Tabachnik, Stephen E. "Lawrence of Arabia as Archaeologist." *Biblical Archaeology Review* 23 (1997): 40–47, 70–71.

Thurlow, Matthew D. "Protecting Cultural Property in Iraq: How American Military Policy Comports with International Law." *Yale Human Rights and Development Law Journal* 8 (2005): 153–87.

Trivedi, Bijal. "U.S. Military Working on Ultimate 'Stink Bomb.'" *National Geographic Today,* January 7, 2002. http://news.nationalgeographic.com/news/2002/01/0107_020107TVstinkbomb.html.

UK Department for Culture, Media and Sport. "Consultation Paper on the 1954 Hague Convention on the Protection of Cultural Property in the Event of Armed Conflict and Its Two Protocols of 1954 and 1999." London: Department for Culture, Media and Sport, 2005.

UNESCO. "Republic of Iraq UN/WB Joint Needs Assessment: Culture Sector." UNESCO Web site (under "Iraq," within the "Culture" sector), October 1,

2003. http://portal.unesco.org/culture/en/ev.php-URL_ID=17322&URL
_DO=DO_TOPIC&URL_SECTION=201.html.

———. "UNESCO Survey." http://portal.unesco.org/culture/en/ev.php-URL
_ID=14658&URL_DO=DO_TOPIC&URL_SECTION=201.html.

U.S. Committee of the Blue Shield. "ICOM-US Announces 2007 International
Service Citation." USCBS news release, May 22, 2004. http://uscbs.org/
news/?p=8.

U.S. Department of State. "Iraq Cultural Heritage Update," July 14, 2003.
http://www.state.gov/r/pa/prs/ps/2003/22388.htm.

U.S. Department of State Office of the Spokesman. "Iraq Cultural Heritage
Project (ICHP) Fact Sheet." October 16, 2008. http://www.state.gov/r/pa/
prs/ps/2008/oct/111017.htm (accessed October 24, 2008).

Vikan, Gary. "An Obscure State Department Committee . . . " Director's Blog,
Walters Art Museum, April 16, 2007. http://www.thewalters.org/blog/
comments.aspx?b=19.

Vinall, Casie. "Profile of Joseph Collins." *Defend America: U.S. Department of
Defense News about the War on Terrorism,* June 23, 2003. http://www
.defendamerica.mil/profiles/june2003/pr062403a.html.

Wadum, Jørgen. "ICOM-CC chair report, May 2003–January 2004." The
Hague, January 2004. http://www.icom-cc.org/index.php?page_id=50.

Waldbaum, Jane, and Patty Gerstenblith. "Tracing Iraq's Lost Treasures."
Washington Post, April 27, 2003, B7.

Wallace, Lt. Gen. William. "News Briefing." News Service, May 7, 2003. http://
www.defenselink.mil/transcripts/transcript.aspx?transcriptid=2573.

Wegener, Corine. "Assignment Blue Shield: The Looting of the Iraq Museum."
In *Antiquities under Siege: Cultural Heritage Protection after the Iraq War,*
edited by Lawrence Rothfield, 163–74. Lanham, MD: AltaMira Press,
2008.

Westervelt, Eric. "Baghdad Museum." NPR's *Weekend Edition,* April 20, 2003.
http://www.npr.org/templates/story/story.php?storyId=1237927.

Wilkie, Nancy C. "Governmental Agencies and the Protection of Cultural
Property in Times of War." In *Antiquities under Siege: Cultural Heritage
Protection after the Iraq War,* edited by Lawrence Rothfield, 237–48. Lan-
ham, MD: AltaMira Press, 2008.

Williams, Sharon A. *The International and National Protection of Cultural
Property.* Dobbs Ferry, NY: Oceana Publications, 1977.

Wiltenburg, Mary. "A Fertile Crescent for Looting." *Christian Science Monitor,*
June 12, 2003. http://www.csmonitor.com/2003/0612/p03s01-woiq.html.

Winter, Irene J. "Babylonian Archaeologists of The(ir) Mesopotamian Past." In
*Proceedings of the First International Congress on the Archaeology of the Ancient
Near East,* vol. 2, edited by P. Matthiae et al.. Rome: Dipartimento di
scienze storiche, archeologiche e antropologiche dell'antichità, 2000.

Wolfowitz, Paul. "Wolfowitz Says U.S. Warred on Saddam's Regime, Not Iraqi
People." Interview on Egyptian TV, April 16, 2003. http://www.america

.gov/st/washfile-english/2003/April/20030419181303ynnedd0.3930475
.html.

Woods, Christopher E. "The Sun-God Tablet of Nabû-Apla-Iddina Revisited." *Journal of Cuneiform Studies* 56 (2004): 82.

Woodward, Bob. *Plan of Attack*. New York: Simon & Schuster, 2004.

Yasiri, Hussein Ali al-. "Plundering the Past." *ICR* 82 (September 6, 2004). Posted on IraqCrisis listhost, September 18, 2004. https://listhost
.uchicago.edu/pipermail/iraqcrisis/2004-September/000858.html.

Youkhanna, Donny George, and McGuire Gibson. "Preparations at the Iraq Museum in the Lead-Up to War." In *Antiquities under Siege: Cultural Heritage Protection after the Iraq War*, edited by Lawrence Rothfield, 27–32. Lanham, MD: AltaMira Press, 2008.

Index